New MANAGEMENT™
— Handbook —

*A step-by-step guide for creating
a happier, more productive classroom.*

REVISED THIRD EDITION

Rick Morris
Creator of New Management

Other Books by Rick Morris

Eight Great Ideas: Simple Ways to Transform Your Classroom
Tools & Toys: Fifty Fun Ways to Love Your Class
Class Cards: Putting Your Students in the Palm of Your Hand

New Management Handbook
Revised Third Edition, Copyright © 2010 by Rick Morris

New Management
6512 Edmonton Avenue
San Diego, California 92122

For information, you can call us at:
(858) 455-6000

or send e-mail to:
rick@newmanagement.com

or visit our website at:
http://www.newmanagement.com

I.S.B.N. 1-889236-02-0

Cover design
Len Torres

Illustrations
Alison Owen
Peter Owen

Editor
Diane Lueke

Not that we are sufficient of ourselves to think of anything
as being from ourselves, but our sufficiency comes from God.
—II Corinthians 3:5

for Debbie...
my wife, my life

Table of Contents

LESSON 8: CHECK OFF SHEET

LESSON 9: FIRST AID KIT

LESSON 10: GRADE BOOKS

APPENDIX

Acknowledgements

First of all, I want to thank God for putting me on the path that led to a career in education.

Not many people know this, but I didn't like kids when I was younger. As a pre-med student at San Diego State University, I had an eye toward becoming a veterinarian. I thought that by becoming a vet, I would be able to stay well away from children. It was not to be. A part-time job that I had lined up for my junior year of college fell through at the last minute and—out of sheer desperation—I took an afternoon job at a day-care center. I was in charge of watching elementary students from the time they got out of school until their parents came to get them. I still remember walking in that first afternoon and thinking, "Oh, man. I am *not* going to like this." To make a long story short, I was hooked in just three weeks. Kids and I got along great. Consequently, I changed my major, earned a teaching credential, and entered the profession.

I want to also recognize the fact that God has blessed me with gifts for being creative and for solving problems. (All of our abilities come from God, and it's only right and fitting that He be given the credit.) I've used these gifts with my students when I'm in the classroom and with my fellow educators when I'm presenting workshops and seminars. This handbook, among many other things, would not have been possible without these special God-given talents.

The previous book I wrote, Tools & Toys, was dedicated to my sweet son, Ben. This one is for my loving wife, Debbie. How anyone could be so lucky to have such a wonderful family is beyond me. (Actually, just about everything in my life is beyond me.) Suffice it to say that their love and prayers have literally carried me through the long days of travel and the occasional back-to-back-to-back speaking engagements. What a comfort to know that they're always there at home, waiting for my return, and greeting me with open arms and affectionate hugs. I am truly blessed.

It would be just about impossible to recognize the individuals—friends, teachers, administrators—who have encouraged me in my life's work. To name anyone is to risk leaving someone else off the list. I'm going to trust that the people who have shared their appreciation for my efforts know how much it has meant to me. There's just no way I could've done it without your support.

*The most extraordinary thing
about a really good teacher
is that he or she transcends
accepted educational methods.*

—Margaret Mead

About This Book

It wasn't easy to write.

In fact, I started working on this book way back in March, 1986. I had just finished teaching my first New Management class to a group of 13 teachers. I was excited by the results of that experience and wanted to put into writing what we had covered. (I still have the original note paper I scribbled on while sitting at the local coffee house. It's framed and hanging on the wall of my office.)

GETTING STARTED

One of the truly pleasant aspects of the NM concept is the lack of equipment needed to start.

Well, after banging out about 30 pages, I became overwhelmed by the enormity of the task. And since the workshops were becoming more popular, I had less time for writing. Also, I had come to realize that verbalizing my teaching philosophy and classroom techniques during these workshops was helping me to refine and clarify them. I felt that this teaching experience would actually enable me to write a better book.

So, I set aside the handbook project and concentrated on the workshops instead. Having done that now for over a decade, it seemed that the time was right to produce the written version of the basic New Management workshop.

I'm glad I waited. By not writing the book in '86, I've been able to include all of the experience and insight gained from conducting workshops. Additionally, the feedback and input offered by teachers who have attended New Management staff development sessions have been incorporated into my writing. As a result of my editorial hiatus, this handbook will actually be more complete and, thus, more useful.

Nonetheless, I didn't want to wait any longer. Judging from the enthusiastic comments shared by the thousands of teachers using the New Management system, I felt that there was a real need for the ideas espoused in this book.

Whether you are a first year teacher just starting out, or a seasoned veteran with years of classroom experience, you'll find ideas that will increase your effectiveness and boost the achievement of your students. The New Management techniques you'll read about are not only simple but work for students as well as they do for teachers. The entire system will help you bring about a sense of order, structure, and accomplishment to your classroom.

> *All of that in one little book?*
> *How is that possible?*
> *What makes the whole thing work the way it does?*
> *Why do teachers say they'll never go back to the old way of running their classrooms?*
> *What's the secret to New Management's success?*

Here's the secret: Number your students.

That's it. The cat is now out of the bag.

> Twenty-two kindergarteners cavorting about your room?
> *Number them from 1 to 22.*
>
> Thirty-one sixth grade students in your class this year?
> *Number them from 1 to 31.*
>
> Thirty-seven hormone-crazed ninth graders trying to keep
> their hands off of each other in your fourth period math class?
> *You guessed it. Number them from 1 to 37.*

Each student in your room will receive a number. The first student will be 1 and the last will be n, n representing the total number of students in your class.

Earthshaking? No.

Mindboggling? Not really.

So what's the big deal?

By taking this one simple step, i.e., numbering your students, you will be setting the stage for a major change in how you'll deal with this year's mountain of paperwork and class-related responsibilities. And, with the tools I've created to take advantage of the numbering concept, you won't be the only one attempting to take care of business. You'll have a whole classroom full of eager helpers.

Numbering your students is a tool you, and your students, will use to better monitor, manage, and account for your class and its progress. By having your students add a number to their class identity—which, up to this point in the history of education, has usually consisted of their first and last names—you will be providing yourself with an amazingly flexible framework upon which to build a system for classroom management. The numbers provide the underlying foundation, the very backbone, for the entire New Management system.

This book, then, is my attempt to share the success of that system, and I thank you for purchasing it. More importantly, though, I applaud your willingness to use the New Management techniques contained in these 10 simple lessons.

It's not an easy thing trying new ideas. It requires that you stretch and take risks. It means that you become a student yourself. This role reversal, though, is one of the best things you can do to improve your teaching. As John Cotton Dana so elegantly phrased it, *"Who dares to teach must never cease to learn."* A teacher with a desire to grow and develop is a teacher worthy of the name.

As I've always maintained, the greatest force we have in education *is* the individual teacher. It's not a governance team or a school advisory committee. It's neither the local school board nor some education agenda coming from Washington, D.C. Our strongest force in education is the classroom teacher dedicated to excellence. It's a caring, effective person who can bring out the best in a group of students. And if this book can help fellow educators bring out the best in the kids with whom they spend so much time, then it will have served its purpose.

Revised Third Edition:

The previous three pages were originally written in 2000 as the introduction to the first edition. They remained unchanged for the release of the second edition in 2007. And now, with the publication of this edition, I find that the words still ring true and will leave them in their original form.

Where you will see change is in the body of the book. I was able to incorporate some new ideas that have been born of the experience I've gained recently while presenting seminars. That work, in addition to all of the interactions I've had with teachers during that time, has led to some new insights and understandings. It is my hope that the inclusion of this new material will make a good book even better.

—Rick Morris
   San Diego, California
   June 1, 2010

Post Script

New Management is not meant to be portrayed as a rigid, chiseled-in-stone, do-it-this-way-or-else kind of program. On the contrary, the strength of its design, what gives it such wide appeal and applicability, is that it's a very open-ended system.

In fact, a great deal of the success teachers have experienced with my ideas is that they freely bent the rules to make things work. They didn't limit themselves to just what they read. Instead, they picked up basic New Management techniques and then set off in slightly different, yet equally successful, directions.

Consequently, the descriptions of how I do things are offered merely to give you clear, specific examples of *how it could be done, not how it has to be done.* So I encourage you to be creative with the ideas presented in this book. If an idea doesn't work properly for you and your students, see if you can change it so that it does work. After all, that's how the whole New Management program has grown to be what it is today.

You may find, though, that some of the ideas are not producing results as quickly as you had hoped. It's either taking too long for your students to become adept at the technique or you keep forgetting to use the idea itself. Whenever you feel that way, just relax and practice patience. Remind yourself that education is a process. More than just a series of separate days; it's a continuum in which the whole is greater than the sum of the parts.

My own classroom experience taught me that a new idea sometimes required more time than I thought necessary before it was able to bear fruit. By not giving up too quickly, the idea was given a fair chance to succeed. And given the proper time and a nurturing touch, bear fruit it finally did.

At the same, though, you might find that you need to stop using one of the techniques because it's just not working. If that's the case, drop it and move on. As my grandfather taught me years ago, *"If the horse you're riding on dies, get off. It won't do you any good to adjust the saddle or change the bit."* It's very possible that you'll be able to restart the idea later on in the year and achieve more success.

So, I encourage you to:

> Be creative.
> Be patient.
> Mess around with this stuff.

You never know where you might end up if you just ditch the map and set out on your own.

After all, there is more than one path that leads to success.

Lesson 1

Before We Begin

How It All Got Started

Numbering Your Students

Using Student Numbers

Timers & Sound Makers

Class Chart

Check Off List

Check Off Sheet

First Aid Kit

Grade Books

Education is a wonderful thing.
If you couldn't sign your name,
you'd have to pay cash.

— Rita May Brown

Lesson 1
Before We Begin

◆ ◆

Goals for this lesson:

☑ Become familiar with the symbols used in this book.

☑ Discover that there's a contents guide on the back cover of this handbook.

☑ Figure out how your individual teaching situation affects the way in which you'll use some of the ideas in this book.

☑ Learn ways to find help when you need it.

☑ Make a commitment to be reasonable about how many new techniques you can successfully incorporate at one time.

◆ ◆

*B*efore we get to the heart and soul of this book, I'd like to cover a few quick points. One of the points has to do with margin notations while the other, more important ones, have to do with you.

Margin Notations

Throughout this book, in the left-hand margin, you'll come upon three types of notations—icons, if you will. Since these icons are designed to help, it would be best if I explained their significance before you actually saw them.

Five Basic Student Needs

The first icon relates to the student needs identified by Bill Glasser in his book *The Quality School Teacher*. Glasser states that there are five basic student needs—power, love, fun, freedom, and safety—that he feels must be met in the classroom in order for students to really become active participants. He goes on to say that if these needs *are* satisfied—by the activities in which you engage or the manner in which you conduct your class—you'll experience a significant rise in student involvement which will lead, in time, to an increase in student achievement.

Since I wholeheartedly agree with Glasser's premise, you'll find these needs woven into the very fabric of the New Management system. In an effort to highlight this fact, I've placed student need icons in the margin next to the passages that allude to them.

Here's a sample passage from Lesson 5 and the margin notation:

power
love
fun
freedom
safety

So, if we take a fun-type tool and call it a toy, not only does it help with the management, but it makes it fun in the process. Your students will begin to develop a very positive attitude toward classroom management. The attitude can be summed as: "We get things done in here and have fun at the same time." This is definitely a good awareness to perpetuate.

The reference above was rather obvious; however, some of them are a bit more subtle. The icons will help to uncover the subtle, more obscure references. Also, you'll sometimes find a passage that actually refers to two or more of the needs. Consequently, the margin notation will indicate this.

Tools & Toys

The second icon, a symbol that looks like a small book, indicates a reference to my second book, *Tools & Toys: 50 Fun Ways to Love Your Class*. The number above this notation refers to the page on which the idea can be found.

Here's another sample from Lesson 5 and the margin notation:

*It's always a good idea to make sure your students are aware of appropriate activities in which they can engage whenever they finish an assignment early. We have an **E. T. Chart**—the E. T. stands for Extra Time—that lists suggested activities. By referring to the E. T. Chart, students will find something significant to occupy their extra time.*

This margin notation means that the **E. T. Chart** idea can be found on page 6 in the *Tools & Toys* book.

Although the brief references to the *Tools & Toys* book given in this book might not provide you with as much information as you may need, I've kept the explanations short for a reason: I didn't want to repeat any of the material from the *Tools & Toys* book in this one. Not only does time—pages, actually—not permit it, but I didn't want to appear redundant.

If you wish to order *Tools & Toys* , just visit my website, NewManagement.com. The book is just $10 which, as you math teachers know, works out to 20¢ an idea.

Core Principles of Effective Teaching

The third icon has to do with something new. Although I've been sharing the strategies in this book for over twenty years at schools and districts around the country, it wasn't until 2007 that I came up with what I call *Core Principles of Effective Teaching*. I've identified six of them. (There might be a dozen, who knows?) And the more I share them with teachers, the more convinced I am that these principles are vital to our success.

So, whenever I write about a technique or teaching situation that is affected by one of these principles, or would benefit from its application, I'll highlight it. Since the only thing you'll see, though, is a little numbered apple icon, you might want to mark this page with a post-it. Having a bookmark will enable you to quickly reference the list of principles as opposed to just skipping past the apple icon whenever you come upon one.

You have safe relationships with your students.
78% of student achievement is based upon the relationship you have with the student.

Your words equal your actions.
When your words equal your actions, students will learn to trust what you say.

You are fair, firm, and consistent.
Develop strategies that manifest these three traits.

You can focus your attention.
Don't speak to everyone about the actions of a few.

Your classroom is manageable for you and your students.
Break things down into simple, easy-to-accomplish steps.

Your students are problem solvers.
Teaching students how to solve problems is a life-long gift.

Who Are You?

The next order of business deals with you, the reader. I need to ask you a couple of questions:

1. **How much do you already know about the New Management system?**

2. **What is your individual teaching situation?**

If I could answer these two questions, I could offer some specific insight that might make it easier for you to use this handbook.

Here, for example, are the profiles of just three readers.

> *I teach fourth grade. I've been to several of Rick's workshops, but it's been a number of years since I last heard him speak.*

> *I'm a new teacher. I teach seventh grade math. I've been involved in New Management staff development through our BTSA program. (Beginning Teacher Support and Assessment.)*

> *I'm a high school social studies teacher who was given this book as a present. I know nothing about New Management except that other teachers really like Rick's ideas.*

As you can see, there is a wide range out there. Given the fact that I couldn't possibly address all of the different backgrounds and present situations—one size *does not* fit all—we can look at some of the more common ones.

New Management Workshops

Some of you have been to one of my seminars and some of you haven't.

If you have attended one, read Section A.

If you haven't, read Section B.

Section A: Workshop Participants

As a former seminar participant, you will find the material in this book comfortably familiar. You'll read about how student numbers can help you become a more effective teacher. You'll also read about how to number your students and how to make a Class Chart. You'll find information about digital timers and how sound makers can be used to communicate with your students. In Lessons 7 and 8, you'll discover how to collect assignments with Check Off Lists and Check Off Sheets. You're going to read about my early days of teaching when I was a pirate and hear me tell some of the same sad stories I told during the workshop. Later on, you'll find lessons on how to handle unfinished assignments and techniques that make grade keeping a heck of a lot easier.

Many of these ideas you're already using with great success. Revisiting them will help to improve and refine your technique. Other ideas, which may have gone by too quickly—as you already know, I do talk fast—are here at your fingertips. You'll be able to work your way through the material at your own pace.

Bear in mind, though, that much of the material in this book was not covered in the seminar. This is partly due to the fact that, in certain ways, information presented in written form is superior to information given verbally. Consequently, I'm able to offer a bit more depth. The printed page allows me to offer teacher/student dialogues, step-by-step directions, samples, photos, and numerous variations that can't be adequately addressed in the seminars.

On the other hand, some of the material that may seem new to you was actually presented in the workshop. That's just the result of memory overload. Sadly, the adult mind can only assimilate so much information before it shuts down. In fact, according to most studies, people can only remember about one-fourth of what they hear.

This auditory limitation was one of the reasons I produced this book. I wanted to offer workshop participants an opportunity to have the information in their hands as a reference. By capturing the seminar thoughts in writing, those teachers can now have access to 100% of the information and not just the normal 25% that they retained from the seminar.

Section B: What's New Management?

For those of you who have not experienced one of the workshops, don't despair. This book was actually written with you in mind. As I told the readers in Section A, this book follows the same format as the workshops and contains the same basic information.

The advantage of the book, though, is that you can take your time and digest the material at a slow, steady pace. (Anyone who has been to the workshop will tell you that I talk fast and cover a lot of ground.)

The disadvantage to the book is that you're kind of on your own. I won't be there to answer your questions or clear up any misunderstandings. It's just you and this book. If you do get stuck—which I don't think is going to happen very often—you can do one of three things:

1. **Look in the Frequently Asked Questions appendix.**
   In the back of this book you'll find a section called *Frequently Asked Questions*. It contains a few of the questions that are commonly asked at seminars and the answers I normally provide. Although I can't anticipate all of the questions teachers may have, I've included the most frequent ones.

2. **Talk to someone who has New Management experience.**
   See if you can find someone, either on your campus or within your district, who has been using these methods and ask them for guidance.

3. **Get in touch with me. (rick@newmanagement.com)**
   Email is by far the best way to go. Not only can I get back to you quickly but I can also use your question and my response to help other teachers who have the same question. So, please don't hesitate to write. Answering questions is just a part of my mission to help improve education.

Teaching Situations

Your teaching situation can have an effect upon how you begin to use some of the ideas described in this guide. Here are the three basic models:

Elementary; self-contained classroom
> One teacher; one class; all subjects

Elementary; redeployment or departmentalized
> Several teachers; several classes; students rotate among teachers

Secondary (middle school, junior high school, or high school)
> One teacher; several classes

Elementary Teachers

This is what my teaching situation looks like:

> I'm an elementary teacher.[†]
> I work with just one group of students all day; no redeployment to other classes and no team-teaching with other teachers.
> I teach every subject.

Consequently, the teaching strategies in the New Management system have been shaped by this "laboratory" in which I've been working. As you know, form follows function. Thus, the very design and implementation of the simple techniques described in this book have been shaped by my years of trial and error in the elementary self-contained classroom.

If your teaching situation matches mine, you'll feel right at home. The ideas and their explanations should make sense because we share a common ground. That's not to say that you won't change things around a bit to fit your style or student population. It's just that much of the material can be directly imported into your room with little modification and a great deal of success.

For Those Who Redeploy or Team Teach

As a result of my experience in a self-contained class, I am able to provide specific examples of how I've used these techniques during my thirty plus years of teaching. As you read through this book, you might want to keep in mind that it was written from that perspective.

Since I don't do what you do—team teach or redeploy students—I haven't spent much time reworking things to fit that style of teaching. Rest assured, though, that it can be done. There are a ton of teachers out there working together at school sites who are cur-

---

† I've actually had classroom experience in kindergarten through high school. (I taught eighth grade for two weeks—more than enough for me—and spent a month at a vocational high school.) The majority of my experience comes from teaching grades 2 through 6.

rently using the New Management system. It just took them a bit of fine-tuning to get things dialed in. To get you started in the right direction, I'll share some ideas given to me by other teachers in your situation.

Number 1 Suggestion

Start with your core group of students.

They are referring to the ones they see first thing in the morning. Some teachers call this their Home Room. Apply the techniques you'll learn in this book to just those students. Then, after coming to some kind of agreement with your partner(s), you'll be able to incorporate all of the students with whom you work throughout the day.

Number 2 Suggestion

Have each teacher in your team start numbering from 1.

Although you could number the students in the first class from 1 to 30, the students in the second class from 31 to 60, and the students in the third class from 61 to 90, you wouldn't be able to take advantage of the student number tools described in subsequent lessons.

By having each class use the numbers 1 to 30 or 1 to 25 or 1 to 20 or 1 to *n*—whatever your actual class size is—you'll be creating a stronger, more flexible platform on which to structure your system.

To differentiate between student number 4 in one class from student number 4 in another class, most teachers use a prefix. Prefixes can be anything from your room number to the first letter of your last name.

FIG. 1-1
Adding a prefix to the number is an easy way for team teachers to identify their core students.

Example:

Three teachers working together are named Hagan, Tripp, and Brown. Hagan teaches literature, Tripp teaches math, and Brown teaches social studies. To help prevent student numbers from getting mixed up, they've decided to use the first initial of their own last names as a prefix.

Hagan's Class	Tripp's Class	Brown's Class
H-1	T-1	B-1
H-2	T-2	B-2
H-3	T-3	B-3
etc.	etc.	etc.

I personally think that color coding is a better way to go. Like the numbers themselves, colors provide a foundation on which you can create a workable system. For example, imagine that the teachers in the previous example, Hagan, Tripp, and Brown, used the colors yellow, blue, and green to differentiate their groups. The three students who were #1 would be Y-1, B-1, and G-1.

They could then use those colors for something as simple as a collection folder for assignments. The advantage for the students is that they would be able to find the folder based upon color alone. From across the room, Hagan's students could spot their yellow folder and know where to place their assignments.

The choice of prefixes, or even if you want to go that way, is up to you and your partners. Live with the basic system for a while. Use it with just your own students before you begin to build a larger, more comprehensive system.

No matter which way you decide to go, though, you'll most likely find yourselves doing the same thing I've done for years and years: playing around with techniques to get them to do what you want. As I mentioned in the introduction—you did read the intro, didn't you?—teachers working with the basic New Management strategies and modifying them to fit their own teaching styles and classroom situations is how this whole thing got to be what it is today.

Secondary Teachers

If you are teaching at the secondary level, you are most likely teaching more than one group of students each day. With that factor in mind, let's start with this suggestion:

Start with just one class.

This thought is based upon the successful experience of other secondary teachers who are now using the New Management system. They've told me to tell other secondary teachers to select just one class and apply the New Management techniques to that one particular group.

By focusing on just one class, you will be able to more effectively introduce and incorporate the ideas presented in this book. Although the system is a simple one, attempting to use it with five different classes and one hundred fifty different students may overwhelm you. The enormity of the task might cause you to overheat and break down before you have had an opportunity to master the system.

If, however, you start small, you will be more inclined to stay the course. Your continued efforts will reap benefits in the long run. Eventually, with just a bit of practice and experience, you'll be able to incorporate your other classes into the New Management fold. There's just no need to try to do it all at once.

Suggestion: Relax and go easy at first. Realize you'll be working with your students all year. (They're not going anywhere.) Take your time. Ponder the tortoise.

Which Class Should I Choose?

When selecting the actual class with whom to begin, some teachers have chosen their most enjoyable class so that their own introduction to New Management is a rewarding one. Others have wanted to start with their most challenging class so that they can make some positive changes. The choice, of course, is yours.

If I were at the secondary level and was choosing a class, I'd pick my best one. The students in that class will offer me encouragement as they respond positively to my new ideas. This reinforcement will foster an environment which will motivate me to incorporate even more ideas.

Later on, after the New Management techniques have proven themselves to be effective with your pilot class, you'll be able to incorporate this system into the management of the other four or five classes with whom you work.

How Do I Keep All of Those Numbers Straight?

I told the elementary teachers who departmentalize—which is similar to your situation at the secondary level—to color-code their different groups of students. I think you should do the same thing. The colors will help you and your students keep materials organized and easy to locate.

If you are going to use colors, you might as well use the rainbow: red, orange, yellow, green, blue, violet. It's easy to remember the order of these colors if you tell your students, like I do, that the man who invented the rainbow is named ROY G. BIV. (*Note:* The "I" in BIV stands for indigo, which is not a color we use. Red, orange, yellow, green, blue, and violet are enough.)

First, assign a color to each period.

Period 1 = RED
Period 2 = ORANGE
Period 3 = YELLOW
Period 4 = GREEN
Period 5 = BLUE
Period 6 = VIOLET

Then, within the period groups number your students in blocks of 100. By that I mean that the first period class, the red group, would be numbered from 101 to 140. The digit in the hundred's column would represent the period number while the rest of it would be the part that identifies the actual student. Period two would go from 201 to 240, etc.

Hotel Analogy

If it helps, think about how hotels are organized. That is, the floor and room number is contained in a single number.

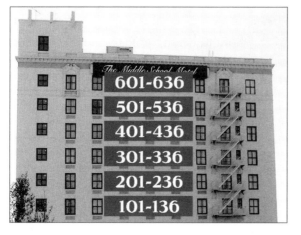

FIG. 1-2
Hotels use 3- and 4-digit room numbers for a reason: they don't want anyone getting confused about where the room is located.

The room key to the right makes it easy for a guest to find the proper room. The numeral in the hundred's column represents the floor number. The rest of it is the actual room number. Put it all together and the guest knows, at a glance, that he's on the 4th floor in room 17.

Think about how difficult things would be if the guest had been handed a key with just a 17 on it. The uncertainty this would create in a hotel with multiple floors would quickly lead to frustration and then annoyance.

In similar fashion, assigning number 17 to six different students might just lead you to abandon student numbers before they were even given a chance to work. And not because student numbers proved to be less than helpful but that it was just too difficult to keep track of which student 17 belonged to which period.

As you can already imagine, though, the use of the extra digit—in this case, a 4—would make it readily apparent that the 417 on the assignment you're holding in your hand belongs to student 17 in Period 4.

The Student Benefit of Using Three-Digit Numbers

Think, for a moment, about how the use of a three-digit number would work on the students' side of the equation. Although they would have written their student numbers in their planners, the hundred's place period designator would help them to more easily remember which number was associated with which class.

The example below shows both three-digit and two-digit student numbers that have been assigned to a hypothetical high school student.

The Recommended Way	*Not So Good*
121	**21**
218	**18**
320	**20**
417	**17**
519	**19**
622	**22**

FIG. 1-3
The numeral in the hundred's column will make it easier for students—and their teachers—to remember which number goes with which period.

Look at how much easier it would be for the student to keep the three-digit numbers clear and organized in his mind. The two-digit numbers are just too similar to be distinct.

The Big Picture

Put it all together and you end up with this remarkably simple structure for success:

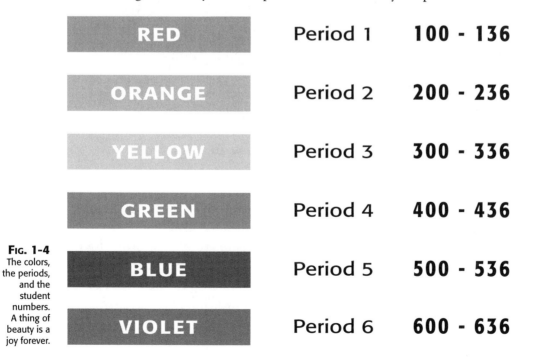

RED	Period 1	**100 - 136**
ORANGE	Period 2	**200 - 236**
YELLOW	Period 3	**300 - 336**
GREEN	Period 4	**400 - 436**
BLUE	Period 5	**500 - 536**
VIOLET	Period 6	**600 - 636**

FIG. 1-4
The colors, the periods, and the student numbers. A thing of beauty is a joy forever.

Why Colors?

In addition to helping to differentiate the periods you teach, colors can make it easier for students to locate materials that pertain to them. Students in your fourth period class, which is the green group, would be able to quickly locate the green folder that contains the activity sheets they need without having to search around the room.

Additionally, you could set up a series of color-coded collection boxes. By doing this, the papers in the red box[†]—the assignments from your first period class—won't get mixed up with the assignments being placed in the blue box that is being used by your fifth period students.

Colors work for the teacher as well as the students. How nice it would be, as your third period class comes streaming in the door, to quickly scan your desk and be able to identify, and fish out, the yellow folder that contains everything you're going to need to begin the day's lesson. Ah, ain't that nice.

Or how about keeping that blizzard of office paperwork in a hanging file crate?

FIG. 1-5
Although this black and white photo doesn't do it justice, the color-coded hanging file crate is a great way to keep papers organized.

With one of these bad boys sitting on your desk you'd have a simple paper organizer that will save you hours of grief.

What I'm trying to convey is that colors can make your room a more manageable place. Making things manageable for you and your students is Core Principle #5. (And that's the last time I'm going to spell out the principles. You're on your own with just the apple icons from here on out. But that's going to be manageable because you book marked page 1-5, right? Of course you did.) Anyway, like most New Management ideas, the more you use colors in your room, the more ways you'll find for using those colors.

[†]   I've found that the best "box" to use for collecting assignments is actually the lid that comes on a case of xerox paper. These are shallow enough to be stackable but deep enough to keep the papers from spilling out. To color them, just glue stick a strip of colored construction paper to one side of the lid.

Okay, just a few more things to discuss and then we can move on to Lesson Two.

Conversational Jargon

You'll find numerous dialogues throughout this book. For the most part, the interaction is a fictional one between my students and me based upon real life experiences.

What some readers might find awkward about the conversations is how I address my class when speaking to them as a group. The following phrases just don't work well for me:

"Boys and girls"   *"Ladies and gentlemen"*
"Class"   *"People"*

What I use more than any other is what comes naturally: "guys." I don't mean any disrespect for the girls in class; it's just my generic way of addressing a group of students.

Dialogues and Thoughts

Dialogues are used throughout this book to: 1) help clarify procedures; and 2) provide some modeling of how I interact with students. Sometimes, though, I'm not showing what a person is saying but, instead, what that person is thinking. To indicate that the words are a thought, they will be preceded by three little dashes.

---Hmmmm. I hope I made myself clear about showing thoughts.

3-Ring Binder

If you feel that a 3-ring binder version of this handbook would be more usable, here's what you do:

1. Go to Staples and buy a 2" view binder. (The view binder is the type that allows you to insert a page in the front and back covers.)

2. Take your book and new binder and visit your local Kinko's.

3. Ask the friendly Kinko's clerk to cut off the spine of your book.

4. Take the front and back covers and insert them into your binder.

5. Give the body of the book back to the clerk and ask him to "drill it." (That's Kinko-speak for 3-hole punch a stack of papers.)

6. Insert your newly punched pages into your binder.

Tip: Be sure to ask for your 10% educator's discount. If they ask for a faculty card, which I've never had to use, show them this book. They should be able to figure out from the front cover that you're a teacher.

Option: If you prefer, you can have them make it spiral bound.

Do What You Can

Accept the fact that there are a lot of ideas in this book and that you won't be able to do them all at once. In spite of your overachieving attitude and enthusiastic outlook, that's just how it is sometimes.

It would be manageable for you—and actually contribute to your long-term success—to start with just a few simple ideas and then plan on slowly adding additional techniques as you gain much-needed practice and experience.

So, make an effort to:
1. Keep your expectations realistic.
2. Be reasonable.
3. Take your time.
4. Proceed slowly but surely.

Bear in mind that it might be better to light one little candle and bring illumination to a dark corner of your classroom than it would to light a hundred candles and end up burning down the place.

A Second Table of Contents

Last thought. On the back cover of this handbook, you'll find a second table of contents. It's nothing more than a list of the titles of each lesson. It was designed to provide a quick and easy way to locate information.

If you need to find a specific section, use the more detailed Table of Contents found at the front of the book.

"I can't believe how much easier it is to run my classroom!"
–Barbara Van der Linde, Fifth Grade Teacher
(one week after learning New Management techniques)

NEW MANAGEMENT HANDBOOK
Effective Student Management in just
TEN EASY LESSONS

1 BEFORE WE BEGIN
2 HOW IT ALL GOT STARTED
3 NUMBERING YOUR STUDENTS
4 USING STUDENT NUMBERS
5 TIMERS & SOUND MAKERS
6 CLASS CHART
7 CHECK OFF LIST
8 CHECK OFF SHEET
9 FIRST AID KIT
10 GRADE BOOKS

Mentor Emeritus Rick Morris is the creator of New Management: a highly-acclaimed program of student management, motivation, and engagement.

A former teacher with over thirty years of classroom teaching experience, Rick now devotes his time to sharing New Management strategies with educators throughout the country.

EDCATION
US $24.95
ISBN 1-889236-02-0

A New Management Production

Lesson 2

Before We Begin

How It All Got Started

Numbering Your Students

Using Student Numbers

Timers & Sound Makers

Class Chart

Check Off List

Check Off Sheet

First Aid Kit

Grade Books

We might cease thinking of a school as a place,
and learn to believe that it is basically
relationships between children and adults,
and between children and other children.
The four walls and the principal's office
would cease to loom so hugely
as the essential ingredients.

—George Dennison

How It All Got Started

◆ ◆

Goals for this lesson:

☑ Realize that most new teachers struggle in the area of student management.

☑ Begin to see the power of using student numbers.

☑ Be able to verbalize the teacher benefits of the number system.

☑ Be able to verbalize the student benefits of the number system.

☑ Accept the fact that student numbers are just a tool.

◆ ◆

*D*uring my first five years of teaching, I was lost and confused. Although I felt I was doing a good job of teaching the subject matter, I didn't have a clue as to how to handle the non-academic part of our day. From taking attendance to passing out materials, from transitioning out of one activity to beginning a different one, from collecting assignments to record keeping, from morning bell to dismissal, things always seemed to be slightly out-of-control. Nothing dangerous, mind you, just a feeling that there had to be a better way of doing things than the way I was doing them.

Being a graduate of San Diego State University and a recipient of a teaching credential from their Department of Education, you would think that I would have been better prepared to run a classroom. Alas, that wasn't the case.

As I think back to my student teaching experience—and that wasn't yesterday, if you know what I mean—I don't recall that we spent much time or effort in the area of classroom management. In fact, about the only tidbit I do remember is this one:

You need to be fair, firm, and consistent.

That sounded good to me. How does one do that?

For some reason, none of the professors spent much time on specific techniques. There just weren't enough hours in the semester to permit this. Plus, everyone had his own specialty—reading, math, language, social studies, art—and guarded his allotted classroom time jealously. Classroom management, the unwanted step-child of education courses, was neglected more often than not.

As it turned out, we were encouraged to ponder the concept of being fair, firm, and consistent on our own when we had the time.

Speaking of fair, it's entirely possible that the professors were thinking that the classroom teachers to whom we'd be assigned during our student teaching practicums would provide the necessary guidance. Then again, maybe they did offer something and I was absent that day. Who knows? Suffice it to say that my student management skills were not what they needed to be.

It should come as no surprise, then, that I ended up in my own classroom with little experience at how to run the show. It wasn't too long before I began to get frustrated at my lack of organizational skill. My days at school just weren't going the way I thought they should be going.

> *Sad reality:* It didn't help that there were veteran teachers at my first school, in classrooms near mine, who seemed to have no problems at all. Everything was one big smoothly choreographed tea party. I still remember observing in their classrooms and thinking: *I'll never be this organized.* Now I think: *Why wasn't I shown a systematic way for managing my classroom and my students? Why does every teacher have to reinvent this wheel?* (In case you weren't teaching in the 70's, you should know that we didn't have a mentor department or a new teacher support program. We were on our own, and it was sink or swim.)

By my third year, I found myself resorting to the use of negative emotion to handle misbehavior and noncompliance. I would raise my voice, yell, and threaten. Before I knew it, I stopped being a Mr. Rogers kind of guy and found myself acting more and more like a pirate.

Whenever I wanted to show my students that I was serious about doing things the right way, I would rant and rave. Little did I realize that getting emotional can establish a dangerous precedent. After all, this type of emotional interaction is played out at home between parent and child on a regular basis.

Here's a typical example:

DAY 1   DAD
  Speaking in a calm fashion:
    Calvin, have you cleaned your room yet?
  CALVIN
    Oh, not yet, Dad. How about if I do it after soccer practice today?

DAD
> Not thrilled, but agreeable:
> *I guess that's okay.*

DAY 2   DAD
> Still the gentle parent:
> *Hey, son, how's your room looking?*

CALVIN
> *I ran out of time yesterday, and I need to go to the library right now to work on my report. You want me to get good grades, don't you? I'll do it after the library.*

DAD
> Still hoping for Calvin to be responsible:
> *Okay, just don't forget this time.*

DAY 3   DAD
> Starting to get bugged but maintaining his cool:
> *Did you get that room cleaned up yet?*

CALVIN
> Ever ready with an excuse:
> *You know, Dad, I completely forgot. I'll do it right after school today.*

DAY 4   DAD
> No more Mr. Nice Guy:
> *GET IN THERE AND CLEAN UP THAT ROOM!* †

Lo and behold, Calvin does what he should have done days ago. Granted, the objective is being met: the room is being cleaned. Unfortunately, though, Dad and Calvin are beginning to lock themselves into a dangerous cycle.

By resorting to yelling at Calvin, Dad is unwittingly emasculating Mr. Nice Guy. In essence, Calvin learns that the calm voice Dad used during the first three days does not really need to be taken seriously. He'll know when things are getting critical because Dad will start to yell.

Calvin's contribution to the problem is that, by finally complying with Dad's request, he reinforces the fact that screaming works. The thoroughly predictable conclusion to this series of interactions is that Calvin will have learned to put off doing things until his Dad raises his voice.

Without realizing why, I was experiencing the same thing with my students. I had to continually jack up my emotions to convince them that I was serious. Over time, even the emotional sledge hammer of a raised voice wasn't enough to keep things from falling apart. By the end of my third year of teaching, I was a mess and so was my class.

---

†   To avoid this, Dad needs some kind of system for following through on his stated expectations. With a bit of consistency and a means for monitoring compliance, Calvin will eventually learn to do what he is told the first time.

Five Long Years

Fast forward to year five of my budding teaching career. It was June, and I was cleaning up the classroom as I prepared for summer vacation. Having completed three items on my yard-long list of Things To Do, I started on number 4: *Clean off labels from flashcard rack.*

Things To Do

✓	Return books to back shelf
✓	Leave overhead w/custodian for repairs
✓	Throw out old clay under sink
	Clean off labels from flashcard rack
	Inventory P.E. equipment/replace
	Ask about new wall map

FIG. 2-1
My end of the year list of Things To Do.

We had been using a sheet of pegboard and cup hooks to hold individualized sets of flashcards. Each hook had an adhesive file label attached above it. Student names were written on the file labels; one hook and label for each student. The flashcards, held together by a metal split ring, hung from the hooks. All in all, it was an easy way to organize the sets of sight words.

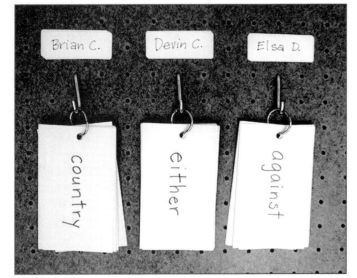

FIG. 2-2
Individualized sets of flashcards hang on the pegboard.

Since my school had a tremendously high transiency rate—it was located in a Navy housing area where a lot of families transferred in and out—some of the hooks would end up with 3 or 4 labels stacked on top of each other. At the end of each school year, I'd faithfully scrape off all of the old labels so that the board would be fresh for my new students.

Anyway, I was standing there scraping away, scraping away, scraping away, and I got to thinking that there had to be a better way to organize this flashcard thing so that I didn't have to scrape off the labels every year.

And that's when, of all the funny things, I got to thinking about my seventh grade P.E. coach, Mr. Biden. I remember that we used to start each class by meeting on one of the blacktop basketball courts. The courts were unusual in that they had numbers painted on them. Our court looked something like this:

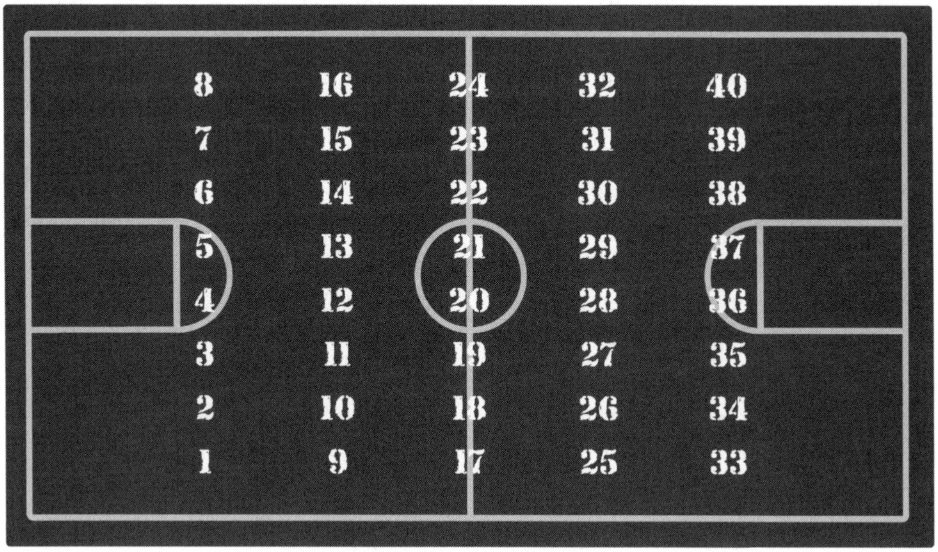

FIG. 2-3
The numbered basketball court on which we would gather for attendance.

8	16	24	32	40
7	15	23	31	39
6	14	22	30	38
5	13	21	29	37
4	12	20	28	36
3	11	19	27	35
2	10	18	26	34
1	9	17	25	33

On the first day of school, Coach Biden walked our class down to the basketball courts and had us stand on the perimeter of one of the courts. He then read the first name from the attendance sheet and called out, "One." The student named went and stood on the number 1. After everyone had been assigned a number, he then had us clear the court and play some hoops.

On the second day of P.E., I was hanging out with my friends on the basketball court. As soon as we saw Coach coming our way, we stood on our numbers so that Coach could take attendance. By the time he joined us, thirty-five boys were occupying thirty-five places on our grid. (Numbers 36-40 were empty because there were only thirty-five boys in our class.) Attendance took all of eight seconds—an empty number meant that the student was absent—and we were ready to play. It was such a wonderfully simple system.

What struck me during my moment of reflection, since I was looking back with a teacher's perspective, was the fact that the numbered court never had to be changed or updated. Coach Biden would just reassign numbers for each new group of students. Then I looked down at the label I was scraping off—Devin C.—and I thought:

---You know, if I numbered these hooks and assigned each student in my class a number, I'D NEVER HAVE TO SCRAPE LABELS AGAIN!

In the business, they call that an epiphany: a moment of thinking that produces a monumental change in life.

The wheels started to turn, and I realized that I could number all kinds of things in the classroom that had, in the past, been identified by names. Almost stunned by the possibilities, I resolved then and there to try the student number idea in September with my new class. I finishing scraping off the labels from the flashcard rack, applied new labels, and then numbered them from 1 to 36. Wow, it was already working! The flashcard rack was ready to go. I didn't have to wait until September when I received my roster of student names. Not only that, but when a student transferred in or out, I wouldn't have to apply new name labels, I could just reassign the number. Incredible.[†]

The New School Year

I'll tell you right now that there was a bit of resistance from some of the other teachers at my school when they learned that I was using student numbers. After all, none of them were using student numbers, and some of them had been teaching for almost thirty years. Who does this new kid think he is?

Their objections were something along these lines:

> *Cold.*
>
> *Heartless.*
>
> *Sounds like a factory to me.*
>
> *Aren't your students going to lose their identities?*

As it turned out, their objections were unfounded. They were based upon projection—what they thought would happen—and not on any actual experience. There was enough skepticism, though, that I thought maybe I was making a mistake trying to use student numbers in an elementary classroom. However, when I thought about my newly redesigned flashcard rack and all of the other student number uses I had planned for the year, my resolve grew strong. I was going to use numbers *and* make sure that none of the teacher's predictions came true. I wanted it to work, so I was going to make it work.

I'm happy to report that, from the beginning, it was an unqualified success. Life in the classroom was so much easier that year because we now had a foundation on which to organize the students and their materials. As the year progressed, we discovered more ways to use student numbers. By the end of that year, I was convinced that I would never try to run my classroom any other way. Student numbers just made too much sense.

The other teachers, though, were still not sold on the idea, and I found myself trying to defend the system. You might encounter the same thing at your school when the parents

---

†   Please bear in mind that I was a new teacher and somewhat easily impressed. Also, I hadn't seen any elementary teachers using this system, so I kind of felt as if I was blazing a new trail. It all seemed so fresh and exciting. Now that I think about it, I have to admit that it still is fresh and exciting. It's just not new; it's been around for a while.

of your students or the other teachers realize your intention to use the New Management system and the numbering that goes along with its use.[†]

It is understandable that they don't want the classroom to become sterile or depersonalized. No one wants to see that, especially you, the teacher. Nonetheless, a lack of understanding about the ultimate goal of the numbering concept could produce a bit of anxiety on the part of the uninitiated. By sharing the well-founded reasons for using numbers—which we'll cover in the rest of this lesson—you'll begin to dispel their apprehensions. And, as soon as the system moves into high gear, they'll become converts.

Teacher Benefits

Let's start with how student numbers will help you do your job so that the students can do theirs.

It's Really Quite Simple

Number one, it's simple. Hallelujah. There are enough complicated things going on in the classroom that we don't need to add to it. And, as you've no doubt already experienced, it's the simple ideas that you'll end up using.

The student number system will really simplify classroom management procedures in your room. And, since you can pick and choose how you wish to incorporate student numbers in your room, you can keep the whole process as simple as you wish.

In my room, there's a rather rich complexity; however, this is mainly due to the fact that I've been using this system for so long now, I've been able to develop more and more applications of the basic numbering format. Bear in mind, though, that you can start simply and build your own New Management program to meet not only your needs but also the needs of your students as well.

It's Extremely Efficient

The next point in favor of the student number system is that it's efficient, and efficiency feels good. (Personally, I've had a long relationship with efficiency. When I was in fourth grade, we had a career fair. Each student was supposed to make a presentation to the class about what future job he or she planned to have. When it was my turn, I got to share that I wanted to be an efficiency expert. I just thought it would be a cool job to figure out how to make things work better.)

In the classroom, efficiency is not a cold, scientific laboratory kind of thing; we're not talking white lab coats and clipboards. We're talking about being able to quickly com-

---

† *One reassuring note:* The use of student numbers has really increased over the past decade. It's no longer relegated to the lunatic fringe; it's gone mainstream. The reason it's gone mainstream? It flat out works. End of discussion.

plete tedious tasks so that you've got more time and energy to spend with your students.

Student numbers, and especially the tools created to put those numbers to work, will have you taking care of business like never before.

> *Major Benefit:* The speed and ease of grade keeping alone is worth the price of admission. I still smile and shake my head in disbelief when I think back to my early years of teaching. Before I started using student numbers, grade keeping was *so* time consuming. The stack of assignments I needed to record never matched the alphabetical order of my grade book. I'd have to scan up and down looking for each student before I could enter a grade. With things in numerical order, grade keeping is downright painless.

You'll find yourself using a system that will streamline your paper handling, improve your record keeping, and eliminate that overwhelming buildup of paperwork. You just won't believe the difference.†

It Will Reduce Your Stress

Raise your hand if you could use a bit of stress reduction in your position as educator. If you've been teaching for any length of time, it's likely that your hand is held high. Job-induced stress is the number one complaint of educators throughout the country.

> *The Reality of Stress:* According to the latest studies, stress is not brought about by how much pressure you have on your job. As you already know, educators have a massive amount of pressure. Believe it or not, the stress actually comes from feeling that you can't control the pressure.
>
> *Conclusion:* Control the pressure and you'll control your stress.

When the day begins to overwhelm us, our stress level can go through the ceiling, and we leave at the end of the day feeling overworked and under-appreciated. Before you are done with this book, you will have a set of tools in your possession which will reduce your stress and keep it in check.

It Will Put You in Control

Your students will see you as the kind of teacher who knows what's going on. This will be the result of having a system that provides you with student-by-student, subject-by-subject accountability on a daily basis. Nothing beats that kind of intimate knowledge for showing your students you're in control.

And the kind of control I'm talking about is a calm, non-emotional kind of control. It's a level of control that allows you to say something once to your class and they know that

---

† Look on the back cover of your book to see a typical comment shared by a veteran teacher just one week after attending a New Management workshop. You'll soon feel the same way.

you mean business. This will only be possible because of the support provided by your student number system. Your words will be the velvet glove; your system will be the iron fist.

Student Benefits

When speaking with parents or teachers about the advantages of using student numbers, don't over explain. Make it matter-of-fact. Talk to them as if student numbers were the most natural thing in the world. While you're talking, try to include these student benefits.

Student Responsibility

63

Tools & Toys

The numbering system is going to enhance responsibility. (Our *Class Pledge*, which we recite every morning, embodies this key trait. *As a member of Room 12, I pledge to: Respect myself by making good choices, respect my classmates by treating them kindly, and take responsibility for all of my actions.*) Experience has shown me that if you haven't got a student's head on straight, there's not much you can pour into it.

Imagine, if you will, that you've been selected as your district's Teacher of the Year. You possess exciting and motivating teaching techniques. You are well prepared and thorough in presentations. Your assignments are appropriate and your evaluations provide nurturing feedback. Nonetheless, you've got a Calvin—of Calvin and Hobbes fame—in your room this year, and Calvin is being irresponsible in a variety of ways. He is not engaging in the learning process. His assignments are late, incomplete, or missing. His sense of involvement is almost nonexistent. Consequently, most of your fine efforts are going to be wasted on Calvin unless we can do something about his rather anemic sense of responsibility. To do that, we need to give him a chance to develop it.

Now responsibility, we need to realize, is not something you can just talk about. Neither is it something that happens to kids merely because they are getting older.[†] Responsibility comes about through repetitive opportunities to exercise and practice it. Your most responsible students, the ones you usually call upon to take care of some bit of class business, are that way mainly because they've been given many opportunities to practice responsibility. And, since the majority of practice occurred in the home, they enter school with a lot of experience under their belts. The unfortunate outcome is that the students who aren't responsible when they first enter your room—the ones who need the most practice—are the ones given the fewest opportunities to work on it.

Let's use math to illustrate this point. It would be unfair to say to your eighth grade

---

† During seminars, I've asked sixth grade teachers if all of their students are responsible. This almost always gets a laugh. It does, however, drive home the point that one of the determiners of responsible behavior is not age but the issue of opportunity. How many opportunities has a student had in his life to practice responsibility? The answer, as we know, varies with each child.

algebra students that they should know how to reduce fractions based upon the fact that they're old enough to know how. The only reason your students would be able to perform this math skill is that they were given lessons and feedback at an appropriate time in their academic career. Knowledge of fractions came about through direct instruction and repetitive practice. Consequently, to assume this knowledge is a function of age is to misunderstand the fundamental principles of learning.

As ludicrous as it may sound, we sometimes take this position when it comes to responsibility. The child who messes up some classroom task is generally denied the chance to perform it again. It's so much easier to have someone more reliable take care of it. Unfortunately, we are denying these needier students some much needed practice.

You'll find that the student number system is loaded with simple, easy-to-use tools that any of your students can use to help take care of class business. And by having them help take care of things, you'll be providing them with the opportunities they need to develop their sense of responsibility.

Student Numbers Will Maximize Student Potential

I think everyone is aware of the fact that each student possesses strengths and weaknesses. The challenge to today's educator is how to become aware of these traits as quickly as possible. As you will soon experience, the numbering system—and especially the tools for tracking the completion of assignments—will put you in direct, immediate touch with your students and their needs.

And with this awareness will come the ability to reward or remediate. Your personal awareness of the individuality of your students, which will be projected in how you interact with them, will go a long way to convincing them that you have their best interests at heart.

Student Numbers Will Promote Involvement

power
love
fun
freedom
safety

Students, for the most part, want to be involved. They want to feel important and necessary. To promote this attitude and feed their need, I've learned to enlist their active participation in running the classroom.

Granted, there are many tasks that you, because of your experience, could take care of more expediently. Nonetheless, by trying to do everything, you end up depriving your students of those precious moments of involvement and, consequently, achievement.

What's needed are fail-safe techniques that the students can use to not only become involved in the management of the room but to do it efficiently. Since the New Management system provides these tools, everyone ends up winning. You win because important tasks are being taken care of, and the students win because of their heightened sense of responsibility, importance, and involvement.

In a very short while, you'll find yourself benefitting from one of the pleasant developmental corollaries of their involvement in your classroom: a reduction in what I call Teacher Welfare. Teacher Welfare occurs whenever the teacher is doing everything while the students sit back and watch. This natural tendency on the part of the teacher to be prominent and dominant actually hinders involvement which, again, hinders student achievement.

By promoting student involvement, you'll decrease the degree of Teacher Welfare in which you engage. At the same time, you'll be establishing an environment in which all of the members of the team—teacher *and* students—feel that their active participation, the very role they play, their contribution, is a crucial part of what makes your classroom such a successful place.

Student Numbers Are Fun

Let's face it: learning requires enthusiasm. One of the best ways to generate enthusiasm is to enjoy what you're doing. Student numbers will inject a much appreciated sense of excitement and energy into your classroom.

power
love
fun
freedom
safety

Now, I realize that fun is one of the five basic students needs that was identified in the Lesson 1. Redundancy notwithstanding, fun is such an important need that I just thought it deserved a bit more emphasis.

It's Just a Tool

Probably the safest point to make regarding this entire numbering process is that the number itself is just a tool. I never think of my students as numbers. They are Dick and Jane, Melody and Juanito. The concept that Dick is #3 and Jane is #14 is only a method we will be using in class to help create an environment that leads to student achievement: one of my major responsibilities as the teacher.

So let's get rid of any notions that this numbering idea is depersonalizing or insensitive. Nothing could be further from the truth. In fact, I've found that most students get quite attached to their numbers. I've even had high school kids—former students of mine—drop by to visit. While they're hanging out, they almost always want to know: "Who has my old number?"

The Bottom Line

In all of the years I've been using student numbers, only one parent has come in to complain. Like the teachers at the school where I first started using numbers, he knew nothing about the student number system and its amazing benefits. All he knew was that his son, Josh, had come home from school to announce that he was #17, and the father didn't want Josh to be thought of as a number.

After taking the time to carefully explain that this was not the case, I asked him to give the student number idea a month or so. It wasn't until parent/teacher conferences, two months later, that we got to talking about the student numbers. By that time, he had come to experience, through his son, how the numbers actually worked. And once he realized that student numbers enabled me to better help his son, he was all for it.

Review

Here's a brief review of the benefits of using student numbers. Keep in mind that, as you use student numbers, you'll soon be adding new benefits to these lists.

TEACHER BENEFITS
Simple
Efficient
Reduces Your Stress
Puts You in Control

STUDENT BENEFITS
Boosts Responsibility
Maximizes Potential
Promotes Involvement
Adds Some Fun

Lesson 3

Before We Begin

How It All Got Started

Numbering Your Students

Using Student Numbers

Timers & Sound Makers

Class Chart

Check Off List

Check Off Sheet

First Aid Kit

Grade Books

*What office is there
which involves more responsibility,
which requires more qualifications,
and which ought, therefore,
to be more honorable,
than that of teaching?*

— Harriet Martineau

Lesson 3
Numbering Your Students

◆ ◆

Goals for this lesson:

✓ Discover the two categories into which most student numbering procedures fall.

✓ Learn about a variety of student numbering procedures.

✓ Decide how you are going to number your students.

◆ ◆

The actual numbering part is fun because you get to involve your students right away. As I've already mentioned, one of New Management's main themes is that the students will become a working part of your classroom management system. An increase in the level of student involvement is one of the reasons why teachers who use New Management say the degree of effort required to handle their paperwork tasks goes down tremendously while student motivation and engagement goes way up.

The procedures used for numbering students fall into two categories.

1. **Alphabetical Order**

2. **Random Order**

Although many teachers give out student numbers randomly, the majority use alphabetical order. Both methods have their advantages and disadvantages. Let's start with alphabetical order.

Alphabetical Order

During my first ten years of using student numbers, the students were given their numbers according to the alphabetical order of their last names. The fact that I used the last name/alphabetical order method was the end result of the conditioning I had experienced as a student, a student teacher, and a new teacher. Just about everything pertaining to students was handled in alphabetical order. It seemed only logical to do the same with my own students.

On the first day of school[†], I would have my students form a line inside the room based upon the alphabetical order of their last names. After the students were in line, I checked to see how they had done. As soon as we had everyone in the proper place, I would have them count off. It was a simple way to assign numbers that also provided for a bit of student involvement.

One of the advantages to alphabetical order by last name was that my records lined up with the office records. If I needed to send something to the office in alphabetical order, I simply collected it in numerical order, and we were in business.

One of the disadvantages to alphabetical order by last name was that, whenever a new student was assigned to our class, our carefully crafted order was forever disrupted.

Since realphabetizing and renumbering seemed like a lot of work for very little gain, we learned to add new students to the end of our list. Or, if a student had transferred out, we could reassign the former student's number to the new student. The out-of-order student, of course, goofed up things alphabetically, but not by too great a degree. It was something with which we could live.

A second disadvantage to last name order was the fact that the students who were normally at the end of the list because of their last names were last yet again. Now, for me, this was never a big deal. Rick Morris was always in the middle; never first, never last. However, for the Zoltan family, it's back-of-the-bus time once again.

> *Reality:* I remember reading an op-ed piece in Newsweek regarding this issue. The woman who had written the article told about her daughter who was in fourth grade. Apparently, the daughter was in a classroom in which the teacher numbered students by alphabetical order. However, instead of using last names, the teacher alphabetized the students by their first names. For the first time, this particular family was able to move from the bottom of the list to the top. It was such a significant event that they actually held a family celebration on the night that the daughter, Alison, came home and made her announcement.

A Better Way to A, B, C

For the past ten years or so, I've switched from using last names to create alphabetical order and have been using first names instead. I've found that there are a few advantages to alphabetical order by first names.

---

† Rest reassured that you can start using the number system at any time during the school year. It doesn't have to be limited to the first week. Even if you only have another month with your students before your year is over, I'd recommend that you get started. The comfort base you've established with your current class during the course of your year together will help to make the transition to student numbers an easy one. Also, the experience you'll gain during that last month will enable you to start the system with your new students with a degree of confidence.

Advantage One

If you'll think about it for just a moment, you'll realize that, in the classroom, we use first names much more than last names. Doesn't it make sense, then, to base a management system on what we actually use as opposed to one based on tradition?

Advantage Two

With an order based on first names, it's actually easier to learn everyone's number. The alphabetical order becomes a bit of a mnemonic device. For example, during my last year of teaching I had two students named Jack and Karena. And although I was certain that they were using numbers 7 and 8, the fact that everyone was organized by first name eliminated the confusion about which one was Student #7 and which was Student #8.

A

Tara
Stephen
Matt
Iliana
Anna
Melissa
Jennifer
Marwa
David
Chi
Bobby
Andrew
Tammy
Nicholas
Malcolm
Erica
Elsa
Dustin
Sheryl
Waleed
Samantha
Shane
Briann
Kevin
Michael
Katie
Stephanie
Keir
Jonathan
Jaclyn
Brittany
Aliya
Cassandra
Lauren
Alric
Peter

B

Aliya
Alric
Andrew
Anna
Bobby
Briann
Brittany
Cassandra
Chi
David
Dustin
Elsa
Erica
Iliana
Jaclyn
Jennifer
Jonathan
Katie
Keir
Kevin
Lauren
Malcolm
Marwa
Matt
Melissa
Michael
Nicholas
Peter
Samantha
Shane
Sheryl
Stephanie
Stephen
Tammy
Tara
Waleed

Take a look at these two class lists. Although they both use the same student names, List A was created by using the students' last names—which aren't shown—to establish the order. List B used first names.

Notice how much easier it is to locate Andrew in List B than it is in List A.

FIG. 3-1 Alphabetical order by last name (left) versus alphabetical order by first name (right).

Advantage Three

Imagine I'm sitting at my desk getting ready to collect math scores from the students. We've just finished correcting an assignment, and they're sitting at their desks figuring out how many they answered correctly so that they can bring me their results. Even though my math grade sheet is in numerical order (more about this incredible time saver later on in Lesson 10) having their first names in alphabetical order makes it easier for me to find a student.

Here comes Victor with his assignment and his score. Let's see…Victor. (I scan toward the bottom of my grade sheet.) Ah, there he is, as I enter a score for Victor, student number 30.

Mazen	20		
Monty	21		
Nicole	22		
Nui	23		
Paul	24		
Ryan	25		
Sean	26		
Shandelle	27		
Steven	28		
Tuan	29		
Victor	30		
Wesley	31		

FIG. 3-2
Score sheet showing Victor and the ease of finding his name when they've been placed in alphabetical order.

Advantage Four

Accept the fact that you're not going to be able to maintain a list of students organized by last names. As important as that may seem right now—it's not, but appearances can be deceiving—it's just not going to happen. Students transfer in; students transfer out. It's the Classroom Circle of Life. Listing your students by first name, though, will completely eliminate the unnecessary pressure of trying to keep students in last name order.

Easy As 1, 2, 3

There have been a variety of procedures I've used over the years to establish alphabetical order. Every single one of them involved the students in some manner. Here's an example:

On Your Mark...

Although I used to assign student numbers on the first day of school, I no longer do that. There is just so much uncertainty—at least at my school—about my class roster the first day. Have the missing students transferred to another school or will they show up in a day or so? Will I be receiving any late-enrolling students? Etc., etc.

Consequently, I've learned it's actually better if I wait until the end of the first week of school. So, on Friday of the first week, after a brief dialogue about the importance of having a student number, I'll explain the basic Get A Number Procedure.[†]

MR. MORRIS

In just a few minutes I'm going to ask everyone to get in line in alphabetical order. We'll be using your first names to make the line. I'd like you to close your eyes and picture your first name. You should really be able to see it.

Modeling with his eyes closed:

I can see my first name. It's R-I-C-K. I can see it written in capital letters on our whiteboard. Keep trying until you can clearly picture your first name.

Dramatic pause:

Okay, open your eyes and I'll show you where we're going to get in line.

Indicating the front of the room:

Let's start the line right here. The A's will be here and the line will go this way so that we end up with the Z's over here.

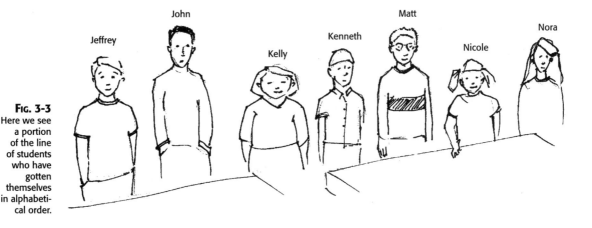

FIG. 3-3
Here we see a portion of the line of students who have gotten themselves in alphabetical order.

---

† If the method I'm describing doesn't fit your needs or seems inappropriate for your students, don't worry. There are a handful of ways you could achieve the same end, several of which are explained later on in this lesson.

On Your Mark, Get Set...

MR. MORRIS

Close your eyes again and picture your first name. Now, imagine I tapped you on the shoulder and asked you to find your place in the line. Where do you see yourself going? Are you going to walk to the front of the line, the middle of the line, or the end of the line? Since my name starts with R, I'd head for the middle of the line. See yourself doing this.

Another pause.

Now, if you're really trying hard, you'll be able to picture other students heading to your same area. Now what? Let's open our eyes and find a few volunteers to demonstrate.

You can always get kids to volunteer. Pick three, and ask them to stand at the front of the room. Remind them about the A to Z orientation of the line and let them organize themselves alphabetically. As they begin to share and compare, I do my standard voice-over.

MR. MORRIS

Notice how all three of them are involved.

power
love
fun
freedom
safety

(If they had been just standing there, they might start to interact with each other. If they continued to doing nothing, I'd give them some private instructions about the need to show the class how this line thing is going to work.)

Notice how they are sharing their names and listening to each other. Look at that, they're getting in order. Let's see how they did.

Stepping up to the first student:

Your name, please.

FIRST STUDENT

Benjamin.

MR. MORRIS

Thank you, Benjamin.

Moving to the next student in line:

And what is your name?

SECOND STUDENT

Kyle.

MR. MORRIS

Thanks, Kyle.

Placing a hand on the head of the last student:

And how about your first name?

THIRD STUDENT

Torey.

MR. MORRIS

Thank you, Torey.

Turning to the class:

Are these three students in the correct order?

Benjamin   Kyle   Torey

First week of school? They won't know. They're wondering why they're not still in their jammies watching cartoons. But, you know how kids are. They'll try to fake it.

STUDENTS
Not sure but knowing they need to respond:
Yeah.

MR. MORRIS
Giving them a quizzical look:
It is???

STUDENTS
Thoroughly confused:
No!

It's a rather sad state of affairs that students have been conditioned to respond not to the question being asked but how the teacher phrases and states it. This is just another example of Teacher Welfare in which the teacher is doing most of the heavy lifting.

MR. MORRIS
Hey, I have an idea. Why don't we pay attention this time. We need to know if these three students are in the correct alphabetical order.

Although school has only been in session for five days, I'm already setting the standard for active participation and intelligent involvement.

MR. MORRIS
Pointing to the handwriting chart on the front wall:
If you wish, you can refer to the alphabet up here on the wall. Okay, here we go. Name, please.

This time, as each student spoke his name, I thanked the child and pointed out the first letter of his name on the handwriting chart.

MR. MORRIS
After hearing from all three students:
Now then, using your fingers, I'd like you to show me what you think about this order. If this is the correct order, hold up one finger. If it is not correct, hold up two fingers. If you're not sure, hold up a fist.

A quick check showed that most of the students thought our volunteers had done it correctly. The three students returned to their seats, and we were ready to have the class get in line.

power
love
fun
freedom
safety

(I know this may all seem like a bit of overkill; nonetheless, I've learned that students need clear, effective modeling before they can successfully engage in a brand new task. It's just part of how I work to keep the classroom safe and loving.)

On Your Mark, Get Set, Go!

MR. MORRIS

Okay, I think we're ready for everyone to get in line. I'll give you five minutes. Remember: we're going to use first names. Make sure you share your name with the students near you in line and listen for theirs. Any questions before we begin? No? Okay, please find your place in line now.

As the students head to the line, I make an effort to stay out of their way. If things are not going as smoothly as I thought they should, I'll give the students an opportunity to figure it out.

As teachers, we have been conditioned to jump in during times of trouble. ("Hi, can I help?") I'm not against helping, mind you, but one of the drawbacks to jumping in too quickly is that the students give up. They're thinking, "Oh, good. The teacher's here. We don't have to figure this out." This is not a good precedent to establish during the first week of school. I'll help if I absolutely need to, but maybe I should wait and see what they can achieve on their own.

As long as we're pondering the possibilities of there being problems, what about Calvin who is still sitting in his seat? Although he heard the lesson on getting in line and he heard me say, "Please find your place in line now," he's still in his seat. He's probably thinking that since I haven't yelled yet, I'm not really serious about what I had asked everyone to do.

In these situations, I recommend that you leave him alone for right now. We can always help him find his place in line later. What I don't want to do is walk over to him and ask him again to find his place in line. I don't want him to get the feeling that I'll be asking him two or three times to do things. As I said, forget him for the moment; we can get him in line later if we have to. Right now, though, I want to focus my energies on the students who are following directions and doing things the right way.

About the only time I do jump in is when I see someone trying to "mother" other students into place.

MR. MORRIS

Guiding a girl away from the two boys she was trying to help:

Excuse me, little girl. Where do you belong? Way over there, huh? Well, why don't you find your place, and we'll let these two boys find their own places. It's nice of you to help, but they need to do it themselves. Okay?

At the end of five minutes, we'll have some kind of a line. I then go down the line asking for names and rearranging them as required. I said, "...rearranging them as required" because, frankly, I'd be shocked if they were able to get themselves in the proper order.

> *Fair Warning:* Not once, during the first ten years of having students get into line alphabetically, was there ever a group of students who did it correctly. I realize that it seems as if this activity is something they should be able to pull off; unfortunately, experience has shown that this has not been the case. So, don't be too surprised if you have to make adjustments.

Once we've established the proper order, each student is then given a student number.

MR. MORRIS
> *Nice job of getting in line. Here comes your number.*
Pointing at the first student:
> *One.*
Pointing at the next student and pausing:
SECOND STUDENT
> *Two.*
MR. MORRIS
> *Good!*
Pointing at the third student:
THIRD STUDENT
> *Three.*
Pointing at the fourth student:
FOURTH STUDENT
> *Four.*

And on we go until we've reached the last student. We then repeat the count off to help ensure that everyone has his number firmly in mind. After that, they head to their seats and write their numbers next to their names on their name tags.

Do I Have To Do It That Way?

The method I just described may have seemed to you like a lot of effort to number a group of students. You might even be thinking: "Couldn't I just take my roster home and number them myself?" Sure you could but, once again, you'd be engaging in Teacher Welfare. Experience has taught me that I should try to involve the students in even the simple things. I've learned that I can't accurately predict what they're going to find valuable or motivating. So, forego the expedient, do-it-yourself route, and give the kids a chance to participate.

Please don't think, though, that the example just given is the only way you can create alphabetical order. There are, as you might imagine, a number of other ways to not only assign your students their numbers but also involve them in the process.

Letter Groups

First graders would most likely have a hard time organizing themselves into an alphabetical order line. Nonetheless, I'm guessing that they would still enjoy the opportunity to participate in the Get A Number procedure.

Here's how one first grade teacher told me she did it:

Before the procedure:

1. She bought a blue vinyl pocket chart, the kind that has ten rows of clear vinyl for holding sentence strip paper.
2. Using a black permanent marker, she wrote student numbers on the clear vinyl. She started on the third row—which left room at the top for a title or what have you—and working down the left side wrote the numbers 1 through 7. The middle column was for 8 through 14 while the right-hand column was for 15 through 21.
3. When she was done she hung the chart at the front of the room.

During the procedure:

1. She gave each of her first graders a 3 x 8 inch piece of construction paper.
2. She then asked them to write their first names on the cards. "Use a dark crayon and make your name nice and large."
3. After they've had a chance to write their names, she asked any student whose name started with "A" to bring the card to the front of the room.
4. She placed the "A" cards in the blue vinyl pocket chart.
5. She quickly arranged the cards in alphabetical order. (You could ask your students to help you do this if you're feeling brave.)
6. She then repeated steps 3, 4, and 5 for each letter of the alphabet.
7. After she'd collected everyone's card and double-checked to make sure the cards were in the proper order, she showed them the final results.

Bonus: She ended up with an easy-to-update Class Chart. (See Lesson 6.)

Fig. 3-4
Student created name cards displayed in alphabetical order.

Write Names and Tape to the Board

A simple variation of the above method would be to pass out 6 x 12 inch pieces of paper to your students. Have them write their first names in crayon on the paper. Encourage them to write large enough so that everyone will be able to see it. As they finish, have them bring you their names and tape them to the whiteboard. Working with your class, arrange the names in alphabetical order. When finished, write a number on each sheet of paper and transfer them to a bulletin board.

Student Introductions

This technique is a great one—we used it several years ago—but it will only work on the first day of school.

1. Students took turns walking to the front of the room and introducing themselves.

   "Hi. My name is Alex Ramon. I was in Room 8 last year. I like to play soccer and Nintendo. My favorite subject is reading."

2. Alex wrote his name on the whiteboard and then sat down.

FIG. 3-5
Student names written on the board during introductions.

3. Every student copied Alex's name on a sheet of paper.
4. Another student went to the front of the room, introduced himself, wrote his name on the board, and then returned to his seat.
5. After every student had had a turn and everyone had a list of names, the students then worked at putting the names in alphabetical order.
6. Announce numbers after you've compared lists.

Send Home a Roster of Names

This idea is a great one because it can be used at any time of the year.

All you need to do is create a list of student names—make xerox copies of your attendance sheet—and then distribute a copy to each student. The students would then take home the list and figure out the alphabetical order. The lists would be compared in class the next day and numbers given out.

Suggestion: If you do use a xerox copy of your attendance folder, make sure you indicate the actual name each student will be using. Otherwise, you might end up with William's name on your list when, in actuality, he prefers to be called Billy.

How Can I Number You?

Let me count the ways. Once again, it's up to you and your students. Involvement of students, though, should be one of your priorities.

Variations on a Random Theme

If, for whatever reason, you don't want to use alphabetical order, feel free to number your students in some other fashion. There are lots of ways you could do it.

Here are but a few of many possibilities:

Circus Theme

A kindergarten teacher I met through our mentor program was doing a circus theme one year. To assign student numbers, she wrote the numbers 1 through 25 on separate slips of paper. She placed one numbered slip inside of a balloon. After blowing up the balloons, she ended up with twenty-five balloons with numbered slips hidden inside.

power
love
fun
freedom
safety

At some appropriate point in the morning, the balloons were piled in the center of the room. The students were then told to get a balloon, pop it, and find the piece of paper hiding inside. She said the kids loved it. (She obviously has a high threshold for loud noises, or maybe it's just a by-product of teaching kindergarten for twenty years.)

Cups of Punch

A second grade teacher told me she used small Dixie cups filled with grape punch for assigning numbers. Before filling the cups, she took a felt tip marker and wrote numbers on the inside bottom of the cups.

power
love
fun
freedom
safety

She passed out the cups of punch to her second graders and then offered a toast to a successful year.

One of the students, having finished his punch, noticed a number on the bottom of his cup and announced, "Hey, there's a number in my cup." Whereupon everyone else quickly gulped down their punch and found their own numbers.

Numbered Desks

Another teacher told me that he has the desks numbered and in order (very efficient) and that he stands by his door on the first day of school and passes out numbered disks. He then tells the students to find the seat that matches the number they were given.

Being an experienced guy and knowing that his students come to school in little cliques, he has the disks all mixed up. In this way, the three buddies who come walking through the door together are getting 4, 19, and 28 and thus are spread around the room. Very clever.

The Sacred Number

One of my favorite techniques comes from a guy who makes a real ritual out of assigning student numbers. He uses the same basic technique that the kindergarten teacher used with the slips of paper and balloons; however, he put his numbered slips of paper in plastic film canisters. (You can still find these at most photo processing stores.)

He had thirty canisters already prepared for the first day of school. Then, when the students went out to morning recess, he added any extra ones he may have needed to match his class count. He then placed all of the film canisters in a large crystal punch bowl and waited for his students to return from recess.

When his students came back in, they were greeted by a darkened room and a candle burning on each side of the bowl of canisters. To add to the dramatic effect, he turned off the lights.

FIG. 3-6
A punch bowl filled with canisters of numbers sits between two lighted candles.

TEACHER
   With palms pressed together:
      You're now going to get your sacred student number. You may walk past and take one container.
   Pause while everyone walked up to retrieve one from the bowl.
      You may now open your sacred container and find your number.

All in all, it would make for an exciting, if unusual, beginning to the year.

Fishing

I heard about a teacher who was in the middle of the school year when she learned about using student numbers and decided she didn't want to wait for next year to try it out. At the time, her students were involved in an oceanography unit. She decided to use their science theme for their student number procedure.

She cut out paper fish, numbered them, and then attached a paper clip to each one. She put the fish in an empty aquarium and then provided the students with a special fishing pole to use for catching the numbered fish. As you can image, there was a magnet attached to the end of the fishing line. The students took turns "fishing" and ended up "catching" their numbers.

FIG. 3-7
Fishing for numbers with a magnet tied to the end of the fishing line.

Let Them Choose

One year, my students were allowed to choose their own numbers. It was the first year of my job share and my partner, JoAnn, asked me how we should give out numbers.

Not wishing to force my way of doing things on our new partnership, I responded with, "I don't care. What do you want to do?"

power
love
fun
freedom
safety

"How about if we let them choose their own numbers?" she suggested.

Since I had never done it that way before, I said, "What the heck. Let's give it a try."

MR. MORRIS
Addressing his new group of fifth graders:

Okay, guys, we need to give out student numbers now. Mrs. Stoll and I would like you to choose your own number this year. Since we have twenty-nine students, you may choose from numbers 1 through 29. When you have decided upon a number you'd like to have, come up and let me know what it is. You might want to decide upon two or three numbers in case your first choice has already been taken. Anyway, think of a number and come on down.

I had eight students at my desk in a heartbeat. These eight students had been with me two years earlier when I was teaching third grade.

Guess what they wanted? That's right. They wanted their numbers from third grade.

> *Reality:* It's amazing the attachment students develop for their numbers. I remember flying home to San Diego from Phoenix one Friday night after having conducted a week's worth of seminars. Sitting next to me in the back of the plane was a young man in his early twenties. As we got to talking about what we had been doing in Phoenix——he had been building custom fireplaces; I had been working with teachers—he got a funny look in his eye. "You're Mr. Morris, aren't you?" he asked. It turned out that he had been one of my students years ago. When I told him that I was now showing other teachers how we ran our class—student numbers, etc.—he smiled. "I still remember my number, Mr. Morris. It was 6. It's been my lucky number ever since fourth grade."

The first student in line was my little buddy, Marshal.

MR. MORRIS
   Marshal, I'm just guessing, but, would you like number 19?

MARSHAL
   Yeah, Mr. Morris.

MR. MORRIS
   It's all yours.

I then wrote "Marshal" next to the 19 on my Check Off List. (The blackline master is in the appendix.) Five minutes later, everyone had a number, and we were ready to go.

```
19 Marshal
20
21
```

It's Up to You

As you can see by now, there are as many ways of assigning numbers as there are teachers reading this book. My one suggestion is:

power
love
fun
freedom
safety

Involve your students so that they are a part of the process.

Recommended: If you're not sure which method you should try, use alphabetical order by first name. All-in-all, I truly feel this is the best way to go. However, like every other part of this New Management business, it's your call.

A Class Roster

In order to make a Class Chart in Lesson 6, you're going to need a master list of student names and the numbers they were assigned. In a few of the "Get A Number" procedures you just read, the teacher didn't end up with such a list.

On the next page you'll find a review of the different methods and whether or not the teacher ended up with a written list of student names and assigned numbers.

Alphabetical Order

Students Form a Line
Students were given a number which they wrote on their desktop name tags; teacher did not end up with a master list.

Letter Groups
Index cards with first names were placed in a numbered pocket chart which could be considered a master list.

Write Names and Tape to the Board
Student names (written on 6″ by 12″ paper) were arranged on the board in alphabetical order; a number was written on each sheet. The now numbered name strips were transferred to a bulletin board which created a master list.

Student Introductions
Students were given a number; teacher did not end up with a master list.

Send Home a Roster of Names
Students were given a number; teacher created a master list.

Random Order

Circus Theme
Each student held a numbered slip of paper; teacher did not end up with a master list.

Cups of Punch
Each student had a paper cup with a number written in it; teacher did not end up with a master list.

Numbered Desks
Each student ended up sitting at a numbered desk; teacher did not end up with a master list.

The Sacred Number
Each student held a numbered slip of paper; teacher did not end up with a master list.

Fishing
Each student held a numbered paper fish; teacher did not end up with a master list.

Let Them Choose
Each student chose a number; teacher wrote the student's name next to the number on a Check Off List.

And let's not overlook the very real possibility that you went your own way and came up with a unique method for assigning student numbers. Do you have a master list?

Making a Roster

If you used one of these methods and did not end up with a master list of names and numbers, you should probably make one after all the numbers have been assigned. The information on this roster will be used in Lesson 6 when you make your Class Chart,† a bulletin board display that shows the names and numbers of your students.

Class Roster
ASSIGNMENT

Sept. 10
DATE DUE

1 Amanda	19 Marshal
2 Andrew	20 Michelle
3 Cara	21 Moises
4 Chris	22 Nickie
5 Daniel	23 Oscar
6 Derick	24 Peter
7 Emily	25 Rick
8 Eric	26 Ryan
9 Gina	27 Tamara
10 Gwen	28 Tim
11 Heather	29 Torey
12 Jenny	30 Yolanda
13 Justin	31
14 Karen	32
15 Kell	33
16 Laurie	34
17 Louie	35
18 Mark	36

✗ finished   ⊕ not finished   ⚠ absent

FIG. 3-8
This list of student names and numbers will be used later to build a Class Chart.

1. Make a copy of the Check Off List found in the appendix.
2. Cut it in half.
3. Write "Class Roster" on the ASSIGNMENT line.
4. Add today's date on the DATE DUE line.
5. Announce to your students that you are going to make a class roster by writing their first names next to their numbers.
6. Call out the first number.
7. Write down the name you hear.
8. After you've written down all of the names, save your roster for making your Class Chart.

The Chinese character at the top of the Check Off List is a 12, the number of our classroom. It was painted by my teaching partner, JoAnn Stoll, a noted Chinese brush artist. We use this logo throughout the year on notes, posters, and correspondence. We even silk screen it on T-shirts. You might want to consider asking your students to design a logo for your class.

---

† If you wish, you could skip the class roster step and write the names directly on a large sheet of butcher paper. You would just have to have it up on the wall before you began the "Get A Number" procedure.

Brace Yourself

Although making a roster may have seemed like a simple thing to do, you might want to prepare yourself for the following situation.

> Mr. Morris
>> *Number 1?*
>
> Student 1
>> *Alicia.*
>>> Writing Alicia's name next to the 1 on my Check Off List:
>> *Thanks, Alicia. Number 2?*
>
> Student 2
>> *Bradley.*
>
> Mr. Morris
>> *Do you want to be called Brad or Bradley?*
>
> Student 2
>> *I like to be called Bradley.*
>>> Writing Bradley's name next to the 2 on my Check Off List:
>> *Thank you, Bradley. Who has student number 3?*

No response.

> *Who has student number 3?*

Again, nothing.

It happens almost every year. One of my students is just not paying attention to what we are doing and, therefore, does not hear his number being called. This probably has more to do with the fact that it takes a bit of time before students "take ownership" of their numbers. It's really nothing to worry about. I've learned to just skip over number 3 and come back to it later.

What you wouldn't want to do at this point would be to express your displeasure or frustration at student number 3's lack of attentiveness. Remember that you told your students that this numbering idea was going to be fun? There's nothing fun about being spotlighted for not paying attention.

power
love
fun
freedom
safety

So, go easy on anyone who doesn't respond the first time you try to use his number. After all, it does take a bit of time for them to develop their number awareness, and we wouldn't want anyone's initial interaction with the New Management system to be a negative one.

After you've called everyone's number and have written a name beside each one, set your Check Off List aside. You'll be using it in Lesson 6.

Name, Number, Date

Now that your students have their numbers, you'll want them to start writing their numbers on their assignments. To help facilitate this process, you should make a sample chart and hang it on the wall for reference.[†]

FIG. 3-9
A tagboard poster for reminding students to write their numbers on their assignments.

As the sample above shows, I have my students write their numbers next to their names. To me, your number is a part of your class identity, and I like to see them together.

Many teachers have told me, though, that they actually prefer to have the students write their numbers in the upper right-hand corner of their papers. This makes the number stand out a bit more.

FIG. 3-10
Alex has written his number in the upper right-hand corner of his assignment.

Another teacher, who plays bridge with her friends, told me that she likes the number in the upper *left-hand* corner. With a stack of papers in her hand, she can fan them out like a hand of cards and see everyone's number. Once again, we see a clever teacher variation of a basic technique.

Regardless of where you decide to have your students write their numbers, accept the fact that some students will take longer than others to develop the "name/number" habit. Try not to let it get to you. Concentrate on the students who are doing a good job, and console yourself with the fact that the others will eventually get on board.

---

† Check out Music Central on my website for a slick little song you can play as a reminder to your students about writing name, number, and date on assignments. It's the old NBC station identifier that used chimes. I merely reconditioned my students to think Name-Number-Date instead of N-B-C when they hear the three notes. Works like a charm.

Last Thoughts

A quick review of Lesson 3 shows that you have:

✓ *Numbered your students,*

✓ *Made a class roster on a Check Off List, and*

✓ *Put up a poster to remind your students to write their numbers on their assignments.*

Now that you've completed those tasks, I'd like you to think about a couple of things.

power
love
fun
freedom
safety

1. Ensure that your interactions are name-based.
2. Make an effort to keep the student number system non-threatening. (Don't expect them to respond instantly when you call out a number.)
3. Give your students a week or so to get used to having a number. (Be patient as they slowly learn to write their numbers on their papers.)
4. Practice simple number procedures such as lining up in numerical order.
5. If you're feeling brave, try a "count off" in which each student will say his number out loud.

   Note: Since the students each have a number, I felt I should have one also. My number has always been zero.

   MR. MORRIS
      With everyone's attention:
        Count off, please...Zero!

   STUDENT 1
      One!

   STUDENT 2
      Two!

   ETC., ETC.

6. Remember that you've got your students all year and that there's no need to build an elaborate number system right now.

   By the way: If you're concerned about how to handle a new student who enrolls after you've numbered everyone, don't be. It happens. Experience taught me that it just wasn't as big a deal as I had thought it might be. Check out Frequently Asked Questions, Lesson 3, for some suggestions and encouragement.

Other than that, you're done with Lesson 3 and have set the stage for some truly exciting changes in your classroom this year.

Lesson 4

Before We Begin

How It All Got Started

Numbering Your Students

Using Student Numbers

Timers & Sound Makers

Class Chart

Check Off List

Check Off Sheet

First Aid Kit

Grade Books

Coming together is a beginning;
Keeping together is progress;
Working together is success.

—*Henry Ford*

Lesson 4
Using Student Numbers

◆ ◆

Goals for this lesson:

☑ Organize your textbooks and materials by number.

☑ Organize your students during disaster drills and field trips by number.

☑ Establish order and fairness when taking turns or playing games with numbers.

☑ Create some wonderfully simple, yet extremely effective, student number tools.

☑ Realize that there are a million ways you can use student numbers.

◆ ◆

One of the joys of the New Management system of student management, motivation, and involvement is that it will improve with age. Unlike other classroom innovations that seem to run out of steam in a year or two, you'll soon discover that the more you use student numbers, the more useful they'll become. The time and effort you spend creating a management system based upon student numbers will pay off for years to come. With that reassuring thought in mind, let's begin to put those student numbers to work so that you and your students can take advantage of the power of numbers.

In this lesson, I'll describe a boatload of ways you can use student numbers in your classroom. Eventually, though, you'll find yourself—and your students!—coming up with your own variations and spin-offs. To get us started, though, let's take a look at how student numbers can help you take care of your classroom materials.

As you already know, one of your jobs is to effectively manage the materials that have been provided for your students. From textbooks to crayons to dictionaries to glue sticks, it's your job to make sure that you conserve and protect these items. If you don't have an efficient, systematic way to keep track of everything, the stress of lost books, unclaimed scissors, and the stray crayons left on the floor at the end of the day will wear you out. It's just one more source of stress in an already stress-filled situation. As we learned in Lesson 2, though, if you can control the pressure of your situation, you can reduce your stress.

Here, then, are a handful of ways that student numbers will help you to manage your materials more effectively.

Classroom Books

Classroom books fall into two categories:

1. Books you will keep all year
   textbooks

2. Books you will only have for a short period of time
   core lit books
   library sets

Let's take a look at the permanent sets of books first.

Textbooks

There are several sets of textbooks—literature, math, and social studies, for example—that have been allocated to my classroom. Since I'll be using these books for many years, it's important that I make an effort to ensure that they are well taken care of by the students to whom they are given. As you can probably guess by now, one of the best ways to get a handle on textbook maintenance is to number each book.

Whenever I receive a new set of textbooks, I sit down with a marker[†] and number them all. The books are then given to the students. All extra copies are placed on one of the bookshelves in our back closet.

Fig. 4-1
Numbered textbooks and shelf where extra copies are stored until needed.

[†]   I like to use a Sharpie felt-tip, permanent marker. Sharpie's are cheap and dependable. The fine tip seems to work the best.

Although I've tried placing the numbers in various locations, I've found that writing it on the page edges seems to work the best. Since the pages are always white, the number stands out clearly. Also, there's no wear and tear on that part of the book, so the numbers won't fade or wear off as the books are used.

An additional advantage to writing the number on the outside surface of the book (as opposed to the inside cover) is that it will enable you and your students to spot the number quickly. A book that has been left lying around the room gets back to the owner with little hassle or delay. This means you'll no longer find yourself holding up an abandoned math book as you plaintively wail the never-answered question: "Whose book is this?"†

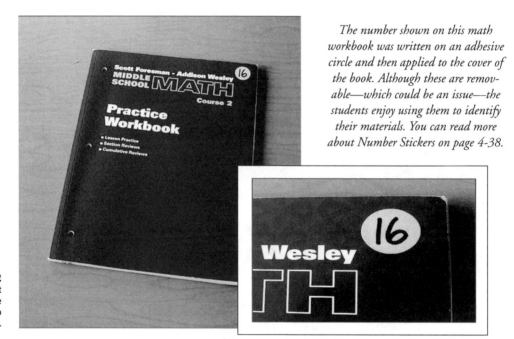

The number shown on this math workbook was written on an adhesive circle and then applied to the cover of the book. Although these are removable—which could be an issue—the students enjoy using them to identify their materials. You can read more about Number Stickers on page 4-38.

FIG. 4-2
Book left out on a table waiting to be returned.

At the end of the year, I'll collect the books in numerical order and store them in the closet until the beginning of the next school year. Anyone who does not return his book—which will be glaringly obvious during the collection process—will be required to pay for a replacement book.

> *Suggestion:* Make sure that your students and their parents understand your book replacement policy at the beginning of the school year. My students are all required to sign a form which states that they are responsible for all textbooks given to them. After signing the form—what we call a *Teacher/ Student Agreement*—the students take home a copy of the agreement for their parents to read and sign. By apprising the students and their parents in this fashion, no one will be surprised later on when they receive a bill for a lost book.

75
Tools & Toys

---

† What you're really saying to your class is, "I don't know what's going on in here. Haven't got a clue. Things are out of control." Not a good message.

Having the books numbered will also make it easier for you to deal with book handling whenever a student transfers out of the room. A couple of years ago, Andrew—who was student number 2 that year—moved to another school. Before he left, I gathered up his textbooks and placed them together on the shelf in our closet. There they sat until March.

Around the middle of March a new student, Nestor Gonzales, was assigned to our classroom. After a brief introductory moment, during which he was assigned number 2, I walked over to the closet, scooped up the stack of books he was going to need, and placed them on his desk. Nestor was up-and-running is no time flat.

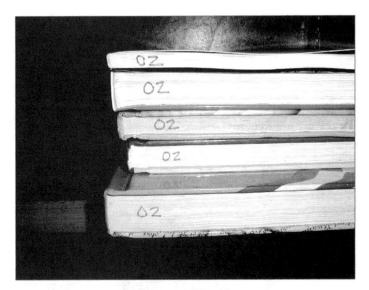

Fig. 4-3
Nestor's new set of books.

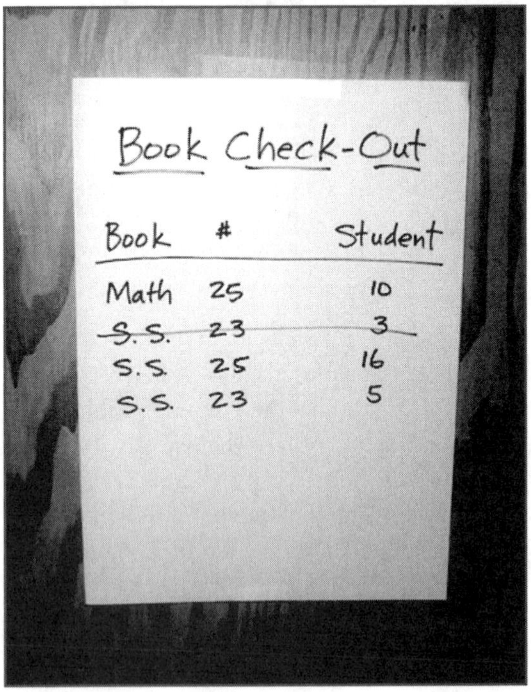

Recommended: Taped to the inside of the closet door where we keep our textbooks is a chart listing the extra copies available. For those times when someone needs to borrow a book, all I have to do is grab a copy and jot down the student number and date next to the book number. When the copy has been returned, the borrower's number is crossed out.

Fig. 4-4
Closet chart of unused books.

Teacher Tip

Here's an idea for the last day of school when you're gathering everyone's textbooks to store until the beginning of the next year.

1. Clean 'em out.

Have the students go through their books and remove old papers.

2. Stack 'em up.

After the books have been purged, the students then stack their books on their desks for you to check.

3. Verify and record.

Check that each student is returning the entire set of books given out and record this information on a grade sheet.

4. Bag 'em.

Give each student a large, brown grocery bag. The students then place their set of books in the bag.

5. Write a letter.

Each student writes a letter to next year's student. For example, Student #12 would write: "Dear #12, Let me tell you a bit about your number." The completed letter is laid on top of the books, and the bag is taped shut.

6. Decorate 'em.

power
love
fun
freedom
safety

As a final touch, the students decorate the bags with crayons to look like birthday presents. At the beginning of the next school year, each of your new students would receive a brightly colored bag o' books.

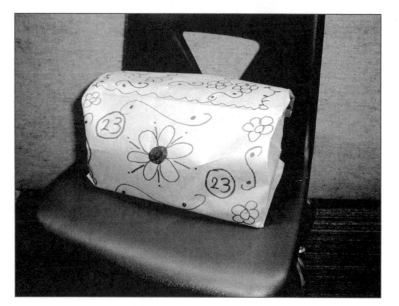

FIG. 4-5
Bag of books to be distributed at the beginning of the new year.

A Temporary Set of Books

Some of the books I use, novel sets, author sets, or core lit readers, for example, are only kept for a brief time and then returned to our district's central library. Thus, a small set of books is able to circulate so that many classes can use them. Unfortunately, so many sets had been sent back incomplete because of lost or missing books, schools are now being billed for each unreturned book. Since the bill is paid out of the school site's material fund, the principal is given a copy of the bill and a list of missing books. As you can imagine, it's critical that I manage these sets of books with diligence.

Since I don't want to deface the books by writing numbers on the outside, I'll place the numbers in a more discrete location: the inside back cover.

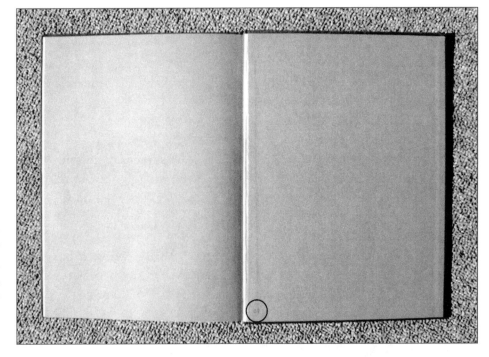

Fig. 4-6 Book opened to the back cover and close-up of the number written discretely in the bottom corner.

For these numbers, I'll use a fine tip ball-point pen. The ink is permanent while the fine point allows me to keep the numbers small.

Notice how I wrote number 7 as 07. I do this with all numbers less than 10. This will prevent someone from changing a 4 to a 14 or a 24.

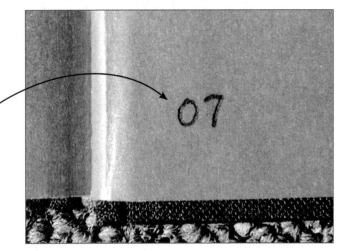

power
love
fun
freedom
safety

This simple step will not only promote responsibility in taking care of things, but will also help to create an environment of safety: one of the five basic student needs.

To illustrate this point, let's go back to my first five years of teaching when I was using the "Who Knows What's Going On" method of management.

The core lit books would be delivered to my school like clockwork every three weeks.

The rules were simple:
1. Use these books for three weeks.
2. Return them to the central library at the end of the three-week period of time.
3. For every book you don't return, we'll send a bill to your school.
4. Enjoy the books.

Mr. Morris (Rookie Teacher)
Thinking to himself:
Enjoy the books? How were we supposed to do that and still get them all back in three weeks? Surely we're going to lose one or two. Wouldn't it be a whole lot easier to just keep the books in the box for three weeks and then return the whole set? That's the only way I was going to get them all back.

Actually, it would be easier to do that; but, of course, I couldn't. I needed to pass them out and use them in the way they were intended to be used.

At that time, though, I didn't have a system in place for managing the classroom. This lack of organization meant that there was not going to be a reliable way for me to maintain our collection of books. About the only tools I had to bring about compliance were fear and intimidation: my fear that I wouldn't have all 36 books to give back to the district's central library, and my intimidation of the students, based on my fear, to hang on to their books.

Mr. Morris
Waving a copy of the newly arrived books:
Okay, guys. Here are your new core lit books. It's really important that you hang on to them. They're due in just three weeks. If you don't have yours, the school is going to charge you $18.00 because that's how much these books cost. Please take care of them.

Two-and-a-half weeks later, as we're reading aloud from our core lit books, I notice that Calvin doesn't have his book. He's looking on with another student.

Mr. Morris
Calvin? Your book? Where is it?

CALVIN
Oh, I took it home last night and forgot to bring it back.

MR. MORRIS
Starting to get worried about the fact that the books need to be returned in just a couple of days:
Hey, you need to bring it back. We have to send them all back this Friday, remember? $18.00?

Now what if Calvin can't find his book. Do you think he's going to bring in a check for $18.00? Not bloody likely. There's no way he could ask his dad for that much money. Dad would backhand him across the room. So, what's he going to do?

Well, if you've been teaching for awhile, you're most likely thinking, "He's going to steal someone else's book."

And you'd be right.

Calvin, in an attempt to escape his responsibilities, will most likely try to snag someone's book to replace the one he took home and can no longer find. He'll scope out the room to see which students normally leave their core lit books on their desks.

Choosing one of those confusing transition times in the classroom—leaving for recess or lunch, lining up for an assembly, coming and going to the library in small groups—Calvin will weasel over to Veronica's desk and, when he's sure no one is watching, take her book. (This was before I developed a system of management. Since the books weren't marked, Veronica's book looked exactly like the one that Calvin had lost.)

Later that week, when I went to collect the books, I got out one of my first classroom tools. It was a list of student names. I thought this list would help me take care of class business.[†]

I announced to the students that I needed to collect the core lit books. I would then read a name and draw a line through it when the student brought me the book. After collecting several books, I eventually got to Calvin.

---

† Using a list of student names as a classroom tool helped at first. After a bit of time, though, I realized that there were a couple of flaws to the name list tool, one of which was how quickly it became obsolete. Whenever a new student transferred in or out, the list had to be redone. With numbers, though, you just reassign the unused number and all of the number tools are still usable.

MR. MORRIS
 With his name list in hand and a concerned look on his face:
  Calvin?

Lo and behold, Calvin brings me his book. It's actually Veronica's book, but I wasn't aware of that nor would I ever figure it out.

MR. MORRIS
 Beaming with delight and relief:
  Alright, Calvin, you found your book. Nice job.

I drew a big line through Calvin's name.

Things were going great until I came to Veronica's name.

MR. MORRIS
 Veronica. Book please.

VERONICA
 With a look of panic:
  I can't find it.

And here was the failure I had foreseen three weeks ago. It has come to fruition. I *knew* I wouldn't get all of the books back. AAAARRGH!

MR. MORRIS
  Can't find it? Come on, Veronica. It was right on your desk. You always have it out. Did you check inside your desk?

VERONICA
 Almost in tears:
  I checked everywhere. I can't find it, Mr. Morris.

MR. MORRIS
 Beginning to sound like a pirate as he addressed the entire class:
  Didn't I tell you guys to hang on to them?
 Turning to Veronica:
  You need to find that book or bring in eighteen bucks.

VERONICA
  But, Mr. Morris…

MR. MORRIS
  Hey, don't you start crying. I need the book or I need the money.

My harsh treatment of Veronica stemmed more from frustration about not being more organized than from feelings of ill will. Unfortunately for my students, though, my frustration was usually vented on them, as if it was *their fault* that I wasn't more organized.

Compounding this tragedy was the damage done to the level of safety in our classroom. If Veronica had to pay for a book she hadn't really lost, it would result in a major loss of trust. As I mentioned in Lesson 1, one of the five basic needs identified by Bill Glasser is a need for safety. Safety is a feeling that someone is taking care of you.

As you've just witnessed, though, my Who Knows What's Going On School of Management was not doing a good job of promoting a safe environment. Veronica has just been victimized by Calvin. Within a month or so, she'll begin to see this classroom in a new light. She'll be thinking: it's me against them.

This means that when she is given her new core lit book for the next three weeks, she won't be leaving it on her desk. Tragically, she's learned to hide her copy. Although this will help to ensure that the book is safe, it also means that she won't be able to read it as often.

> *Recent Finding:* According to the latest research, time spent reading is one of the leading contributors to reading improvement. The more you read, the better you get. (Gee, who'd of thought that?) If your students are having to hide their books so that other students don't take them, not only is their sense of safety being compromised, but they're also losing out on valuable reading time. After all, it's much more likely that a student will engage in independent reading if the book is readily available than if he has to dig through his desk to find his book.

And what did Calvin learn throughout this scenario? That's right. Why be responsible? Deceit works great.

So, let's check the scoreboard:

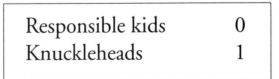

Responsible kids	0
Knuckleheads	1

A lack of organization on my part was causing one of my students to slowly withdraw from the class. At the same time, Calvin was figuring out that duplicity and deception are workable alternatives to being responsible.

There's got to be a better way.

By writing a number in the back of the core lit books, Veronica—and everyone else, for that matter—will be able to safely keep her book on her desk. And if Calvin *were* to take Veronica's book to replace the one he's lost—which he might try once—a quick check in the back will point out that Calvin, for some strange reason, has Veronica's book.

MR. MORRIS
> Checking the inside back cover as he's collecting the core lit books:
>> *Oh, look at that, Calvin. There's a number 29 in this book. This is Veronica's. She's been looking for it. Thanks.*
>
> Turning to Veronica:
>> *Veronica, Calvin found your book. I'll mark you off.*
>
> Returning his attention to the slightly stunned Calvin:
>> *Now then, where's your book? It has a 6 in the back.*

power
love
fun
freedom
safety

Due to the awesome power of student numbers, we will know with complete certainty who should be paying for the missing book. This mini-lesson on taking care of your things will be reinforced on Monday when Calvin receives his new core lit book for the next three weeks.

CALVIN
> Looking in the back of his new book and seeing a 6:
>> *---Oh, no. They're marked. I'd better hang on to mine.*

And that, my friends, is how students learn responsibility. It doesn't happen by talking about being responsible; it comes from daily practice. And of all the funny things, I'll use the student number system to develop, promote, and reinforce responsible behavior.

Student Materials

An obvious extension to the use of student numbers for identifying books would be to apply the same technique for the various materials used during the course of the day.

Think about all of the student items in your room that could be marked with numbers.

Crayon Boxes

Write the number on the inside of the lid and the bottom of the box.

FIG. 4-7
Crayon box lid marked with student number.

If you want to be a real fanatic about it, you could also number the individual crayons.

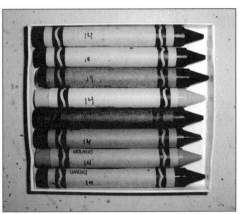

Fig. 4-8
Individual crayons with the student's number written on each of them.

For some strange reason, there always seems to be at least one crayon on the floor at the end of the day. If the crayon has a number on it, you'll be more inclined to save it for the student and not just toss it into the nearest trash can. The reason crayons get tossed is twofold:

1. We get sick of picking them up, and
2. We get frustrated not knowing whose it is.

Rulers

Mark the numbers on the backside of the rulers.

Suggestion: Have a lost-and-found for student items. Find something like an empty, clear plastic Tootsie Pop container and label it "Have You Seen My Owner?" or "Help Me!" or "Free Stuff!" or anything clever or eye-catching. Place loose pencils, stray crayons, rulers, etc., in the container for the students to get on their own when they finally figure out that they're missing something.

Scissors

These are somewhat difficult to mark due to the surface on which the numbers are written. Whether you use a permanent marker on the metal blade or the plastic handles, you'll find yourself having to rewrite the numbers every couple of months because, with time, the felt pen number will slowly fade away.

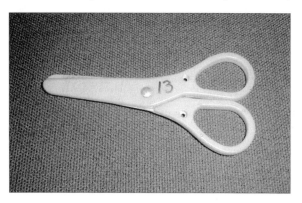

FIG. 4-9
Scissors marked with permanent ink pen.

Suggestion 1: If you use all-metal scissors—ours are the Fiskar type that have plastic bodies and metal blades as shown in Fig. 4-10—see if your custodian has an engraving pencil. This is an easy-to-use electrical device that will "write" on metal.

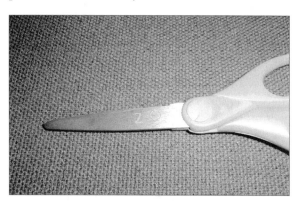

FIG. 4-10
Although you can't see it well in this photo, the engraving is easy to see in real life.

Suggestion 2: Get some white adhesive tape, the kind found in first aid kits. Attach a piece of tape to one of the handles. Write the student number on the tape with a permanent marker.

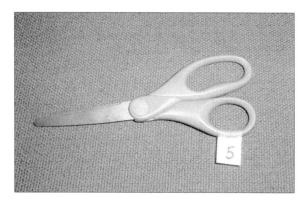

FIG. 4-11
Number written on tape attached to scissors.

Pencils

The bane of just about every teacher, pencil maintenance can suck the life out of you. From losing pencils, to sharpening pencils, to fighting over ownership of a pencil, it's just one big on-going, never-ending Advil event.

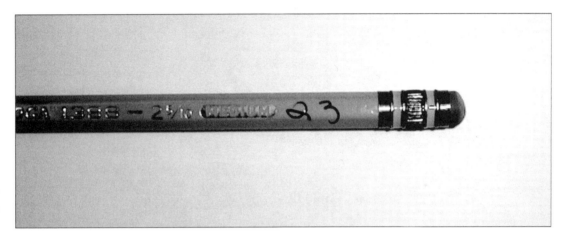

FIG. 4-12
Numbers written on barrel of pencil.

Three Different Suggestions for Dealing With Pencils

1. Number each pencil on the barrel.
   This will help to reduce the fighting over pencil ownership.
2. Have a numbered shoe box where students "store" an extra pencil.
   This will provide them with a "back-up" pencil when their first one loses its edge. A student helper—read: pencil manager—could be in charge of sharpening the pencils at some non-academic appropriate time.
3. Accept the fact that pencils are a hassle, buy a 100 of them, sharpen them, and dump them in a tub so that students have easy access to a fresh pencil.

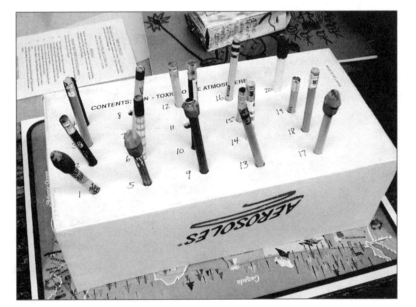

Reality:
You've got to choose your battles in order to survive.

FIG. 4-13
Shoebox with numbered holes for holding pencils.

Organizing Your Students

Before we spend any more time numbering things in the classroom, let's take a moment to look at some of the ways in which student numbers will enable you to more efficiently deal with some typical student maneuvers.

Disaster Drills

During my first five years of teaching, when I was lost and confused, I soon realized why they called these things "disaster drills." For me—and my students—it was almost always that: a total disaster.

Whenever the bell would ring—three repeating rings for fire—we would stop what we had been doing and head out to the dirt field. Once there, I was required to quickly verify that everyone was accounted for. A student was then dispatched to the principal who was standing in the middle of the playground with a stopwatch in her hand. (No pressure there.)

Since I never seemed to have my attendance folder or a seating chart with me during these drills, I found myself having to come up with some type of "Is everyone here?" procedure.

MR. MORRIS
Somewhat rattled:

Okay, everyone gather together. Now stand still; I need to count you. 1, 2, 3...I SAID HOLD STILL...1, 2, 3, 4, 5, 6, 7, 8, 9, 10, 11, 12, 13, 14, 15, 16...

Having a great time now, aren't we?

17, 18, 19, 20, 21, 22, 23, 24, 25...WOULD YOU GUYS QUIT FOOLING AROUND BACK THERE!
26, 27, 28, 29.

MR. MORRIS
Instantly realizing that something's wrong and thinking to himself:

Twenty-nine? We're supposed to have thirty-one. We're missing two students.

Quickly now, Mr. Morris. Who are the missing students and where the heck are they? The principal is waiting for your report and just about every other class has already sent over a runner.

Arrrrggghh!!!!!!!!

(Pirate talk for "I hate moments like these!")

With student numbers, of course, disaster drills are a piece of cake.

At the sound of the disaster bell, I'll walk my students out to the field[†] and then pick an appropriate spot for our line to begin. I'll then hold up the "zero order" sign.

Fig. 4-14
This hand signal, which looks like the letter "o," is our sign for "Please line up in numerical order."

As I mentioned earlier in the book, since every student has a number, it seems only right that I have one. Although I used to put myself at the end of the list— number 36—it didn't work the year I had thirty-six students. So lately, I've put myself "outside" of the list. I'm number 0.

My students will then rearrange themselves in a single-file line so that they are in numerical order with student number 1 at the front.

Now that the students are in line, I'll be able to walk down the line counting off students. If I don't have a name/number roster in my head—it usually takes a couple of weeks—my students will help me with the names and numbers.

Mr. Morris
    Calmly walking down the line of students:
    1, 2, 3, 4, 5, 6, 7, 8, 9, 10, 12.

10, 12???

    ---Where's Fabian?

Thinking, thinking. Puzzled looks from the students.

    ---Oh, wait a second. He went to the resource room before the drill.

Looking across the playground, I see Miss K, our resource teacher, with four students standing near her. Fabian is one of the four. Sweet.

    Continuing to walk down the line:
    12, 13, 14, 15, 16, 17, 18, 19, 20, 21, 22, 23, 24, 25, 26…

Student 27 is missing.

Mr. Morris
    Where's Stephanie?

---

† We don't worry about the order of the line as we head to the dirt area. The primary task is to get out there ASAP.

HELPFUL STUDENT
She's absent, Mr. Morris.

MR. MORRIS
That's right. Thank you.
Counting the last four students at the end of the line:
28, 29, 30, 31.

5 And in a matter of moments, I'm done. Not only was I able to quickly figure out that two students were missing, I knew exactly who they were and where they were.

MR. MORRIS
Speaking to his student room manager:
Dayna, please tell the principal that Room 12 is present and accounted for.

Patience please: The first time you try this organizational procedure, you'll find most everyone crowding to the front of the line. This is mainly due to the fact that they have been conditioned to always try to be first. In fact, it usually takes my students about two weeks to be able to get in line numerically without a lot of fumbling and delay. So, be patient with yours as they come to terms with this somewhat confusing process. The complexity of having to interact and work cooperatively might cause some difficulty at first. By the third or fourth week, though, it will become automatic.

Suggestion: You might want to give this "zero order" thing a try when you're not facing the pressure of a fire drill. Just pick an appropriate moment and explain the routine. Then, take them outside, hold up the sign, and don't budge from your spot or say a word. Very entertaining.

Field Trips

While you're thinking about the disaster drill, think about applying the same numerical order procedure when you're out on a field trip.

I remember taking my students on a whale watching field trip one year. Before we got on the boat to motor out into the bonnie blue, I stood on the pier and held up the zero order sign. They quickly got into line, attendance was checked, and we boarded. As soon as the boat came back to the dock and we disembarked, I again held up the zero order sign to ensure that everyone was off the boat.

The buddy system—students are assigned partners who hold up joined hands to verify everyone's presence—is okay but not completely reliable.

Imagine, for example, that you and your students are at the zoo. As you all exit the House of Reptiles, you have buddies get together and raise their hands.

Teacher
  Seeing all of the raised hands:
    Everybody have a buddy? Great! Let's go.

Unfortunately, two buddies were still checking out the giant green anaconda when you had everyone raise hands. Consequently, you and your students will head off to Monkey Land leaving behind the two buddies who will eventually exit the House of Reptiles and then wander around trying to figure out where everyone went.

A line of students in numerical order beats the buddy system hands down.

Lining Up

It should be noted that I'm not real big on lines. Whenever I need to have my students walk from our room to the library, cafeteria, or playground, I prefer a more relaxed form of group migration. Some schools, though, require that students stay in lines. If this sounds like your school, you might as well do it well and have your students line up numerically.

If, however, you do the predictable thing and have student 1 at the head of the line, you're not being very fair to student 31 who will always be riding in the caboose. A simple way to promote equity would be to use the date to determine who should be the line leader.

power
love
fun
freedom
safety

Example: Today is the 16th
1. Your line would start with student 16.
2. Lined up behind student 16 would be students 17 to 31.
3. The line would end with 1 through 15.

Student 16 is our line leader today.

Teacher Tip

Here's an idea from a kindergarten teacher regarding "seat" assignments.

I meet with my students on the carpet at the beginning of each day. To provide them with their own space, which will help get them settled down and focused, I marked off a grid using masking tape. Each square is 24 inches wide, and the grid is set up to be six squares wide and five squares deep.

The student whose number matches the date introduces the day, leads the flag salute, and then sits in the first square. We then practice counting as the students, one by one, sit in their squares.

A Word from the Author:

What a great technique. Although it would be easier for the teacher if the students always sat in the same place, they would eventually get bored with their assigned square. This would be especially true if the student happened to be sitting in one of the back rows.

It's kind of like playing volleyball. Who wants to spend the entire game in the back row? Nobody I know. If you're really into the game, you want everyone to rotate around so that you get to be in the front. I think it's the same thing for students. They would appreciate the opportunity to sit in a new seat every morning. It would provide them with a different perspective on the day.

power
love
fun
freedom
safety

A Word to the Overachievers: Lining up or sitting down according to the date sounds like a fine idea, but you're already realizing that certain students will have their numbers appear on a Saturday or Sunday and will miss their turn to be leader. How fair is that?

As it turns out, it's not as big a deal for the students as you may think. There are so many days in the year that everyone will be skipped several times.[†] To help ease any hurt feelings, you could always allow someone who was skipped to take the place of a student who is absent on the day he should be the line leader.

Filling in for Absent Students

18
Tools & Toys

At the end of morning recess, and again at the conclusion of lunch recess, my students gather together on a painted circle on the blacktop. (See Tools & Toys, *Lining Up After Recess.*)

power
love
fun
freedom
safety

I've found that the circle arrangement is a much more effective way for students to organize themselves. With the circle, as opposed to the standard line, there's no first or last. Thus, you'll never hear a single student complain, "He cut me!" Also, since the circle enables students to stand side-by-side, they can continue to be social as they wait for your directions to return to the room.

power
love
fun
freedom
safety

The normal procedure is that the student whose number matches the date steps away from the circle. He then signals one of the two students who were standing next to him to follow as he leads everyone back to the classroom. On days when the student who should be leading us back is absent, or you don't have enough students to match all of the days of the month, other students vie to be the leader. All they have to do is come up with a math equation that: 1) uses their student number; and 2) equals the date.

AMANDA
Realizing that today's "line leader" is missing, she raises her hand with two fingers forming a "V" indicating that she'd like to volunteer for something.

MR. MORRIS
Yes, Amanda?

AMANDA (STUDENT #2)
2 times 7 plus 1 equals 15.

power
love
fun
freedom
safety

MR. MORRIS
Nicely done, young lady. Today is the 15th and Ryan is absent. Amanda, please show us the way to our room.

[†]   You could even make it a math project. Provide them with calendars, indicate holidays for the year, and have them calculate how many days they'll be at the front of the line.

Dismissing Students

You can reinforce math skills in a playful way by dismissing your students according to their student numbers.

MR. MORRIS
Wanting to hammer home the just concluded lesson on factors, products, and multiples:
If your number is a multiple of 3, you may line up at the door for recess.

Several students would get in line. Several others would be thinking:

---Multiple?
---What's a multiple?
---Dang. I knew I should have been listening.

STUDENT
Turning to his neighbor:
Juan...what's a multiple?

JUAN
As patiently as possible since Mr. Morris just taught this lesson:
Remember? It's like the answer to a multiplication problem. Hey, your number is 24. 3 times 8 equals 24. You should be in line, 'mano.

A sixth grade math teacher told me about a lesson he taught on prime numbers. A part of the assessment process was that each student had to indicate whether his number was a prime number or not and then show proof of his reasoning.

In the ensuing weeks, to help reinforce the concept of prime numbers, he would have students line up at the door by number. Some days, the prime numbers went first. On other days, it was the non-primes who lined up first.

Even though they took turns, he said it wasn't long before the students with prime numbers got a bit of an attitude.

TEACHER
Dismissing his students for recess:
If your number is a prime number, you may walk to recess.

STUDENT
To his desk partner whose student number is 16:
Excuse me, but I need to go. I'm a prime.
A bit louder now:
Prime number, comin' through. Outta my way, composites.

Taking Turns

It is so easy to have your students take turns for activities when you use their student numbers as the ordering determiner. All of the confusion, all of the complaining, all of the unintentional bias that resulted whenever I would arbitrarily call upon students are gone. In its place: a calm, sensible system for ensuring that everyone receives a fair turn.

Let's look in on some first graders at my school to see this in action.

It's independent reading time, which means that the teacher is meeting with students individually to go over their *Frog Words.*[†] The students are sitting at their seats studying until it's their turn to go see the teacher. Since the students know that the teacher is calling students in numerical order, they can relax and wait patiently. Not only is this a fair procedure, but the students actually learn to anticipate their turn and prepare themselves for it.

In an old school classroom, you'd have students sitting at their desks wondering why they haven't been called over yet. If they were thinking rationally, they'd realize that everyone gets a turn eventually. Unfortunately, though, students—especially first graders—don't always think rationally.

STUDENT
   Sitting at his desk and studying his Frog Words:
      ---*Gee, she hasn't called me up yet.*

That's right, little buddy. She also hasn't called up a dozen other students either. But you're not thinking about them, are you? You're only thinking about yourself.

      ---*Gee, maybe I should go remind her I haven't had a turn.*

Walking to the front of the room and interrupting the teacher and the student with whom she is currently working:

   Is it my turn yet?

TEACHER
   Smiling patiently:
      No, honey. Not yet.

[†]   On a bulletin board in the room was a large frog pond. The frog pond was composed of water and lily pads. The students were paper frogs. Everyone's frog was placed on the first pad, and each of the students was given a paper lily pad with a list of sight words printed on it. To move from one lily pad to the next, you had to be able to read all of the words. Although the first pad contained only a few short words, the lists got longer and the words got more difficult as you hopped your way through the frog pond. First grade sounds like fun, doesn't it?

The student returned to his desk and studied his Frog Words.

Two minutes later:

> STUDENT
> Back at the teacher's desk interrupting her time with another student:
> *Is it my turn now?*

> TEACHER
> Smile beginning to fade, voice losing her friendly edge:
> *No, dear. Don't worry, though. You're on my list. Please wait your turn.*

The student again returned to his desk. After the teacher has seen another student or two, he's back.

> STUDENT
> *Is it my turn now?*

> TEACHER
> Finally fed up with the interruptions:
> *All right! It's your turn.*

This little soap opera is played out on a daily basis in a thousand classrooms across the country. The sadly predictable outcomes were these:

1) The teacher ended up getting frustrated and
2) The student learned that interrupting the teacher eventually got him his turn.

However, by using student numbers to establish the order, every student knows that he'll be given a fair turn with the teacher. Instead of bothering the teacher, Mr. Pushy Boy is now staying at his desk and studying. Being student 17, he knows he's always after Thomas, student 16. There's no need to worry about a missed turn; there's no need to interrupt the teacher. The numbers create an order that is as predictable as the days of the week.

Bonus: Mr. Pushy Boy would eventually get to the point whereby he would appear at the teacher's desk as Thomas, student 16, finishes. The teacher wouldn't even have to call him over. This time, though, he would be showing up at the proper time. What a great thing: students using the number system to help maintain a smoothly running classroom.

power
love
fun
freedom
safety

Physical Education

As opposed to spending valuable P.E. time trying to figure out who is going to be chosen last, why not use student numbers to divide your students into teams?

YOU, THE CALM, RELAXED TEACHER USING STUDENT NUMBERS

Addressing your students at the backstop:

Numbers 1 through 16, you're in the outfield. 17 through 31, your team is up.

Or...

Odds in the outfield, evens are up.

Or...

We need to make four teams. 1 through 8, 9 through 16, 17 through 24, and 25 through 31.

It's just so easy to do.

I used to coach the sixth graders every year and help them prepare to play the teachers in the end-of-the-year softball game. (I was the only male teacher on campus, so I was the coach. Go figure.) The first thing I would do was call a meeting in the auditorium. After explaining the basic rules of conduct, I had everyone fill out a simple sign-up card. On the card was the student's name and room number. The cards were collected by gender: girls in one container and the boys in another. Cards were then drawn from the container, one at a time, and numbered. After drawing all of the cards, I gave them to one of the students who produced two rosters. These rosters were then used during practice to ensure order and fairness.

FIG. 4-15
Sign-up card, numbered pile, roster.

During morning recess, I'd meet with the sixth graders at the softball diamond and conduct batting practice. On even days, the girls would bat and the boys would be in the field. We wouldn't keep track of outs or runs. It wasn't a game; it was just practice.

On the odd days the boys would bat and the girls would field. And, by having the students bat in numerical order, there was a wonderful atmosphere of calm organization because everyone had a fair turn at the plate.

In my pre-number days, boys' batting practice was like a scene straight out of *Lord of the Flies*. The boys would all rush to the front of the line where a pushing match would ensue. The biggest and baddest always got to bat first. The dweebs were shipped to the back of the line. Other than being grossly unfair and violating a student's need for safety, this Every-Man-For-Himself behavior was counterproductive to building a sense of team spirit.

power
love
fun
freedom
safety

With numbers, there's no fighting for your place in line. In fact, you could come out to practice a few minutes late and yet still be able to find your proper place in line. That spot was sacred. Not even the toughest kid in school could deny you your place.

General Rule: Similar to lining up, we'd use the date to establish which student actually batted first. So, on the 8th, for example, batter #8 would be at the front of the line. It would then go 9 through 27 and end with 1 through 7.

Student Number Tools

As you are beginning to see by the examples in this lesson, the opportunities for using numbers in managing your students are almost limitless. Before too long, you'll be adding your own spin to the system.

To get the juices really flowing, let's conclude the lesson with a few student number tools I use in my room that you can easily reproduce or adapt to meet your own needs.

Cubbies/Post Office

I took an old bookcase and, by adding some particle board, subdivided the space into little compartments and assigned one space for each student. As you can see in the photograph below, I used student numbers to indicate which space belongs to which student. This means, of course, that I'll never have to redo the labels on this handy classroom tool.[†]

FIG. 4-16
The Room
Twelve Post
Office.

Our "Post Office" is a great spot for placing items that need to go home.

> **To be sent home:**
> - finished, corrected assignments
> - office memos to the parents
> - PTA flyers and announcements
> - cafeteria menu for the month
> - the ton-and-a-half of stuff I get in my mailbox promoting:
>   Boys' Club activities
>   soccer leagues
>   vacation reading programs
>   community events
> - etc., etc., etc.

---

† Although this may not seem like a big deal, it's the cumulative result of all these little time savers and stress reducers that will contribute to your effectiveness as a teacher.

In keeping with the New Management theme of student involvement, the best way to get the stuff in the mailboxes would be to have a student do it for you. The procedure I use is a simple one.

1. **Find a student to be in charge.**
    See if you can get one of your "fringe kids"—a student who isn't completely connected to what's going on in your room—to be your Post Office manager.

    Reminder: If you can, avoid the very real temptation of only using a select group of overachievers to take care of extra tasks and classroom jobs. I realize it's important to have these things taken care of correctly—which is why we rely on these students—nonetheless, it's equally important to involve as many students as possible.

    Opportunity: Use these simple classroom jobs to build personal relationships with your students. I've found that it's much easier to establish a working relationship with an underachiever than it is an academic one. And, once I *have* created a personal connection, which only takes a couple of interactions, the academic relationship always follows.

2. **Decide on a procedure the two of you will use.**
    I usually place the necessary items on the student's desk in the morning. My Post Office manager knows that anything he finds on his desk needs to be put in the mailboxes. Although the actual placement is usually done in the morning, it can be done at any time as long as it's done before dismissal.

3. **Have your students empty their mailboxes at the end of the day.**
    Either the Post Office manager will remind them or I will. Either way, all of the things I've been given to pass along to my students will go home in a timely fashion.

Variation: My students now use two colored folders, green and red, to help keep their papers organized.

The green folder is for papers that go home and then come back to school. Samples of green folder papers would include unfinished assignments, book logs, and activities to be completed at home.

The red folder is for papers that go home and stay home. Red folder papers— corrected assignments, school announcements, etc.—are to be shared with the parents.[†] The now empty red folder is returned to class the next day.

[†]   Parents have told me over and over how much they appreciate not having to dig through the backpack to see if there is anything important that they should be receiving.

Numbered Clothespins

A set of numbered clothespins makes a wonderfully versatile student number tool. The clothespins are easy to manipulate, can be clipped to a number of places—a large chart, a length of rope, the rim of a cardboard box—and will endure years of active service.

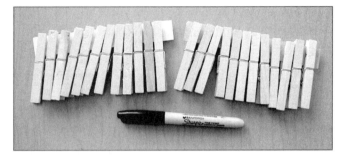

Fig. 4-17
A bunch of wooden clothespins and a permanent marker is all you need.

Here are a few of the many, many ways you could put a set of numbered clothespins to work in your classroom.

Attendance Taker

1. Clip your clothespins around the top edge of a cardboard box.
2. Place it near the door of your classroom.
3. As students enter your room, they remove their clothespins and drop them into the box.
4. At the morning bell, a student helper will verify that the clothespins still clipped to the rim of the box indicate absent students as opposed to someone who has forgotten to remove his clothespin.
5. The student will then report the results to you.
6. When appropriate, the student attendance manager will reset the clothespins for the next day.

Fig. 4-18
Clothespin attendance taker.

Opportunity: Put a Burger King or McDonald's bag inside the box. Have the students who will be buying a cafeteria lunch drop their clothespins in the bag. A quick count by your student assistant will provide you with the lunch count for the day.

A Clothesline for Art Projects

1. Run a length of clothesline near one of the walls of your room.
2. Have students attach their art projects to the clothesline with their clothespins, or ***Art Hangers***, as we call them.
    Suggestion: Place newspapers on the floor under the clothesline if there is the possibility of dripping.
3. After the art has dried, have students sign their artwork and place it in their cubbies to go home.

67
Tools & Toys

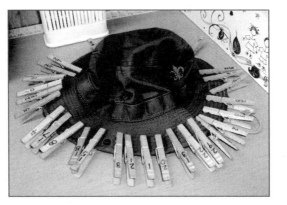

Fig. 4-19
Using a hat is an easy way to keep the clothespins organized.

I've found that a hat works best for displaying the clothespins. I used to use a small cardboard box for holding the pins. The problem was, you had to dig through the box to find your clothespin.

The hat, as you can see at the left, shows everyone's clothespin in an easy-to-get-to fashion. Also, when you aren't using them, the hat will hang on the wall looking kind of cool.

Student Input

A kindergarten teacher told me that she uses a set of numbered clothespins as part of their morning start-up activity.

1. Before the day begins, the teacher writes a question on a large sheet of newsprint and attaches it to her chart.
2. After the morning bell rings, the students gather together on the carpet facing the chart.
3. The teacher and the students then read through the posted *Question of the Day.*
4. The students are given an opportunity to verbalize their feelings about the question.
5. Later in the morning, when students have an extra moment

during their activity center rotations, they will clip their clothespins to the YES side of the chart or the NO side of the chart.

6. Just after snack time—which would give any students who still hadn't placed their clothespins on the chart a chance to do so—the class would reconvene on the carpet and discuss the results.

Forming Groups or Committees

As part of a Social Studies activity one year, I wanted my students to work on one of four different committees. To make the "Choose a Committee" process bearable, I used our set of numbered clothespins.

1. I found an empty cardboard box in the supply room.
2. Using a permanent felt marker, I wrote the names of the four committees on the outside of the box, one committee per side.
3. During Social Studies time, I held aloft the cardboard box and discussed the four committees and what the members of these groups would do.
4. After this committee preview, I placed the hat with the clothespins and the box in the back of the room.
5. The students then clipped their clothespins on the side of the box that represented the committee on which they wished to work.
6. After every student had chosen a committee, the box was given to two students who then made committee rosters.

Advantage #1: Looking at the clothespins left on the hat will alert you to the students who have yet to make a choice.

Advantage #2: Looking at the box will tell you if the committees are balanced or in need of some adjusting.

Advantage #3: Switching committees will be easy to do if a student decides that he didn't like his first choice.

Fig. 4-20
A cardboard box and your set of numbered clothespins makes committee organization a breeze.

Overachievers: I suppose that I could have typed up committee descriptions with a listing of responsibilities and requirements. Then, after printing out the four sheets, I could have glued them onto the sides of the box. This would have allowed anyone who wasn't clear about one of the committees an opportunity to review the information.

Bonus Idea: Get some gold spray paint and spray a dozen clothespins gold. During times when the committees are working on their projects, you can give a gold clothespin to a committee and have one of the members clip it to the box to indicate they had been working especially well. (The numbered clothespins had been removed during step 6.) The gold clothespins could then be incorporated into the final assessment procedure at the conclusion of the activity.

Pegboard and Golf Tees

Talk about a marriage made in heaven, golf tees and pegboard go together like peanut butter and jelly. The tees fit perfectly into the small holes of the pegboard while the grid-like layout of the holes in the pegboard is well suited to charting or organizing information.

68
Tools & Toys

In its simplest form, a small piece of pegboard (12 inches x 24 inches) can be used to take attendance. The one I used for years, the *Roll-A-Matic*, was attached to a bookcase facing the door. The procedure was similar to the one for taking attendance using numbered clothespins that was described on page 4-30. The only difference was that, instead of dropping the golf tee into a box or bag, students would move them from the first column to the second.

Holes 21 and 25 don't have a golf tee because those students are no longer enrolled in our class.

FIG. 4-21
The Roll-A-Matic: a simple attendance taking tool.

If you wanted to, though, you could get really creative with the pegboard/golf tees thing because the materials are cheap and durable.

Homework Board

Pegboard would be a great way to show which students are completing homework assignments during a two-week period of time.

1. Set up the student number column.
2. Label eight columns with the days of the week. (We're using only eight because we don't collect anything on Mondays.)

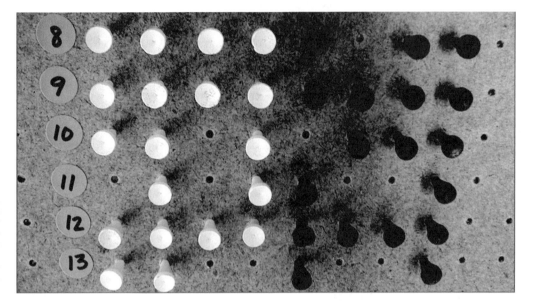

Fig. 4-22
An easy-to-use tool for documenting the completion of homework assignments.

3. Students are given a golf tee as they turn in their assignment for the day.
4. The golf tee is then placed in the proper column.
5. At the end of two weeks—the amount of time for which the board has been labeled—all golf tees are removed and a new two-week period is begun.

Important factor: What's nice about this tool is that it only covers two weeks. Thus, a student's irresponsibility in completing homework assignments will only be on a display for a short time. When the tees are all removed at the end of two weeks, everyone will be given a "fresh start" and an opportunity to show improvement. If, on the other hand, you had a homework completion chart that showed months worth of assignments, some students would have to live with the shame of the poor work skills and study habits they had displayed at the beginning of the year. Two weeks seems like a more manageable amount of time.

power
love
fun
freedom
safety

Bonus: Have some kind of incentive or recognition for students who bring in all eight assignments during the two week period. A short note or a simple certificate would be appropriate for recognizing the student's efforts while also keeping the parents apprised.

power
love
fun
freedom
safety

Numbered Popsicle Sticks

I use a cup of numbered popsicle sticks to randomly select which students will take out the play equipment at recess. One end of the stick has a student number. The other end has been dyed red.

FIG. 4-23
A popsicle stick that has been dyed on one end and numbered on the other.

After calling upon four students, I return their sticks to the cup so that the numbered end shows. I'll keep drawing sticks that have the red end up until they've all had a chance. The sticks then get turned over, and we start again.

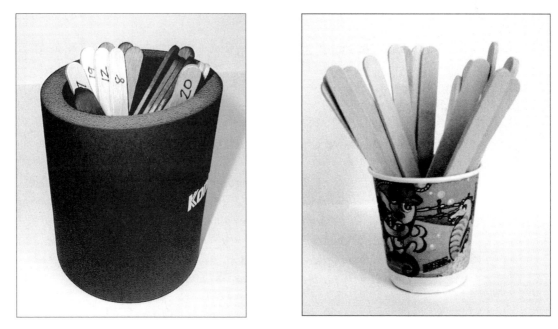

FIG. 4-24
The dyed end enables me to just use one cup to hold them all. I used to have one cup for the ones that had been chosen and one cup for the ones that had already had a turn. One cup makes more sense.

I dye one end of the stick in a small paper cup that contains about a half-inch of red food coloring and water. Don't let the sticks stay in there more than a few minutes or the dye will wick its way up the sticks.

Common myth: Popsicle sticks are good for calling upon students randomly during lessons and discussions. Uh, not true. Since the question will have been asked *before* a stick is pulled, what do you do when the name on the stick belongs to a student who can't answer the question on his own? Better, in my opinion, to use a set of playing cards or 3 x 5 index cards instead of the sticks. With the cards in hand, you'll be able to stagger the top four or five cards and see which students are coming up next. This will eliminate the uncertainty of who's next and leave you better able to handle the many and diverse needs of your students.

Miscellaneous Thoughts and Ideas

At this point in the lesson, you are either:

      A. Feeling excited about the possibilities for using student numbers in your classroom,

      B. Feeling overwhelmed by the broad range of applications we've covered so far,

      C. Feeling a little bit of both, or

      D. Feeling elated.
      (I'm thinking about all of the veteran teachers out there who are reading this book. With all of your experience you'll be able to quickly apply these ideas and take your classroom to a whole new level.)

Well, here's what I'm hoping: I'm hoping that you're feeling excited.

Nothing beats that feeling of adventure and discovery when you're trying new ideas and exploring new areas.

If you *are* feeling a bit overwhelmed, just take a deep breath and repeat to yourself:

      ---Rick's been doing this number thing for over twenty years. The ideas he's shared didn't come to him overnight. Since this is my first attempt at using his techniques, I'm going to do what I can and relax in the knowledge that the more I use the New Management system, the better it's going to get. I'll bet that by my second year, I'm going to be sending him ideas on how to use student numbers.

Now that we've stopped to make sure everyone's okay, let's push on. How about if we talk about three more variations, and then we'll put this lesson to bed? Sounds good to me.

Here comes:

1. **a student number idea**
    (A Roster in Your Head)
2. **a student number tool**
    (Temporary Number Stickers)
3. **a toy to randomly select students**
    (Pick-A-Student)

A Roster in Your Head

I can't begin to tell you the number of times I've found myself needing to mentally run through my list of students for some type of evaluative process.

For instance, at a staff meeting a couple of years ago, the principal asked the third grade teachers to submit a list of students who should be considered for next year's recess game leaders. With neither a seating chart nor an attendance folder at hand, I was able to mentally go through my list of students—numerical order providing the mnemonic structure—and give each student a brief review.

1 Anna
2 Carrie
3 Crystal
4 Danny
5 Devin
6 not being used
7 Erica
8 Fabian
9 Heather
10 Jenni
11 Lisa
12 Melanie
13 not being used
14 Nick
15 Rachel
16 Rick
17 Robyn
18 Seth
19 Tricia
20 Valencia
21 Van

Three minutes later, feeling good that I hadn't unintentionally overlooked anyone, I handed the principal a short list of qualified candidates.

Once again, this may seem like a small matter. Bear in mind, though, that it's the cumulative effect of many small steps that makes for large strides.

Temporary Numbers

69
Tools & Toys

There are times when you only want to mark something for a brief period of time. In this case, I'd use *Number Stickers*. (See the photo of the math workbook on page 4-5 for a sample of how the number sticker looks in action.)

Number stickers are made from small adhesive circles. Numbers are written on the stickers with a permanent marker and given to the students to use. They can be peeled off when no longer needed.

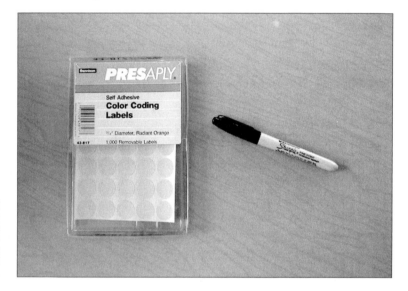

FIG. 4-25
Number
sticker kit:
Sharpie
marker and
a sheet of
circles.

I usually give the students a strip of four circles at the beginning of the year. They're given a new strip every couple of months after that.

power
love
fun
freedom
safety

Helpful: You might want to have a sheet of adhesive circles and a Sharpie available so that your students can get a circle whenever they feel they need one.

FIG. 4-26
A set of
number
stickers. I
use the ones
that are a
half-inch in
diameter.

Warning: Removable stickers might not be a good way to identify the core lit books we talked about earlier in the piece about inventory control. If he chose to, Calvin could take advantage of the removable nature of the stickers by peeling off Veronica's number 29 and replacing it with one of his own number 6 stickers. Although this may seem like a stretch, bear in mind that Calvin's had years and years to work on his strategies for avoiding responsibility. It might actually be better for him if you removed the temptation by holding off on the stickers until he's had a chance to adjust to his new reality.

Random Helpers

I found a little toy called Quick Pick *(shown below)* in a Sav-On drugstore one day. It's a hand-held device that's powered by a AA battery. There's a button in the handle that causes the little numbered balls inside the globe to swirl around. (Although it came with 55 numbered balls, I was able to remove the ones that didn't match the numbers of my students.) After a swirl or two, some of the balls would exit the globe through a small opening and end up in the tube next to the handle. As you can imagine, the numbers that ended up in the tube represented the students who would be chosen.

MR. MORRIS
Looking at the Quick Pick in his hand:
It looks like Alicia, Erika, and Tony will be helping in the snack shop today.

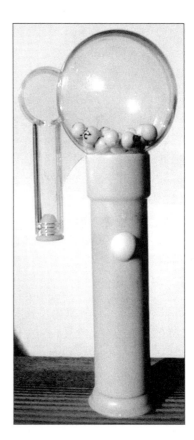

FIG. 4-27
Quick Pick lottery toy (far right) and a close-up of the three numbered balls that ended up in the tube.

In the sample to the left, students 3, 11, and 28 were selected. When I announced the "winners," I quickly translated the numbers and identified each of them by name.

Another nice aspect of this little number toy was that when you pushed the button to get the balls moving, you'd hear an unusual, but pleasant, whirling sound. The sound was so distinctive, in fact, that I didn't even have to announce that I needed some student helpers for a task. I just picked up the Quick Pick, pushed the button, and their heads would pop up. They'd all be thinking, "Mr. Morris is about to select someone to help! I wonder who's it going to be?"

Okay, now for the bad news. The company no longer makes them. Yeah, I know. I was pretty bummed, too, because I had sold thousands of them at workshops and knew that teachers loved using these little toys in class.

Crisis or opportunity? My son, Ben, saw it as an opportunity and created a product called Pick-A-Student[†] which is the new and improved Quick Pick. Basically, it's a clear plastic

---

† All of the proceeds from the sale of Pick-A-Student go to Ben. I'm happy to say that he deposits 60% into a savings account and gives 10% as a tithe. The rest is his to use as he sees fit.

jar that contains 40 numbered tokens. (The tokens were printed on plastic and then die-cut using a design he created.) It's wonderfully simple and easy-to-use.

Ben's design enables you to quickly orient your eye when viewing numbers. Thus, it's easy to see that the number at the top-left of the pile is a 6 and not a 9.

Directions:
1. Open the jar and remove the tokens that don't match the numbers of your students.
2. Screw the lid back on. [no need to open again = no lost tokens]
3. Give the jar a vigorous shake. The sound alerts your students that you are about to select a helper or two.
4. Turn the jar upside down.
5. The numbers you see are the ones from which you make your selection.

Advantages:
1. No more on/off switch to go bad or batteries to replace.
2. The numbers are large enough to be read easily.
3. Several numbers will be showing which affords you some discretion as to who you actually choose.

Reality: I used to get jammed up every now and then using Quick Pick when the number that came out first belonged to a student who, for whatever reason, really shouldn't be the helper. Pick-A-Student enables me to temporarily overlook that student and choose one of the other numbers. At the same time, though, I am able to create the appearance of equity which eliminates anyone from complaining, "You always pick her!"

Etcetera, Etcetera

As you can now see, there are a world of possibilities for putting student numbers to work in your room. This lesson was designed to get you started and moving in the right direction. In no time at all, you'll be off and running.

Lesson 5

Before We Begin

How It All Got Started

Numbering Your Students

Using Student Numbers

Timers & Sound Makers

Class Chart

Check Off List

Check Off Sheet

First Aid Kit

Grade Books

*To know how to suggest
is the great art of teaching.
To attain it we must be able to guess
what will interest;
we must learn to read the childish soul
as we might a piece of music.*

—H. F. Amiel

Lesson 5
Timers & Sound Makers

◆ ◆

Goals for this lesson:

☑ Learn how "definition" can lead to "control."

☑ Understand the importance of sharing a common language with your students.

☑ Discover the power of using a digital timer.

☑ Find out how to have fun with some simple sound-making toys.

☑ Learn how to utilize the power of the right-brain.

◆ ◆

Let's take a break from numbers and have some fun. Actually, Lesson 5 involves a bit of philosophy and a bit of play. First, we're going to develop an understanding of the power of specific communication and how it can improve your teacher/student interactions. Then we'll play with some New Management tools and toys: specifically, timers and sound makers. Before we break out those tools and toys, though, let's do some deep thinking.

Back in my college days, I was fortunate to be in a political science class taught by a guest lecturer by the name of Milton Silverman. Silverman was a lawyer by trade and a brilliant one at that. He's probably the brightest man I've ever been around. The class, conducted as a Socratic seminar, was amazing.

Each week he would toss out an idea or thought and then encourage us to debate and discuss it from all possible angles. The most memorable one was this:

The power to define is the power to control.

Silverman actually made his living by applying this principle to his cases. If he could go into a courtroom and, through his carefully reasoned definition, determine motive or explain evidence or identify who's a credible witness and who isn't, he would be able to establish a certain amount of control over the outcome of that trial.

Since I wasn't planning to enter the field of law, I didn't do much with this philosophy. It wasn't until I had been a classroom teacher for a number of years that I began to apply Milton's Principle. During the past fifteen years or so, I've been living by this philosophy. The more I adhere to the Law of Define and Control, the more successful I've become at communicating with my students. The advantage gained in my interactive effectiveness has been rather significant. Here's a simple case in point.

"Clear desks, please."

Imagine that it's almost recess time. Now, before my students head outside for a bit of sun and fun—I teach in San Diego—I want them to put away their books and organize the materials on the tops of their desks. With that simple goal in mind, I would address the class.

> Mr. Morris
> *Okay, let's get ready for recess.*

Seems like a logical request, doesn't it? After all, it was clear in my mind what I meant. Unfortunately, the ambiguity of the phrase produced a variety of responses. As it turned out, there were as many different definitions of "Let's get ready for recess" as there were students in my room.

For some students, it meant:
Run to the equipment box and get your hands on a ball before the other kids take everything.

One or two students thought it meant:
Line up at the door right now.

The neurotically compulsive students, upon hearing my rather vague request, would ponder the possibilities.

> --- *Get ready? Gee, maybe I should clean out my desk. While I'm at it, I'll get the cleanser and buff off a few pencil marks.*

And at the other end of the spectrum was the student who wouldn't even budge. He's thinking:

> --- *Hey, I've been ready since 8 o'clock. Let's go.*

The confusion resulted from their uncertainty of what I really meant by "Let's get ready for recess." Although I knew exactly what I wanted my students to do, they were left to draw their own conclusions.

This sounds like a perfect opportunity for using some Define and Control.

How about clearly defining my instructions and then giving this oft-used instruction set a specific phrase of some kind? This combination of consistent language/consistent meaning will make the verbal directions I give to students easier to understand.

We should start by getting rid of the not-very-clear "Let's get ready for recess." In its place we'll create a phrase that is unique yet understandable.

MR. MORRIS
Writing the words "Clear Desks" on the whiteboard:
From now on, when I say "Clear desks," I want you to do three things:
Writing each step on the board:
1. Put your books in your desk.
Pause to make sure students aren't putting away books right now. Encourage them to wait until they've been given all three steps and the command "Clear desks" before beginning.
2. Place your papers in your green folder.[†]
A brief pause so they can visualize it.
3. Give me your attention.
Stepping back to verify that the instructions were written correctly and then turning to the class:
Let's try it and see how it works. Pretend you're still working.
Waiting until they're "working" on something:
Clear desks, please.

Armed with a clear definition of what I meant by what I said, my students were able to comply with my directions. I was pleased to see that everyone in class was putting away their books and papers and then giving me their attention.[††]

[†]   Introduced on page 4-29, you'll find "paper folders" in the Class Glossary located at the back of the book.

[††]   If you have students who are not complying with your stated wishes, jot down their names on a piece of paper. Then, as you're about to dismiss the class for recess, announce that you'd like to see some students before they leave.

After everyone else has left, and you are alone with just the students who made little effort to comport themselves in a proper manner, restate your expectations of behavior. You won't need to get mad or raise your voice. Just make a point to let them know that they need to improve their "Clear desks, please" routine.

As I normally ask during these types of interventions: "Did you think I was kidding about the 'Clear desks' thing.?" Student response: "(Mumble, mumble, denial, deflect.)" Me: "What are you going to do the next time I say 'Clear desks, please?' " Student response: "Uh, do it the right way." Me: "That's all I'm asking for. Thanks for listening. You may go now."

Note: To keep things light, I'm smiling the whole time I'm talking.

MR. MORRIS
Showing his pleasure with a large smile:

> Wow! That was great. I'll use that phrase from now on when it's time for recess or lunch or whenever we need to head to the auditorium for an assembly. Why don't we add "Clear desks" to our Class Glossary?

> Define and Control[†] has added so much to the success I've experienced in the classroom that I've formalized the process by having each year's group of students produce a written Class Glossary. (Check Appendix for suggestions.) Since the terms included in the glossary have remained rather constant over the years, it's been an easy procedure to maintain, and the time spent in creating it has paid dividends with each new group of students.

As you can image, the more terms you define, the more successful your students will be at understanding your messages. And by sharing a common language, you'll find that everyone within the unique culture being created by you and your students will share in the control of a smoothly-running classroom.

With that in mind, let's define two more terms: *tools* and *toys*.

Tools and Toys

By definition, *tools* are things we use in the classroom that enable us to more easily deal with the various classroom tasks we face during the course of a normal school day. Some of these tools were created to harness the power of the student number system. (Assigning the student numbers was only the start. The real fun begins, as you saw in Lesson 4, when you actually put the number system to work.) Other tools, though, are not number-dependent. They're merely classroom procedures that act like the oil in your car's engine: they help make things run smoothly while cutting down on friction.

You don't have to call them tools if you don't wish. You could call them "things I use in my class." Call them whatever you wish. For some reason, though, just calling them tools seems to make them more useful. Also, I've found that the students are inclined to take them more seriously if you use a serious word such as tools.

Toys, on the other hand, are another matter entirely. By definition, toys are fun to use. Consequently, if we take a fun-type tool and call it a toy, not only does it help with the management, it has the added advantage of making the process or procedure a bit more fun. Your students will begin to develop a very positive attitude toward classroom management. The attitude can be summed as: "We get things done in here and have fun at the same time." This is definitely a good awareness to perpetuate.

power
love
fun
freedom
safety

[†]   Although the phrase Define and Control may sound a bit harsh and coercive, it's actually a Win-Win kind of thing. I win because my expectations of student behavior are being communicated to my students in a clear, concise fashion. At the same time, the students are winning because they now have in their possession a Rosetta Stone for removing the uncertainty of frequently used commands.

So, let your students hear you call them tools and toys. They're quick at picking up on the way you look at things. Call something a tool, and they'll use it seriously. Call something else a toy, and they'll think they're having fun. Sounds strange, I know, but that "define and control" thinking really works.

But enough theory; let's get back to some practice.

Classroom Tool: Digital Timer

Here's a classroom tool that has proven to be indispensable. It's a digital timer.

FIG. 5-1
This is the first digital timer I purchased years ago. It's still going strong. (It's shown here in actual size.)

This is my old Westbend Triple Timer. I really liked it because I could time three separate events concurrently.

The little "arrow" pointing at the 2 means that timer #2 has been set for 15 minutes.

Timers #1 and #3 are not being used.

(I've since found a better timer for classroom use. You'll find a picture of it on page 5-19.)

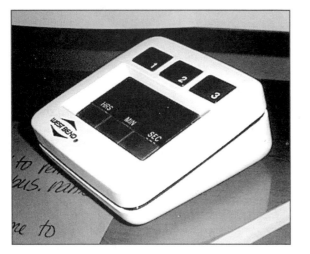

FIG. 5-2
As you can see, this is a desk top model.

I bought the timer shown in Fig. 5-1 about twenty-five years ago. Although the price has since risen to somewhere around $35, it was $14 when I bought it.[†]

After laying down my hard-earned teacher dollars, I took my new timer to the classroom and gladly retired my old, non-digital timer. What a welcome relief that was.

You see, in my early days of teaching, I had one of those white, circular, spin-the-face, tick-tick-tick-DING! kitchen timers.

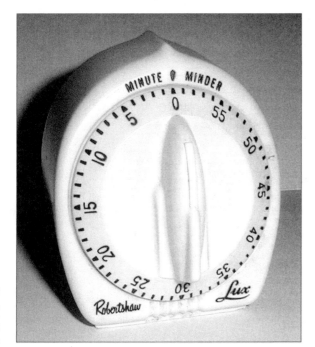

If you do happen to have one of these analog-type kitchen timers where you twist the circular dial and it ticks away the minutes, here's a suggestion: keep it in the kitchen where it works just great.

In the classroom, you're going to want something a bit more functional for alerting everyone that their time is up.

Fig. 5-3
An old, spin-the-face kitchen timer.

Kitchen timers are okay, but they have a couple of drawbacks. For one, it made a loud ticking sound that got to be annoying. (Teachers have told me that they've actually had to put this type of timer in a drawer so that the ticking wouldn't bother their students.)

The other problem, which developed as the timer got older, was the decrease in the volume of the "Time's up!" bell. That pathetic, little DING just wasn't loud enough to carry to the back of the room.

And while we're at it, I dare you to set a kitchen timer for just one minute. You had to: 1) spin the dial past 5 minutes; and then 2) spin it back to the one minute mark. It was so sadly inaccurate for short time spans that "one minute" could be over in 15 seconds or end up running as long as 130 seconds. You just never knew.

---

† Speaking from personal experience, buying a digital timer was, without a doubt, the best money I've spent in all my years of teaching. Fortunately, they've brought out some new models lately that are more affordable. I'll show you what I think is the best timer available in just a bit. It sells for $15, and has a few advantages over the first one I purchased.

With the digital timer, you won't have those problems. First of all, since it's digital—as opposed to analog—you can set it for the exact amount of time you want. Then, when the time has expired, you'll find that the distinctive electronic beep it emits is much more effective than the one-time DING from the kitchen timer. Also, the digital timer will continue to beep until someone presses a button and stops it.

Nice feature: It will stop beeping by itself after thirty seconds.

So basically, the digital timer is better than the analog timer. Both of them, though, were better than what *my* elementary teachers used when I was a student. Back then, the state of timekeeping technology was the clock on the wall or the clock on the wrist—neither of which would alert the poor teacher to the fact that the students should be stopping one activity and moving on to another. To illustrate the shortcomings of the old technology, let's travel back in time to the year I was in fourth grade.

Rick Morris as a Fourth Grade Student

My fourth grade teacher, Mrs. Dye, was a sweet old lady nearing the end of her career. Kind and loving, she was a wonderfully nurturing person. Although she wasn't the most organized thing on two feet, she had a heart of gold.

I can still remember how she would address the class every morning at 9:00.

> MRS. DYE
> *Okay, boys and girls, I see it's 9:00. It's time to work on your spelling assignment. You have 15 minutes. Any questions?*

Since we were a rather responsible little group and were familiar with the spelling workbook, we had very few questions. We knew the plan: work on spelling and have it finished in 15 minutes.

> *All right. You may begin.*

power
love
fun
freedom
safety

And with that, we would begin to work on the spelling assignment. Mrs. Dye, loving teacher that she was, would begin to circulate around the room. She wouldn't retreat to her desk to correct papers or get on the phone and call the office. Neither would she file papers nor prepare materials for some other lesson. If she said we were supposed to work for 15 minutes, she made sure that she was an active member of the work group. This kind of sincere, supportive involvement helps to meet one of the five Glasser student needs: the need for love.

What was especially endearing was that her interactions during the 15 minutes of spelling time were not limited to just academics. She also used the time to build a bond with her students. A lot of her comments, as she walked around, were along these lines:

MRS. DYE
  Wandering amongst the students:
  It's nice to have you back in class today, Jennifer. I'm glad you're feeling better.

  Len, would you thank your Mom for donating the cupcakes for our bake sale. That was very sweet of her to help us.

  Julian, your watercolor looks beautiful back there on our Artist's Board. The colors are really vibrant.

An effective teacher is a teacher who cares, and in Mrs. Dye's class, you were always aware of how much she cared.

In addition to the love she showed was the educational benefit we gained because of her immediate accessibility. By circulating, she made herself available for questions. (It's my feeling that students are more inclined to ask for help if the teacher is within reach as opposed to the teacher sitting in the back of the room grading papers.) Looking back now, from my perspective as an experienced teacher, I can see that half of her time was devoted to academics while the other half was devoted to our social and emotional development: a wonderful balance.

There were times, though, when she would get so caught up in the Love Fest that she'd take her eye off of the clock. This meant that instead of stopping at 9:15—as she had said we would—the actual stopping time turned out to be 9:20 or even 9:25.

This wasn't a problem at first because I was more intent on getting my assignment done than I was on watching the clock. However, I did experience days when I was finished by 9:15, but Mrs. Dye was still involved with a couple of students. As the clock ticked on, I began to think about my situation.

  --- *What do I do now? Maybe I should check over my paper. Wait, a second. I'm a student; I never check over my paper.*

  --- *Gee, I finished faster than I needed to. Am I working too hard?*

  --- *Shoot, look at the clock. Doesn't she know what time it is?*

RICKY
  Turning to his buddy sitting next to him:
  Dennis. Hey, Dennis. Look at the time. It's 9:23, and she doesn't know.
  Seeing that Dennis is about to call out to Mrs. Dye:
  No, no, no. Don't tell her. Let her figure it out. It's so much fun to watch.

And sure enough, as Dennis and I kept an eye on her, she would finally glance at the clock.

MRS. DYE
Hurrying to the front of the room with her hands pressed to her cheeks:
Oh, dear me. Look what time it is, boys and girls. We need to stop now.
Seeing students starting to get up from their seats with spelling papers held in outstretched hands:
No, don't give me your papers now. I'll get them tomorrow. We really need to get started on our social studies lesson.

We made the quick switch from spelling to social studies without a complaint but, the next morning at 9:00, she was at it again.

MRS. DYE
With a sincere smile and the best of intentions:
Okay, boys and girls, I see it's 9:00. It's time to work on your spelling assignment. You have 15 minutes. Any questions?

---Yeah, lady, I've got a question. Is it really going to be 15 minutes? I'd like to know how hard I have to work.

Well, it didn't take long before I began to exhibit a very subtle but damaging shift in my work skills. Although I had spent the first month applying myself to be done in 15 minutes, by the fifth week of school I started to slow down and not work quite so hard.

This change was a direct result of the fact that what she *said* and what she *did* were two different things.

Child Development 101
Jean Piaget discovered that children learn in fundamentally different ways than do adults. Children are all about their experience. It's not what you say to them that shapes their behavior. It's what you actually do that has the greatest impact.[†] To children, action is the only reality.

Although I had heard my teacher state that we had 15 minutes in which to have the assignment done, we didn't always stop in 15 minutes. Granted, it was 15 minutes on some days. On other days, though, we exceeded that time limit.

The fairly predictable conclusion was that I began to ignore Mrs. Dye's admonitions about being done on time. We had extra time so often that I began to anticipate it. And if I'm anticipating extra time, why rush? Slow down, Ricky. Take your time.

---

† Piaget's findings are the basis for Core Principle #2: Your words equal your actions. An excellent book that clearly explains how to make this a reality in your room is Robert MacKenzie's *Setting Limits in the Classroom*. It is, without a doubt, the best book I've ever read on discipline, and I highly recommend picking up a copy.

Sadly, though, there were days when I was in one of my slow-work modes but Mrs. Dye was playing Beat the Clock.

MRS. DYE
>At 9:15 sharp:
>> *I need to collect your spelling now.*

RICKY
>In stunned disbelief:
>> *--- What?!?! I'm not done yet.*

And do you want to know the most troubling aspect of this entire little melodrama? It was the fact that *I had the skills to be done on time.* My teacher, though, had undermined those skills through her inconsistency.

Let's save everyone from falling into this Old School trap by employing a simple piece of technology: a digital timer.

Rick Morris as a Fourth Grade Teacher

If I want my students to work on an assignment for 15 minutes, I'll pick up Max[†], set him for the proper amount of time, and show the class.

MR. MORRIS
>Showing the students that Max has been set for 15 minutes:
>> *We have 15 minutes for this assignment. Any questions?*
>Seeing no question hands raised:
>> *All right, then, I've got a question. What are you going to do if you finish early?*

> It's always a good idea to make sure your students are aware of appropriate activities in which they can engage whenever they finish ahead of the time limit you've established. We have an ***E.T. Chart***—Extra Time—that lists suggested activities. By referring to the E.T. Chart, students will find something significant to occupy their extra time.

>> *That's right. Just check the E.T. Chart, and choose one of the activities listed. Any other questions? No? You may begin.*

I'd then press the button on Max which would begin the 15 minute countdown. With the timer to keep track of things, I no longer had to keep one eye on the clock. I could completely and freely interact with my students. And during the entire 15 minutes I didn't spend a single second worrying about stopping the activity on time. That, you will soon discover, is a major stress reducer.

---

† We had a "Name the timer" contest one year. Max was chosen. I've found that some classroom tools and toys are easier to use if you give them a name. "Has anyone seen Max?" has a better feel to it than "Has anyone seen our digital timer?" But then again, maybe that's just me.

Fifteen minutes later, Max will start beeping. In our room, the beeping sound meant:

Stop what you're doing and get ready for something else.

Consequently, the students would put away their materials as I disengaged from the students with whom I had been interacting. By the time I got back to my desk, a student would have turned off Max—usually after a couple of beeps—and we'd be ready to move on to our next activity. Just the fact that I didn't have to say, "Please stop what you're doing and get ready for our next activity" was worth the money I spent for Max.

Using a Digital Timer

Although the example just given demonstrated the use of a timer to monitor the amount of time students were given to complete an assignment, it shouldn't be limited to just those situations. As I'll explain over the next several pages, there will be many, many ways in which you can put a digital timer to work for you and your students.

Discretionary Time

Imagine, if you will, that you've just wrapped up a grammar lesson. In fact, your students were such hard workers and your lesson went so well, you actually finished ten minutes earlier than you thought you would. The only problem is that the lesson was supposed to last until morning recess. You now have ten minutes to fill until it's recess time. With Max in hand, you'll be able to use those bonus minutes well.

power
love
fun
freedom
safety

Mr. Morris

What a great job you guys did on today's lesson. Take a look at the clock. We finished ahead of time. Tell you what, why don't we work on our seat cover project † until recess. We have about ten minutes to stitch.

Students

Thanks, Mr. Morris!

And with that, they'd dive into their stitching. In less than a minute, they'll be up to their elbows in burlap and yarn.

Fortunately, I've got Max to help keep track of this extra time. Since we only have ten minutes, and we're going to need a bit of time to clean-up, I'll set Max for just eight minutes. With Max minding the store, I'll be free, once again, to circulate around the room to see how my students are doing. I love the freedom to do this without the nagging concern of watching or worrying about the clock.

† You can find the Seat Cover Stitchery project on the New Management website: www.NewManagement.com.

Eight minutes later, Max starts beeping. Without having to say a word, my students will put away their stitchery materials and organize their desks. After their desks are organized, they'll find their independent reading books and begin to read. Then, when the recess bell does ring, we're able to leave for recess in a calm fashion.

If, on the other hand, I didn't have a digital timer to keep track of this extra time, I would have had to monitor the clock. Otherwise, there's a chance the recess bell could catch us by surprise.

> *Sad reality:* Having experienced this in my early days of teaching, I can tell you that students have very little energy for cleaning up at this point. They want to go directly to recess. Feeling somewhat guilty because of the poor time management on my part, I was sometimes inclined to allow them to leave without first cleaning up. Unfortunately, leaving their desks in a mess and then coming back to the mess really interfered with a smooth transition to independent reading.

Time Out

There are times when I need to send a student to another classroom for a brief "Time Out." It's just one of the many interventions I employ to deal with negative behavior. Due to Max's assistance, "Time Out" has become a manageable procedure.

It wasn't so manageable back in my pre-timer days. Other than my memory, there wasn't anything to remind me to bring the student back to the room at a reasonable time.

MR. MORRIS
Meeting his students on the blacktop at the end of recess and seeing one of the students wildly fooling around:
Hey, Mr. Funnyboy. You think that's funny? Oh, that was a riot. You need to wait here. I'll be right back.

I would then lead the others students into the room—which is not too far from where they line up on the blacktop—because I wanted to get them started on their independent reading. Well, independent reading led to Daily Oral Language which then morphed into Word Study and, before I knew it, I'd forget about the student I had left outside. Not that I meant to leave him out there (which is what I'll say to his parents when they call tomorrow to complain) but, you know how it is: "Out of sight, out of mind."

The other students in class, of course, provided very little help in reminding me about the student still outside. Eventually, one of them would ask:

Mr. Morris, weren't you supposed to go talk to Travis?

Whoops.

MR. MORRIS
> Looking sheepishly at his watch:
>> *Well, he's been out there an hour. I guess that's enough. I'll go get him.*

Adding insult to injury, I wouldn't even apologize to the poor kid. I made it sound as if I had wanted to leave him out there that long. (When I was a new teacher, I wasn't very good at apologizing to students for my mistakes. I'm not sure why. I just wasn't. I've since gotten much better at it. It's a Love and Safety thing.)

MR. MORRIS
> Full of gruff bluster:
>> *Well, I hoped you've learned your lesson, young man. You may come back to class.*

To avoid this debacle, I now rely on Max, my trusty sidekick, to keep track of how long a student should spend in the other classroom.

MR. MORRIS
> Having to stop in the middle of a science lesson because Calvin's in one of his "not working cooperatively" modes:
>> *Calvin, come with me please.*
> Walking him to the door with Max in hand:
>> *I've asked you before to pay attention and do your best. You weren't doing either of those things. Please go to Room 11 and sit for the next five minutes. Thank you.*

I'd then set Max for the allotted five minutes[†] and return to my science lesson.

Five minutes later, when I've already forgotten about it, Max will beep. That's the signal for one of my students to go to Room 11 and bring Calvin back to class.

Kaizen: The Japanese philosophy of continuous improvement.

An example:

I used to send our Student Deputy over to bring Calvin back to the room. My mind-set was: the kid's been busted, send the thug to bring him back. Therefore, the Deputy had been chosen for his intimidation value more than his sensitivity. Consequently, when Max beeped, the Deputy—who didn't want to leave the science experiment—would go to Room 11 and, in somewhat brusque fashion, command Calvin to return to the room. The Deputy would then return to his group and resume the activity. Poor Calvin, having been gone from the room for the past five to ten minutes, was left to fend for himself. What are the odds that he would be able to rejoin his group successfully and integrate himself into the activity?

---

† The research seems to indicate that "time outs" of longer than fifteen minutes result in reduced self-esteem and increased anxiety. Five minutes might be long enough. All I'm trying to do is reinforce to my students that certain behavior is not appropriate and will not be tolerated.

Kaizen (continued): I now send over a Social Worker to retrieve Calvin. Social Workers are students who are chosen because of their general popularity with the other students. Social Workers are the students with whom everyone wants to play and eat lunch. They're the kids whose birthday invitations are coveted. Even Calvin wants to be liked by these students and, thus, will be inclined to listen to them.

Now, when Max beeps, one of the Social Workers will go over to Room 11 and get Calvin. The two of them will then go to the back of our room and sit together for a minute or two so that the Social Worker can bring Calvin up to speed. As soon as he feels ready, Calvin then rejoins his team for the remainder of the activity.

power
love
fun
freedom
safety

By using Max to support the Time Out intervention, I was able to deal with the negative—Calvin's behavior—while staying focused on the positive—the science lesson and the students who were doing a good job.

Silent Reading

As I mentioned in the previous section, we engage in ten minutes of Independent Reading immediately after morning recess. Before I started using Max, I was always the one who had to monitor the time by watching the clock. Depending on how well Independent Reading was going, I sometimes extended the time limit. On a good day, I could grade papers for thirty minutes. On a bad day, Independent Reading might only last five minutes.

As the weeks went by, the inconsistency of how long Independent Reading actually lasted caused a problem. Since the students never knew how long it would go, some of them had a difficult time immersing themselves in their reading. They were so preoccupied trying to determine by my expression or behavior when I was about to announce that reading was over that their heads were bobbing up and down: read a bit, check Mr. Morris, read some more, check Mr. Morris again.

With Max in charge of the time, we don't have those problems.

Upon our return to the classroom from recess, a student will set Max for ten minutes. Everyone then reads. (Since the students left their Independent Reading books on their desks opened to the right page before they went out to recess, it's easy for them to have a seat and begin reading. There's no wasted time as students root through desks or wander around the room looking for a book. We're talking high engagement from the moment they sit down.)

Due to the fact that Independent Reading is *always* ten minutes, the students become accustomed to this time frame. Within a month or so, even my underachievers come to the realization that ten minutes is not that long. Although they're not crazy about reading, ten minutes—*and no more than ten minutes*—is bearable.

True to his nature, Max will beep when the ten minutes are up. Hearing the beep, the students put away their books, and we jump into our Daily Oral Language assignment.

Bonus: You may have noted that, from the time we came back into the room from morning recess, I hadn't had to say a word. It was quiet from the time we came in until Max beeped. Ah, blessed silence and a break from my voice for them.

Rotations

If you use learning centers or activity stations as a part of your day, having a timer will help to ensure that everyone is getting a fair turn at each center.

Let's say that you have five student teams, five centers, and forty minutes in which to use the centers. All you have to do is set your timer for 8 minutes, send a team to each center, ask them to begin, and then start your timer. Eight minutes later, the students will hear the timer and, like clockwork, move to the next center. All you have to do is reset your timer and press the start button. At the end of your forty minutes of activity time, you can rest assured that each team had had an equal opportunity at each learning center.

Reality: The time limit might need to be 7 minutes so that you have some "rotation time" built into the process.

Sharing

When I taught second grade, I quickly discovered that, in their eyes, Sharing was a sacred rite. My little second graders would look forward all week long to Friday afternoon's Sharing. I can still remember how they would rush me first thing Friday morning to not only verify that we were going to have Sharing after lunch but also to let me know that they had something to share.

By the third session, though, Sharing had begun to lose a bit of its luster. Or, at least it had from my perspective. We always seemed to have too many students taking much too long to share their personal stories and special events. Sounds as if we need a procedure.

The new Sharing procedure:

On Friday, I would draw a box on the whiteboard and label it "Sharing."

FIG. 5-4
This space on our whiteboard was created Friday morning as the place for students to sign-up for sharing.

By dedicating a small portion of our whiteboard for Sharing sign-up, I was able to reassure the students that Sharing was definitely on our schedule for Friday afternoon.

Students who wished to share would write their names inside the box. They would also indicate whether they wanted one minute or two minutes for sharing. Since we only had fifteen minutes for Sharing, students had to stop and do some column addition to see if we had time left on today's "show" before they added their names to the list.

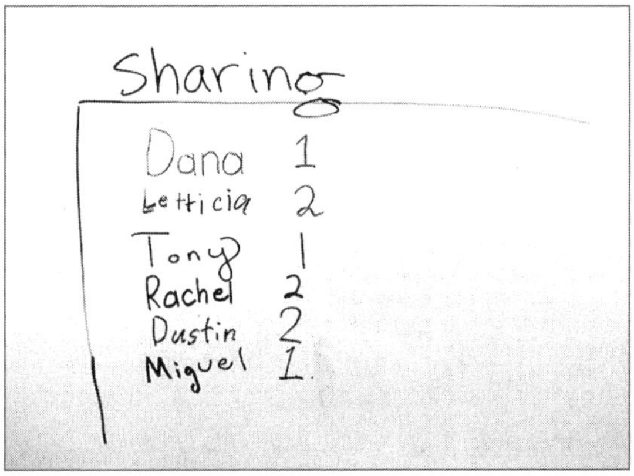

FIG. 5-5
A simple way to keep track of which students wish to share and how much time each one needs.

Sharing

Dana	1
Letticia	2
Tony	1
Rachel	2
Dustin	2
Miguel	1.

As you can see by the example shown here, six students have signed up for Sharing. Altogether, they'll need nine minutes. We still have six minutes available.

If all of the fifteen minutes has been claimed, students would be encouraged to wait until next Friday's show.

power
love
fun
freedom
safety

After lunch on Friday, we'd get ready for Sharing. The students would turn their chairs around so that they all faced the front of the room. One of the students would get Max, check the Sharing sign-up, call the name of the first student, and then set Max for the proper time. The student called would then go to the front of the room and share.

One of two things would happen.

1. The student would finish sharing before Max beeped. (A minute is a long time for some students.) In this case, we would stop Max and thank the student for sharing. The student in charge of Max would then clear any remaining time, call the next student, and set Max again.

MR. MORRIS
   ---Sweet. We just saved thirty seconds.

2. The student is still sharing when Max beeps. (I'm thinking about the kid who signed up for two minutes and is determined to share every painful detail of his recent birthday party at Chuck E. Cheese. Two minutes of this would be more than enough.) When Max started beeping, we would politely thank the child for sharing and move on to the next student.

In all of the years I've used this technique, we never went beyond our fifteen minutes nor did we have to endure someone's rambling, disjointed 10-minute discourse on the Family Vacation to Grandpa's. Not only that, but the students developed the ability to:
   1) assess how much time they were going to need and
   2) modify their "presentation" to fit within that time.

All in all, it was, and still is, one terrific procedure.

Choosing a Digital Timer

Over the years, I've come upon a variety of effective timers. And like most things in life, they each have their own advantages and disadvantages. My main recommendation is that you stick with a brand name such as Sunbeam or Westbend. Some of the off-brand models are so poorly engineered that you'll quickly tire of their shortcomings.

Here's what you want in a timer.

1. Check to see that it times in minutes and seconds. A timer that only displays hours and minutes won't be specific enough for your purposes.

2. Make sure that the beeping sound is loud enough for your students to hear. If they can't hear it, what's the sense in using it?

3. Check to see that the minute and second button have a "rapid advance" feature. This means that, after you hold down either the minute hand or the second hand button for three seconds, the numbers begin to cycle up quickly. Some low budget timers require a push for each minute and emit a beep for each push. Having to set one of those to forty-five minutes is a beepin' pain.

4. A magnet on the back allows you to slap it on your whiteboard. The magnet is more of a bonus feature than an actual necessity.

My Personal Favorite

I've sold a lot of timers to a lot of teachers over the years but this is by far the best digital timer I've ever come across. It's made by CDN—the company that supplies Starbucks with all of their timers—and sells for $15. Shown below in actual size, your students will be able to see the display from across the classroom. That alone sold me.

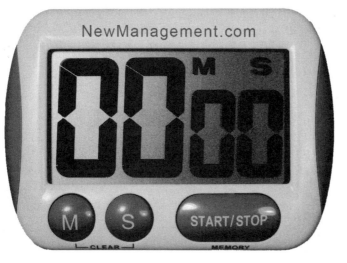

FIG. 5-6
Your students will be able to read the display from across the room.

ADVANTAGES:

- Large, easy-to-read display

- Uses an inexpensive, AAA battery
  Some timers use special batteries that not only cost quite a bit more but are difficult to find.

- Has both a magnet and a stand
  It even has a flip-up loop you can use to secure it to the wall with a screw if you're worried about theft.

- Has a memory feature
  This is especially useful when you are using your timer for rotating groups through activities. After you set the time and press the START/STOP *button, your timer will countdown to 00:00 and begin to beep. When you press the* START/STOP *button again to stop the beeping, it will automatically reset itself for the time you have previously entered. Thus, if your groups are scheduled for 8 minutes per station, the display will reset to 8 minutes after you press* START/STOP.

- Clear, distinctive beep
  The one disadvantage to many timers on the market is that the beep is not very loud. A softly beeping timer is not going to do you much good in the classroom. If, for some reason, the beeping sound is too loud for you or your students—not likely but you never know—a little bit of scotch tape over the opening in the back from which the beep is emitted will muffle the sound.

- Beeps as you set the time
  Every time you press the minute button or the second button to set the time, you will hear a beep. The sound your timer will make when you set it for 10 minutes—beep, beep, beep, beep, beep, beep, beep, beep, beep, beep—will be a subtle, subconscious reminder that: 1) you're about to use your timer; and 2) the time period is not all that long.

- Has a fast setting mode
  This model has that "rapid advance" feature I mentioned on the previous page; therefore, the choice is yours. Beep, beep, beep, beep, beep for an attention-getting five-minute setting or hold the button down for three seconds and then watch the digits quickly scroll up to 30 for a half-hour setting.

- Has a count-up function (just press START/STOP with the display showing 00:00)
  Handy for keeping track of elapsed time. (See "I'm Waiting" on the next page.)

FIG. 5-7
A stand for your desk, a magnet if you want to stick it on a whiteboard, and even a loop for bolting it to a wall so that it doesn't "walk away" from your classroom. That's pretty dang sweet.

"I'm Waiting..."

When you go looking for a timer, try to find one that has a count-up feature. This can be extremely helpful in cutting down on how much time you have to wait in order for your students to come to attention so that you can begin a lesson.[†] If, after waiting a reasonable amount of time—say, fifteen seconds—they're still sitting out there chit-chatting, I'll pick up Max and, with the display reading 00:00, hit the START/STOP button *(beep)*.

I don't announce what I'm doing or even watch the students. I just hold up Max so that he is visible to everyone and keep my eyes on the time.

When they finally quiet down, I'll press START/STOP again which pauses the count-up process. (It will take them a few times before they finally figure out that it's in their best interests to come to attention quickly.) I'll then announce the number of seconds to the class and have a student write the number on the board.

Later on, just before we leave for lunch, we'll add up the numbers on the board.

> MR. MORRIS
>> With Max in hand:
>> *I see by our calculations that we spent forty-one seconds this morning waiting for students to pay attention. That was better than yesterday, but not as good as you'll do tomorrow, I'd be willing to bet.*

I'll then set Max for that amount of time and press START/STOP. The students will then have to wait in their seats until Max beeps before they're allowed to go to lunch.

Although forty-one seconds may not seem like a long time, you'll have to experience it before you realize how long it can seem. This will be especially true for your students who will have to sit there silently waiting to go to lunch as other classes are walking by your room on their way to lunch. Your students will be able to visualize that lunch line getting longer and longer.

It won't take too long before your class comes to attention when you need it.

Assemblies

One of the advantages of the timer shown on page 5-7 was that it could be set to go off hours later. It also had three channels, which meant that it usually had an unused channel available. A great use for one of those unused channels was the ability to set a "Time to leave for the assembly" alarm.

---

† For the record, I don't call for my students attention when I need to start a lesson. Although they've been conditioned to having a teacher do that, I don't. I actually stand in front with my arms crossed by my waist and wait. As I wait, I look for the students who are paying attention and give them some kind of recognition: a wink, a nod, a smile, a sign language "thank you," etc. Before long, I'll have them all. Within a week, I'm able to stand in front of my class and have everyone's attention within fifteen seconds. If, on the other hand, I always call for their attention, I'll always have to call for it. It's all in how you condition them.

First thing in the morning, I'd check our schedule for the day to see if we had any school-wide events scheduled. Sure enough: Assembly, 10:15. I'd pick up Max, calculate how long until then, and set him to beep five minutes prior to that time. After double checking my elapsed time math, I'd press the START/STOP button.

Two hours and forty-seven minutes later, for example, Max starts to *beep*.

> MR. MORRIS
> Who had the quizzical attention of his students because Max was unexpectedly beeping:
> > *Max is reminding us that it's time for the Mad Science assembly.*
> Mild buzzing from the students:
> > *Clear desks, please.*

Room 12 is now guaranteed of arriving at the assembly in a timely fashion. If, on the other hand, I hadn't used Max and I did forget about the assembly, I'd more than likely be the recipient of a phone call from the office.

> OFFICE STAFF MEMBER:
> > *Hey, Mr. Management. Are you bringing your class to the assembly or what? It started five minutes ago. Everyone else is already here.*

Dang.

Medication

Similar to the use of a spare channel to alert us to assembly time would be the use of a channel for a student who needs to take medication in the nurse's office each morning. Although most students in this situation can be counted on to go each and every day unassisted, some need support.

If this is the case for one of your students, show him the proper way to use the timer and then have him set it in the morning. In addition to the fact that the medication would be taken as needed, this student would be getting some great practice at self-sufficiency.

> *Computer Software:* Come to think of it, this strategy would also work for students who need to leave the room to see the resource teacher, speech therapist, counselor, etc. If, however, the student goes to the resource room every day at the same time, it might be easier to download a simple digital timer/alarm clock. If you use a PC, just google "Cool Timer." The Mac faithful should take a look at Alarm Clock 2 by Robbie Hanson. Both are free and work flawlessly. You can even assign a song to play in place of a beeping sound.
>
> *Windows users:* Check out Music Central on my website for a video demonstration of how to create a classroom alarm clock using Task Scheduler.

Secondary Students and the "Pack Up" Routine

A while ago I was invited to visit a couple of former students who are now teaching at the middle school level. Although it was great to see them, it was difficult to witness the rudeness and bad attitudes being displayed by some of the students. You almost got the feeling each of these young ladies was wearing a sign that read: "Kick me. I'm a new teacher." What really bugged me, though, was watching a number of their students packing up well before the end of the period.

At the end of my visit, I mentioned to both of them that they needed to get a handle on the "pack up" routine or it was going to get worse. My suggestion? Set a timer to go off two minutes before the end of the period as a signal to begin to get ready to leave.

By removing the uncertainty of when it's okay to pack up, the teachers would be able to hold their students accountable. Basically, the understanding would be: Don't even think about packing up until you hear the sound of the timer.

And Still More Uses

Even though I've used a digital timer for more years than I care to ponder, I'm still discovering new uses for it. Granted, it's predominantly used for timing lessons and activities; nonetheless, it can be used in other situations to great effect.

Parent Conferences

I don't know how you arrange your schedule for seeing parents at report card time, but my schedule always seems to have bulges wherein I've got five sets of parents coming in one right after the other. In an attempt to provide each of them with some quality time and ensure that I'm seeing each of them at the proper time, I've enlisted Max's support.

After a brief round of introductions and a chance to get settled, I'll show them Max and briefly explain how and why we use it in the classroom. I'll then set him for 18 minutes—we have 20 minutes scheduled for our conference—as I reassure them that this time is all theirs. If it's appropriate, I also mention that I was able to see them on time because I had used Max in the previous conference. (Most parents have no problem with the timer.)

Eighteen minutes later, Max announces the end of our time together. The last two minutes are spent in drawing things to closure and walking the parents to the door. Before they leave, I always offer the following suggestion:

MR. MORRIS
Rising from the conference table:
I'm sorry we don't have more time to talk. Please feel free to call me and schedule an appointment. Or, if you want to, just stop by whenever you wish. The room is always open. Thanks again for taking the time to come in.

It may seem to you that using a timer to monitor a conference is a bit harsh or even rude.[†] As with any sensitive issue, though, it's all in how you present it.

Staff Meetings

Why not take your new timer to your next staff meeting and see if you can impose a time limit on some part of the agenda? (As a courtesy, you should probably check with your principal *before* trying this variation. Also, new teachers might want to bear in mind that I have tenure and, thus, have a bit more freedom to make these kinds of suggestions.)

Maybe your staff is going to discuss some emotionally charged issue. You could bring up the idea that, to keep things moving along, there should be a predetermined time frame for the discussion. Start with ten minutes and see how it goes. Usually, after a heated ten minutes, the majority of teachers will be more than happy, at the sound of the beep, to move on to the next agenda item.

Warning: Using a timer to help keep a staff meeting focused is a little bit tricky. However, if you can pull it off you'll be a hero.

Talking With Other Staff Members

This strategy was given to me by a teacher, and it's a good one. She told me that the counselor at her school uses a digital timer whenever he needs to speak with any of the teachers during their break time.

Being aware of the fact that the time teachers have for breaks—recess and lunch—is precious, he wanted to reassure them that his impromptu, hallway conversations would not take up too much of that valuable time.

Counselor
> With timer in hand, approaching a teacher in the hallway at recess time:
> *I know you're busy. May I have just a minute of your time?*

Come on now. What jaded soul out there could possibly begrudge this guy a minute? You're right, no one does.

The teacher told me two things happened over time.

1. Staff members no longer avoided the counselor during break time. They had learned that, at the most, any dialogue with this counselor would only last for a minute.

---

† Actually, the parents I'm going to be rude to are the ones who are now waiting outside the room for me. Without a timer, conferences can go on and on and on. And even though most parents will wait patiently, I can't help but wonder if some of them are out there thinking:

> ---*This guy can't even meet with parents on time. What must the school day be like?*

2. The counselor noted that many teachers, upon hearing the timer beep, would continue the conversation. This effectively eliminated the need to continue the dialogue at a later time.

This is just another one of those classic Win-Win situations.

Ben's Computer

When my son, Ben, was young, he loved to use his computer before he went to bed. Being the die-hard, ring-every-second-out-of-the-day kind of kid that he is, my wife and I sometimes experienced a bit of resistance when it was time for him to shut down his Mac and head to bed.

I eventually realized that this was due to the rather abrupt and unexpected termination of his beloved computing. Although in the back of his mind he knew that he was going to have to stop at some point, he just never wanted "some point in time" to be "right now."

Having had such great success with digital timers in the classroom, I thought that maybe one would work at home.

It did.

I now use a timer to alert Ben that it's time for bed, and the change has been a pleasant one.

DAD
Walking into Ben's room with a timer in hand:
Son, it's almost time for bed. I'm going to set the timer for five more minutes. When it beeps, you'll need to turn off your computer. Okay?

BEN
Not terribly thrilled but bowing to the inevitable:
Okay, Dad.

Sure enough, five minutes later, when the timer beeps, Ben will shut down his Mac and come find me.

The reason this transition works is two-fold:

1. He was told that the end was near. As simple as this may appear, it enabled him to mentally and emotionally prepare himself to stop.

2. Knowing that his time was almost up, he was fully able to enjoy his last five minutes.

It's kind of like when you're home relaxing, reading a novel, and working on a sleeve of Girl Scout Thin Mint cookies. As you reach for another cookie you're shocked to discover there are no more. You had eaten the last cookie without realizing it was the last one.

CLUELESS COOKIE EATER
Reaching for the cookies only to find that they're all gone:
What?!? I ate the last cookie? Oh, man. If I had known that the one I had just eaten was the last one, I would have enjoyed it so much more.

HAPPY COOKIE EATER
Pulling the last cookie out of the sleeve:
Oh, last cookie. I think I'll stop reading for a moment and just savor your goodness.

It's the same thing with my son and his computer.

BEN
Eyeing the timer:
---Oh, man. It's almost time for bed. Well, at least I still have five more minutes on my computer.

Timer Tips

Experience has taught me a few things about using a digital timer that I'll share with you so that you won't have to experience the same learning curve.

Assessing How Much Time for Activities

It will take a while to get a feel for how much time you need to provide for certain activities. Although ten minutes for independent reading and a five minute "time out" work well, how long should I give my students to answer a set of social studies questions or complete a math activity sheet?

Recommended:
1. Set your timer for what you think is an appropriate amount of time.
2. Announce the time to your students.
3. Allow them to get started.
4. Start your timer.
5. Start to circulate around the room to check on progress.[†]

As you work your way around the room checking on your students, you'll begin to get a feel for whether you've set your timer for the proper amount of time.

---

†   Don't use the pace of your overachievers as you assess their progress. Overachievers will give you a false sense of success and achievement. Look, instead, to the handful of average students.

If, by your observations, you feel that the amount of time you've given them is not going to be enough, it's important that you adjust the time before the timer beeps.

MR. MORRIS
Getting the attention of his students (see pages 5-31 to 5-38 for suggestions):
I think I goofed on how much time you're going to need to complete this activity. In fact, check your papers. If you are on track to be finished when Max beeps, you should be on problem number 12 right now.

STUDENTS
Checking their papers and gasping at their appalling lack of progress:
Oh, no.

MR. MORRIS
Resetting Max:
Everybody calm down. I'm going to add 10 minutes to the time I gave you. You now have 20 minutes to have this assignment finished.

STUDENTS
Thanks, Mr. Morris.

power
love
fun
freedom
safety

MR. MORRIS
Enjoying the appreciation:
You're welcome. Back on task, please.

If, on the other hand, I hadn't intervened when I should have, and Max started to beep as originally set, I'd find myself with a whole host of unhappy-because-their-assignments-aren't-yet-finished students. This would be especially true if they really hadn't been given enough time to complete the assignment.

MAX
Having counted down to zero:
Beep…beep…beep…beep…beep…beep…beep…beep…beep.

MR. MORRIS
Stopping Max and addressing his students:
I need to collect your activity sheets now.

STUDENTS
What?
Already?
I'm not done yet!
That wasn't enough time!

I'm now faced with two options:

1. Add more time to what was originally given.
2. Tell them we'll work on this assignment tomorrow and collect it then.

Adding more time is fine. After all, teachers make mistakes and need to address them with their students. However, if I make a habit of adding time, my students will eventually begin to see Max—and, by association, Mr. Morris—as something that can be ignored rather than obeyed. Extending the activity until tomorrow falls into the same category: fine as long as it's not overdone.

With a bit of practice, though, you'll get good at setting your timer. And, by learning how to judge appropriate time frames, you'll not only avoid the perils of extending the time, you'll reinforce your consistency and fairness.

Breaking Up Long Times

Whenever you find yourself needing to set your timer for a period of time greater than thirty minutes, you might want to think about keeping them apprised of the passage of time.

I've made it a practice to announce the halfway point.

> Mr. Morris
> With Max in hand:
> *You have 40 minutes in which to complete page 2 of your social studies activity packet. Any questions?*

Not a peep.

> Mr. Morris
> *Well, then, I have a question. What are you going to do when you finish early?*

> Student
> *Put your packet in your paper folder and check the E.T. Chart.*

> Mr. Morris
> *That's a good plan. Okay, 40 minutes. Let's get to work.*

And with that, I'd set Max for 20 minutes. The beep we'll hear at the halfway point will enable me to remind them about how much time they have remaining.

> Mr. Morris
> With the now beeping Max in hand:
> *Max is telling us we have just 20 minutes left in which to complete this assignment. If you're stuck or confused about anything on this page, please ask for help. Back on task, please.*

power
love
fun
freedom
safety

This simple technique helps to prevent time from getting away from us. It also enables me to encourage students who now realize that they are not sure about part of the assignment to seek help before it's too late.

Two Minutes Left? Time to Prepare

One of the subtle advantages to using a digital timer is that you'll be able to adjust what you're doing according to the time left. As you near the end, check the display to see how much time still remains.

Less than two minutes...

> Don't get yourself involved in something that will take more than two minutes. You need to be ready to make a smooth transition to the next activity you have planned for your students.

Although most of your time during independent activity periods should be devoted to "working the room" so that you're available for students who need your assistance, there will be times when they are doing fine and you're free to take care of some type of classroom business.

One minute left...

> Write a quick note to a parent regarding something positive one of your students did today.

> Check off your name on the routing slip attached to the announcement sent to you by the office. These things can pile up if you allow them to. Find a student who has finished the assignment, give him the routing slip and announcement, and send him to the next room on the list.

> Check your plan book to reassure yourself that you have already prepared all of the materials you're going to need for later in the day.

> Go sit with one of your underachievers and provide some emotional support.

power
love
fun
freedom
safety

Thirty seconds left...

> Collect your thoughts.

> Think about how you want to transition to the next activity.

> Double-check to see that you have what you're going to need.

> Relax and smile.

Max is beeping...

> Allow them a moment to disengage from their activities.

> Give transition directions in a slow, calm voice.

Transition Music

Speaking of transitions, if you have the book, *Eight Great Ideas*, make sure you read Chapter 4: *Using Music for Student Management.* It describes, in step-by-step fashion, how to use something as simple as the *Jeopardy* theme song as a transition timer.

I've found that TV theme songs are well suited for this purpose. For one, they are usually of a short duration. For another, most of the songs are familiar enough that the students can use the music to pace themselves. By the time the song is hitting its final few measures, they'll be ready for the next activity. You gotta try it to see what I mean.

Music Central: On page 5-22 I referred to Music Central. Be sure to check out the area on my website devoted to using music for management. A brief list of current posts includes:

> Main Music Page
> Classroom Alarm Clock
> Download Instructions
> iTunes Trick
> More Music
> Overhead Spinner
> Sound Effects
> Test Timers
> TV Theme Songs
> Wrap-Up Song

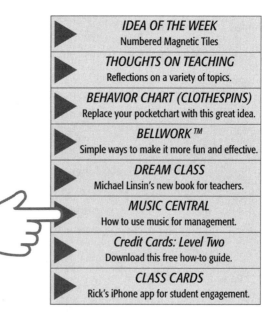

▶	**IDEA OF THE WEEK** Numbered Magnetic Tiles
▶	**THOUGHTS ON TEACHING** Reflections on a variety of topics.
▶	**BEHAVIOR CHART (CLOTHESPINS)** Replace your pocketchart with this great idea.
▶	**BELLWORK ™** Simple ways to make it more fun and effective.
▶	**DREAM CLASS** Michael Linsin's new book for teachers.
▶	**MUSIC CENTRAL** How to use music for management.
▶	**Credit Cards: Level Two** Download this free how-to guide.
▶	**CLASS CARDS** Rick's iPhone app for student engagement.

Classroom Toys

As I mentioned earlier in this lesson, the words *tools* and *toys* are great ones to use with students. Not only is the language easy enough for them to understand, but the words provide a subconscious message which tells everyone that "we take care of business in this room." This attitude is important to convey to your students, especially at the beginning of the year when they are beginning to develop an awareness about what the year is going to be like.

power
love
fun
freedom
safety

My only caveat about the word *toy* is the fact that students can sometimes go overboard on the fun associated with toys. Frankly, though, that's one of the main benefits to using toys in the classroom. Toys will help you meet that critical student need: fun. Learning requires enthusiasm, and just about everybody gets enthusiastic when they're having fun. By using a variety of simple toys to help you take care of business, you'll feed the need while availing yourself of some powerful techniques.

Sound Makers

One of my first classroom toys was a plastic space gun I found at a swap meet. The electronic sound it emitted was distinct and sounded like something a child could relate to. So, I bought it and took it into the classroom. My thought was that I could use the sound to get the attention of my students whenever I needed to make an announcement.

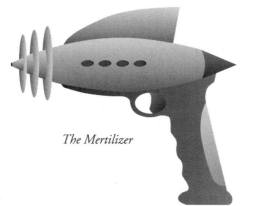

The Mertilizer

BTW: It didn't really look like this, but the photo I had wasn't all that great. I took that as an excuse to take a break from writing and make a cool one using Adobe Illustrator.

It looks a bit like the Mertilizer that Calvin used when he was in Spaceman Spiff mode. (Calvin & Hobbes is my all-time favorite cartoon strip. I still mourn the retirement of author and artist Bill Watterson.)

Although I was a bit uncomfortable waving a gun around the room, I really liked the electronic sound it produced and how quickly that sound got the attention of my students. When my little space gun finally wore out, as electronic toys eventually do, I replaced it with something even better: a dog squeak toy. (See page 5-35.)

I still remember the day I introduced that first toy to my students.

MR. MORRIS
Holding up the space gun:
I found a toy I'd like to use in the classroom. It's this little space gun.

Ooohs and aaahs from the students.

STUDENT

I've got one of those at home!

MR. MORRIS

Waiting a beat before responding:

That's nice. This is not a normal toy, though. We're not going to play with it the way you would at home. This toy is actually going to help us. Here's how. This little guy makes a cool sound.

I squeezed the trigger and produced the sound.

When you hear that sound, it means that I have an announcement to make, and I'm going to need your attention. So, when you hear this noise,

Another blast from the gun,

I want you to "freeze." Okay, let's give it a try. Everyone pretend you're working on an activity. When you hear the new sound, let me see you "freeze."

Well, I had forgotten that to an eight-year old, "freeze" means *assume a contorted position*. So when I pulled the trigger and the students heard the sound, they twisted themselves into these stiff, little pretzel/statue shapes.

MR. MORRIS

Now realizing the language he used was not the best:

Tell you what, let's rethink that one. "Freeze" wasn't the right idea. How about this one: "Stop, Look, Listen." When you hear the sound, stop where you are, look at me, and listen for the announcement.

Pausing:

Okay, now. One more time.

Another sound blast from the Mertilizer brought everyone to a calm stop whereupon they gave me their attention:

There you go. That's exactly how it's supposed to work. Everyone has stopped and is paying attention to what I need to say. We'll use this space gun from now on whenever I need to make an announcement.

Prior to the time I brought in a sound maker, I would use my voice to get their attention. This was primarily due to the years of conditioning I had received when I was a student myself. From the time I entered school as a kindergarten student until the day I received my own credential to teach, almost every teacher used verbal cues for getting the attention of a classroom full of students. Consequently, as a new teacher, I continued the practice.

It was usually something along the lines of...

Excuse me...

Boys and girls...

Eyes please...

I need your attention...

One...two...three...

It used to be so frustrating. I'd have maybe half the class looking at me while the others were still occupied with the task they had been given to complete. I found myself having to repeat the phrase several times as I slowly raised my voice.

> *Generally speaking:* There is nothing inherently wrong with using your voice in this manner. Nonetheless, you should be aware of the fact that you will begin to experience some difficulty if the verbal attention-getter turns out to be the only method you use.

It wasn't until years later, after I had been using sound makers quite successfully, that I came upon the research that explained why voice cues are not the best way to get the attention of your students, especially when they are working independently.

*95% of the independent work students
do in class is left-brain dominant.*

Since I usually need their attention when they are working, I'm actually addressing a group whose left brains are occupied, which means that their left-brain doors are closed. My words—a left-brain cue—are not getting through the closed door. What I need to do is go through the right-brain door because that sucker is wide open and, for the most part, sadly under-utilized.

I say sadly because, according to the research, children stop developing their right-brains at five years of age. Tragically, that's when they enter school: an environment dominated by the left-brain. (You don't have to be too much of a scientist to detect the correlation between the lack of development and the advent of formal schooling.) By activating their uncluttered right-brains, your signalling cue will actually meet with better reception.

Compounding the problem of using verbal cues is that you're adding to the overall amount of talking you do[†] which will decrease the impact and significance of your spoken words.

In a nutshell, you're using your voice when you don't really need to use it. By using a sound maker, you'll not only cut down on the amount of talking you do during the course of the day, but you'll also gain their attention more quickly.

[†] According to the research, 80% of the talking in the elementary classroom is done by the teacher. If you're not careful, overuse of your voice will cause it to become almost invisible by January.

With that in mind, let's use a classroom toy to get their attention.

The Situation:

I've passed out a list of vocabulary words for my students to unscramble as a break from our normally high-octane vocabulary program. I've set Max for 10 minutes. Things are going great for the first minute until I realize that they're not going to be able to figure out word #9 because it doesn't have all of the letters it should.

---Uh, oh. There's a typo on #9. I'd better head them off at the pass.

power
love
fun
freedom
safety

Mr. Morris
Using the Mertilizer to get the students' attention:

Sorry for the interruption; but, I'd like everyone to skip #9 on your vocabulary list. I didn't type it correctly. Just draw a line through it. Sorry about that. Back on task, please.

And with that, I'd leave them in peace so that they could complete the other vocabulary words on their list.

Whenever I need to make a timely announcement and use a sound-making toy to get their attention, the benefits are shared by all.

STUDENT BENEFIT

They get a break from my voice since I no longer have to say, "Boys and girls, I need your attention."

TEACHER BENEFIT

I was able to quickly get their attention and then provide them with the necessary information.

Dog Squeak Toy

Here's the replacement sound maker for the space gun. It makes a great sound, doesn't need batteries, will never wear out, and is almost impossible to break. (The only challenge is to avoid looking ridiculous as you squeeze each of the 50-odd toys in the local pet shop trying to find just the right one.) Everyone knows to "Stop, Look, and Listen" when they hear the squeak-squeak-squeak.

FIG. 5-8
A dog squeak toy is one of the two sound makers I start with each year.

Hotel Bell

This is the second sound maker I introduce each year. It's a simple hotel bell, or call bell. The one shown to the right came from an old card game called Pit. (You can buy a shiny chrome one in our on-line store for six bucks.)

The bell sits on my desk. Whenever I need to pass out material—the activity sheet we're about to do, the kind of paper the students are going to need for an assignment, or merely the reminder note about Picture Day being this Friday—I ring the hotel bell.

power
love
fun
freedom
safety

Each team (we have five teams of students who sit together) sends up a representative. The team rep tells me how many are needed and I hand him that amount. The rep then returns to his team to disseminate the papers.[†] It only takes my new class two days to learn this procedure. After that, it's a zero-effort, no-brainer.

---

†   Part of the procedure is that the students know not to look at what they've received or write their names on it. Since I'm the kind of teacher who waits for the attention of his students, it's important that I make it easy for them to be attentive. Getting distracted by the materials or searching for a pencil interferes with that.

Two is Enough

Before I continue sharing sound making toys, let me stop and make a point.

At the beginning of the year, I only use two of them: the hotel bell for "I need to pass out materials" and the dog squeak toy which means "Stop, Look, Listen." That's it. I don't want to overwhelm or confuse anyone. And, since I've got my students all year, there's really no rush to introduce more sounds than just these two.

However, after the first month, I will slowly add to the sound-making collection of toys we use which will further facilitate my ability to communicate actions and directions to my students. Before Christmas, we'll probably be working with four or five different sounds. By the end of the year, we might be using as many as ten.

Although that may seem overwhelming to you right now, bear in mind that the sounds were slowly introduced and the students were given sufficient practice and support to produce the success I've come to expect. And just think about all of the words you'll no longer need to use.

Rule of thumb: For the first several weeks, I keep it simple and just use two sounds that send two distinct and separate messages.

More "Stop, Look, Listen" Toys

So that you aren't left with the mistaken impression that the "Stop, Look, Listen" sound must be electronic or a squeak toy in order to catch the ear of your students, let me show you a few of the many I've used over the years. Each one has worked because of its unique sound.

Energy Chime

Similar to a tuning fork, this chime will resonate for a long time. It's not the loudest sound but, because of its pitch, it's very effective.

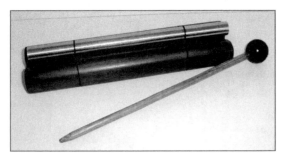

Fig. 5-9
This one sounds kind of like a mellow tuning fork.

The only thing I don't like about it is that it requires two hands to use: one to hold the chime and the other to use the little mallet. I don't always have two hands free. Just one of those little things I thought I'd point out.

Wind Chimes

Here's a soft sound maker. It's a miniature wind chime I received one year as a present from a student. It produces a beautiful sound that really carries.

Helpful Hint: As you seek out a toy for your own "Stop, Look, Listen" sound, make sure you find one that is loud enough. Something that sounded okay in the store might end up frustrating you in the classroom because it's not able to penetrate the ambient sound level of your room. Rain sticks, for example, are nice sound makers but can only be used during quiet times or your students won't be able to hear it and respond.

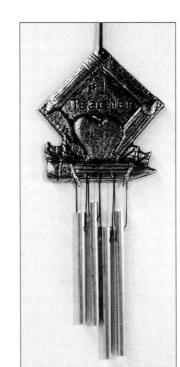

Jingle Bells

Easy to use, won't break, and produces a clear sound. What more could you ask for?

FIG. 5-10
Maybe it's just me, but jingle bells sure do make a happy sound.

Slide Whistle

I found this in a music store where my son takes lessons. Although you will need to use two hands, the sound it produces is well worth the three bucks I spent for it.

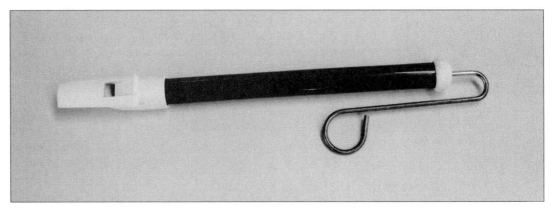

FIG. 5-11
Slide whistles can produce a cartoonish sound kids really seem to like.

Bicycle Horn

Got this one at Toys R Us. It definitely makes a loud sound which can be beneficial when you are in one of those full-body-contact learning activities. You know the ones where the students are working in groups, talking loudly, being productive, and are totally engaged in the project. The bicycle horn cuts through all of the noise.

Fig. 5-12
This one is especially nice when it's a bit loud in your room.

Adding New Sound Makers

Part of using a sound maker effectively is to make sure I don't overuse it. For example, it wouldn't be an effective use of the dog squeak toy—*Stop, Look, Listen*—to get their attention merely to say, "Line up outside." It would be better to use a different sound for that situation.[†]

Train Whistle

I found an old train whistle at a gift shop one day. The whistle makes a softly beautiful sound that conjures images of the old steam engine.

Fig. 5-13
You can find these online or in the catalog.

Although I wasn't sure how I was going to use it, I bought it anyway and took it into the classroom.

---

†   Not only is the right-brain able to differentiate the sounds and their meanings, but I would have eliminated the need to say, "Please line up outside," after using the squeak toy. A specific line-up-outside sound would say it all.

---Hmmmmm. How could I work a train whistle into our routine? Let's see...trains, transportation, train station...(light bulb goes off here)... oh, yeah! That could work.

Before using this new sound, I took my students outside the classroom and showed them what would become the "Room Twelve Train Station."

MR. MORRIS
Gesturing to the proper spot:
This area just outside of the door and along the windows is going to be the Room Twelve train station. We will have two rows of "seats," just like a regular train. "Sit" near the wall if you want to see the buildings; "sit" away from the wall if you want to see the playground.
Holding up the train whistle with a flourish:
From now on, when you hear this sound,
A sweet, gentle sound is produced by blowing on the whistle:
It means, "Stand up, put your chair under your desk, and quietly get on board the train." So we'll use the train whistle whenever we need to line up.
Pointing to the door:
Let's go back inside and give it a try.

I can tell you from experience that by the third or fourth time I use the train whistle, they've got it down. And, from that point on, whenever they see me lift the whistle from my desk, they're already predisposed to be successful because they know the behavior associated with the sound. They see the whistle and think: "We're about to line up outside." They hear the whistle and comply.

Reality Check

One of my concerns as I write about procedures and how my students responded to them is the idea that teachers might not achieve the same success. With that in mind, I'd like to make something clear: it wasn't all rainbows and puppy dogs in my room. There was a lot of trial-and-error, give-and-take, and your basic "How am I going to make this work with the students I've got this year?" before things really clicked. The train whistle is a classic example of the problem-solving it sometimes took to make things work.

Ticket Line
To deal with a rather talkative class one year, I created a Ticket Line for the students who weren't abiding by my spoken request to get on board quietly. After all, it's one thing to ask them to be quiet as a show of respect for the neighboring classes. It's another matter entirely to back it up with action.

With the creation of the Ticket Line, I had an easy way to deal with the loud students. From my spot at the doorway, I was able to call the name of a student or two and motion them toward me. I then stepped aside and asked them to get in the Ticket Line which was just inside the classroom facing the door. Then, when we were ready to go, I'd allow those on board to lead the way as I hung back with everyone in the Ticket Line. As soon as the caboose passed me, I joined the train and brought the Ticket Line with me.

Their line-up behavior was much improved from that point on which goes to show that, even with a tough class, you can achieve success. Just bear in mind that it was the action of putting students in the Ticket Line that produced the change and not my words.

Grace and forgiveness: Students only had to be in the Ticket Line for a day or two; just long enough to make a point. After that, they were allowed to board as usual. However, anyone who was too loud getting on board would hear me say, "Ticket Line, please."

Tone Bars

A long time ago, I found a discarded set of tone bars in our school's storage room and decided to put them to use. I took three of them (D, G, B) and glued them together. By playing a three note pattern, D-B-G, I was able to produce the sound of the television promo for NBC. (It's amazing how many students can recognize that sequence.) But instead of thinking "N - B - C" when they heard those notes, I conditioned them to think "Name - Number - Date." It wasn't long before each student would check for those three pieces of information on their assignments whenever they heard that little three-note song.

Once again, we behold the awesome power of the right-brain.

The same "N-B-C" sequence is available on the CD that comes with the book, Eight Great Ideas.

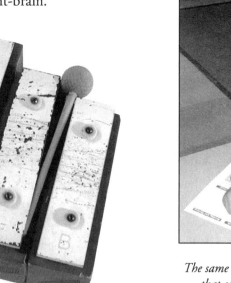

FIG. 5-14
I found these just sitting on a shelf in our storage room gathering dust.

Bicycle Bell

I attached this little bell to the arm of my overhead projector. Since the projector is always next to my desk, the bell is always within reach. Whenever I want my students

to join me on the carpet that is located right behind me, I just ring the bell twice. Without even thinking about it—since these sound signals produce conditioned responses—my students stand up, slide their chairs under their desks, and join me on the carpet.

Within a week, it's automatic.

FIG. 5-15
Since my overhead projector sits right next to me, this bell was always within reach.

Sending More Messages

As you begin to use sound making toys in your room, you'll become convinced of their power and, thus, more aware of how many you come upon in the real world. You'll find yourself at the toy store, wandering through the swap meet, or cleaning out your own children's closet and find one. The difference will be that, instead of passing it by, you'll take it into your classroom and add it to your growing collection of toys.

Tone Bars Revisited

Although I mentioned about the use of tone bars for reminding my students about the name/number/date thing, that wasn't their first use. In fact, years ago, when the set of tone bars was one of the few sound makers I had, I ended up using the heck out them. I taught the students three-note "tunes." Each one represented a different message. One tune meant "put your pencils down," and another one meant "line up at the door." They ended up learning four or five of them.

Clicker

This idea for using a clicker was given to me by a middle school speech teacher.

SPEECH TEACHER
Speaking to Rick at a seminar:

Before the students make their individual speeches, we'll stop and identify a key trait of an effective speaker. Let's use "Eye contact" as an example. The students will then verbalize why "eye contact" is so important in public speaking. After the discussion, the students take turns giving their speeches. If I see a need for more eye contact from the speaker, all I have to do is click my little cricket clicker. The sound is distinct without being distracting. Not only does the speaker get the message that more eye contact is needed, the audience also receives the message. Students who are about to go up begin to prepare themselves for making eye contact.

Need we say more?

Actually, yes, we do. Especially if you're thinking: "Rick, that's a great suggestion, but I'm not a middle school speech teacher. I can't use that idea."

Here's one of the ways I've used the clicker in my room. During those times when the students are reading orally, I'll click it once as a way to indicate that we need a student to take over the oral reading duties.

Upon hearing the click, the student who had been reading looks around the room and chooses a successor. Just be patient since it seemingly takes forever for the student to make the choice. I guess it's a power and freedom thing.

An adhesive magnet attached to the back of the clicker will enable you to keep it handy on your whiteboard.

FIG. 5-16
Check the website to find these handy little sound makers.

Cardboard Accordion

I found this toy in a 99¢ store.[†] The sound means: "Please rise." (Imagine a church choir standing in unison before they sing, and you'll get the picture.)

FIG. 5-17
This palm-sized toy makes a very distinctive sound.

---

† Dollar stores and Big Lots! are two great resources for sound making toys. I just like to wander through them looking for new toys and oddball gadgets that I can take to the classroom.

Final Thoughts

We covered a lot of material in this lesson. Among other things, we talked about:
1. Define and Control
2. Digital Timers
3. Sound Making Toys

Define and Control

As with most new ideas you try in the classroom, you'll get better at this the more you use it. Having your students begin to compile a simple Class Glossary might make it easier to get started. Once started, though, you shouldn't have any problem maintaining your own progress.

Tip: Put a student in charge of writing down words to include in your glossary. By having a student keep a list, you'll be more likely to add new words or phrases as they arise. Otherwise, if you just try to store it away in your memory for inclusion later when you're free, you won't remember half of the words you wanted to add.

Digital Timers

I can tell you right now—without a doubt—that you are going to love having a digital timer in your room. You'll quickly find it to be an indispensable tool for keeping your class on schedule and your stress in check.

Recommendation: Start slowly and have realistic expectations of your students' ability to respond to the rather strict requirements imposed by your new timer. For some of them, it will be a brand new ball game. Before too long, though, your students will see it as a useful addition to the classroom and will be coming up with their own ways to put it to work.

Even now, after almost twenty years of timer use, I'm still coming up with new ideas for using my little digital buddy. I'd be willing to bet that you'll be doing the same thing. And, as you look back over the year, you will: 1) realize that you used it more times than you could possibly imagine; and 2) wonder how you ever got through the day without one.

Sound Making Toys

Go easy at first and, again, have realistic expectations of student compliance. Start with a "Stop, Look, Listen" sound and the hotel bell for passing out materials. Stick with just these for a month or so.

However, don't let your sensibly slow start keep you from incorporating a variety of sound making toys. Remember that their right-brains are starving. By using a number of different sounds, you will be providing them with some much needed nourishment.

Suggestion 1: Ask the students if they have a sound maker at home that they would like to bring to school. You could designate a Sound of the Week and have it as your "Stop, Look, Listen" sound. I think they might support the idea a bit more if they were the ones supplying the actual sound makers.

Suggestion 2: Allow students to use the sound makers. They're going to want to anyway so you may as well redirect that energy. Either that or you have to suppress it. Just have them do it during recess or between periods so that it doesn't annoy their classmates.

Sounds and the Second Language Student

Sound makers provide an added advantage for second language students, or students who don't speak English proficiently.

As opposed to the words you might use to indicate what it is you want your students to do, the sounds will do the same thing. However, the sounds don't really require an understanding of English, merely an understanding of what is expected. Thus, your newly enrolled student from Thailand, who speaks very little English, will be able to achieve a fair amount of success through the use of your sound making toys.

Initially, he'll merely mimic the response of your other students. That is, when he hears the train whistle, he'll figure out that he needs to follow everyone else outside and stand in one of the two lines of students. Very quickly, though, he'll be lining up outside on his own when he hears the sweet sound of your train.

power
love
fun
freedom
safety

When he hears *squeak, squeak, squeak,* he'll know to stop what he's doing, look at you, and listen. Granted, he most likely won't be able to understand all of your words, but at least he won't feel so left out. He'll be able to do what everyone else is doing because of the sounds he's hearing.

Have Fun

More than anything else, tools and toys are designed to make the classroom a happier, more productive place. Make an effort to keep your own tools and toys—and the way you use them—as positive as possible.

When you see your three knucklehead boys not stopping, looking, or listening when they should be, keep a smile on your face. Jot down their names and speak to them later. Give your attention, though, to the twenty attentive faces who *are* following the procedure.

Focus on the positive.

Lesson 6

Before We Begin

How It All Got Started

Numbering Your Students

Using Student Numbers

Timers & Sound Makers

Class Chart

Check Off List

Check Off Sheet

First Aid Kit

Grade Books

Good teachers are glad when a term begins and a little sad when it ends. They remember some of their students for many years, and their students remember them. They never make assumptions about what their pupils know; they take the trouble to find out, and they are tireless in finding new ways of repeating where repetition is necessary.

—Margaret Mead

Lesson 6
Class Chart

◆ ◆

Goals for this lesson:

☑ Learn how a Class Chart will support your use of student numbers.

☑ Realize the importance of making a rough draft Class Chart.

☑ Create your first Class Chart.

◆ ◆

*A*lthough the timers and sound makers presented in Lesson 5 are not essential to the success of using student numbers, the tool discussed in this lesson—a Class Chart—is specifically designed to support student numbers.

Basically, a Class Chart is a roster you'll post in your room which shows the first names of your students and the numbers they've been assigned. Here's a sample from years ago when I was still using last names to create the order.

Fig. 6-1
A Class Chart displayed on a bulletin board will provide name and number information.

By the way, this was the last year I used last names to order the students. After that, I went with first names.

Room Twelve   Class of 1992

1	Robyn	13	Rich	25	Richard
2	Thomas	14	Carrie	26	Shawna
3	Tricia	15	Woo	27	Cesar
4	Crystal	16	Gabe	28	Mike
5	Teresa	17	Seth	29	Paul
6	Jenny	18	David	30	Jennifer
7	Lisa	19	Dylan	31	Mario
8	Rachel	20	Sabrina	32	Anna
9	Sergio	21	Nicole	33	Danny
10	Michael	22	Van	34	Luis
11	Michelle	23	John		
12	Stephanie	24	Melanie		

A Class Chart may not seem important at first glance; however, this easy-to-make tool will help in three critical ways.

1. **The presence of a Class Chart hanging in your room will be a strong visual reminder that student numbers are a significant and permanent component of your classroom management system.**

    Since some people are concerned about student's losing their identities in the student number system, having the names of your students prominently displayed will help to assuage their worries. (You might want to think about writing the names nice and large and keeping the numbers small. This would subconsciously support the fact that, although you're using student numbers, they're secondary to students' names.)

2. **During your first month of using student numbers, as you slowly but surely learn everyone's name and number, your Class Chart will be there to supply you with numbers whenever you're drawing a blank.**

    Granted, you'll quickly learn them—it takes me about a month—but how about substitute teachers or parent volunteers? Your Class Chart will be a convenient way for them to get student number information.

3. **Similar to the support it will provide you, the Class Chart will be a convenient reference tool for your students.**

    As mentioned earlier in this book, student helpers are an integral part of the New Management system. Anytime someone is processing a task that is number dependent and there's uncertainty about another student's number, your Class Chart will provide the necessary information so that the job can be completed by your helper.

Your Class Chart in Action

Imagine that you've asked one of your students to organize a stack of assignments so that the papers will be in numerical order. Since there should be a student number on each assignment, this will most likely be a relatively easy task for your helper to complete. If, however, one of the papers does not have the student number written on it, your student organizer might get stuck.

Without a Class Chart for reference, he'd either:

A *Come ask you for the number.*

B *Go ask the student for the number.*

C *Give up and not finish organizing the papers.*

Option A - Ask the teacher

Asking you for the number would be the typical course of action. Students have been conditioned to seek out their teacher whenever a problem arises. It's unfortunate, though, that they don't always stop to see if they could solve it themselves; they just go find the teacher.[†]

Personally, I don't mind helping my students; it's part of my job and something that I enjoy doing. Nonetheless, I have to be careful about how much helping I do. Too much unnecessary helping—that condition we've been calling Teacher Welfare—will stunt their growth in the area of self-sufficiency.

A simple Class Chart, hanging on the wall for everyone to see, will provide your students with the information they would normally ask from you. It will also help them in their journey to become independent problem solvers: a critical skill for a successful life.

Option B - Ask the student

Asking the student for the missing number would be a bit better. The student, whose paper was missing the student number information, would receive a reminder about the importance of writing his number next to his name on his assignments. Unfortunately, the interruption would take the student off-task while doing little to boost the self-reliance of the student organizing the papers.

Option C - Quit

Giving up and not finishing the task is probably the most damaging choice of all. For one thing, the stack of papers still needs to be put in numerical order. More importantly, though, is the fact that the student helper ended up being negatively reinforced about his ability to successfully complete a simple job.

General rule: For many of these paper processing tasks, I like to use my underachievers. These types of tasks: 1) promote involvement; 2) are manageable; and 3) reinforce the critical skill of "completes work on time." (Work does not have to be academic for this skill to be developed.) If, however, an underachiever is not able to complete the job at hand, it defeats the purpose of involving him in the first place.

As you can see, none of these choices is a good one, especially if the whole mess could have been avoided by making a Class Chart. Which leads to a new choice:

Option D - Check the Class Chart

You have to have one, of course, before they can check it. So, let's make one.

---

† We have a classroom sign that states: "Ask three, then me." This reminds them to ask other students before asking me.

Class Chart Basics

Here are the criteria for your Class Chart. (Secondary teachers turn to page 6-15.)

1. **It needs to be somewhat prominent.**

    Make it large enough to see from most locations in your room or portable.

2. **It needs to be in place as soon as possible.**

    Don't get caught in the "pretty trap" by thinking that your Class Chart needs to be a work of art. Save the pretty version for later on when you've got the time and have had a chance to live with student numbers for a while.

This is going to be easier than you thought, huh?

Making Your Class Chart Visible

Think about making it the size of one of your bulletin boards. (One of the great things about your Class Chart is that it will use up bulletin board space *all year long*.)

> *Recent finding:* According to the research, kids don't really pay attention to bulletin boards unless they are actively involved somehow. Did the students create the actual bulletin board display? Does it showcase their work? Does the bulletin board contain something they need in order to complete an assignment? If it doesn't, there won't be much interaction between your students and your finely crafted bulletin boards. Instead of curriculum-based bulletin boards, try to use that same space to promote your class and what they're doing.

Choose a location that can be seen from as many student desks as possible. This will enable your students to access the information from their seats without having to get up and move. Being able to see it from *your* desk is not as critical. You can always make a small desk-top version for your own reference.

Getting It Up Quickly

It would probably be in your best interests to make and display your Class Chart as soon as possible. To help you achieve this goal of getting it up quickly—keeping in mind all of the other things that demand your time and energy—I recommend that you make a "rough draft" version and live with it for a month or so. Later on, when you've got the time and energy, you can create a work of art and imagination.

Pyschologically speaking, the decision to make a temporary first chart will enable you to construct a rudimentary prototype without worrying about how nice it looks or how well it blends in with your existing room decor. If it helps, think about the fact that the primary purpose of the Class Chart is not form, but function. It doesn't really matter what it looks like at first. The important thing is to have one in place so that you and the students will be able to begin using it.

Making a Class Chart

Now that we've decided to use a highly visible bulletin board and start with a rough draft Class Chart, let's make the thing.

1. **Cover the bulletin board with butcher paper.**

   Get some white butcher paper and staple it to the bulletin board. Don't worry about making a border or anything else. Don't worry about how plain it looks. It's just a rough draft. As my grandfather taught me years ago when we were once again building some goofy thing in his basement shop, "Sometimes good enough is good enough."

2. **Create a heading.**

   I usually use "Class of (year in which school ends)" as a header. If you look back to page 6-3, you'll see that the Class Chart for the beginning of that year was titled, "Room Twelve   Class of 1992."

   Like most of the ideas I share, it doesn't have be that. It could be:

   The Great Room Eight
   Mrs. Johnson's Super Stars

3. **Number your Class Chart.**

   Using a broad-tip marker, number your Class Chart from 1 to *n, n* being the total number of students in your room. You might want to add a couple of numbers if your school has a high transiency rate and you receive new students on a regular basis.

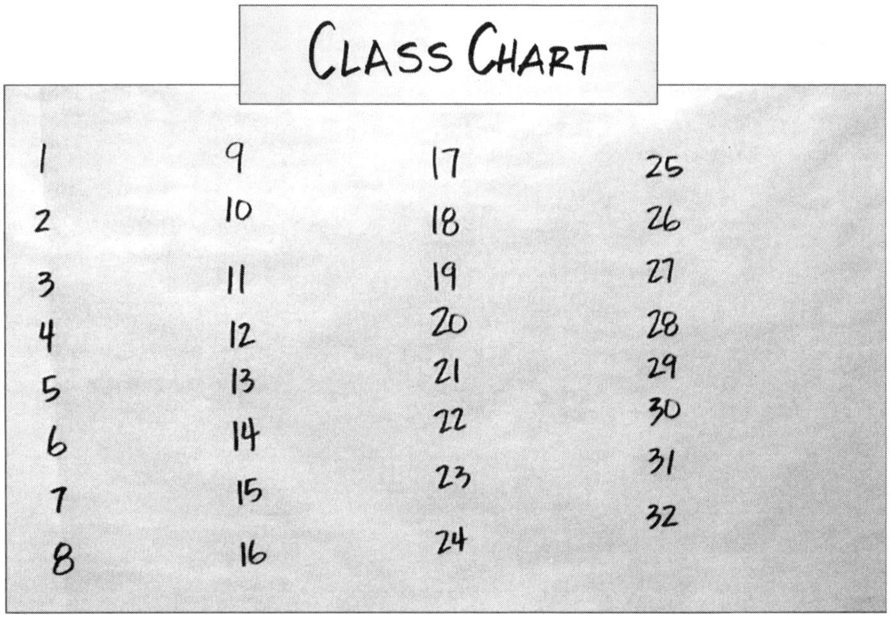

FIG. 6-2
Although the heading "Class Chart" is not terribly creative, this butcher paper and felt marker creation is ready for student names to be added.

CLASS CHART

1	9	17	25
2	10	18	26
3	11	19	27
4	12	20	28
5	13	21	29
6	14	22	30
7	15	23	31
8	16	24	32

4. **Add student names.**

Using the Check Off List roster you made in Lesson 3, write the names of your students next to their numbers. You should probably wait until after dismissal to fill in the names so that you're not using academic time.

Note: If you had completed steps 1 through 3 and your Class Chart was on the wall during your "Get a Number" procedure in Lesson 3, you might want to think about filling in the chart with the help of your students. I realize that you'd be using a bit of academic time; but, it would promote a sense of involvement. It would also help to establish the presence of your new Class Chart.[†]

5. **Enjoy it.**

Even though it wasn't that difficult to make, you should stop and congratulate yourself for your progress. Everything you do in your quest to create a new system of student management takes you one step closer to creating a happier, more productive class. Making a Class Chart is just one of those steps, and you should feel good about the progress you're making.

A More Permanent Chart

The butcher paper chart is fine for a quick start, but you'll eventually want to replace it with something more attractive and functional. By functional, I mean that it should be easy to change the names on your Class Chart whenever a student transfers in or out. Drawing a line through a name (student transfers out) and writing another above it (new student transfers in) is fine until you've done that four or five times. By the sixth time, your butcher paper/felt pen Class Chart will lose some of its initial clarity.

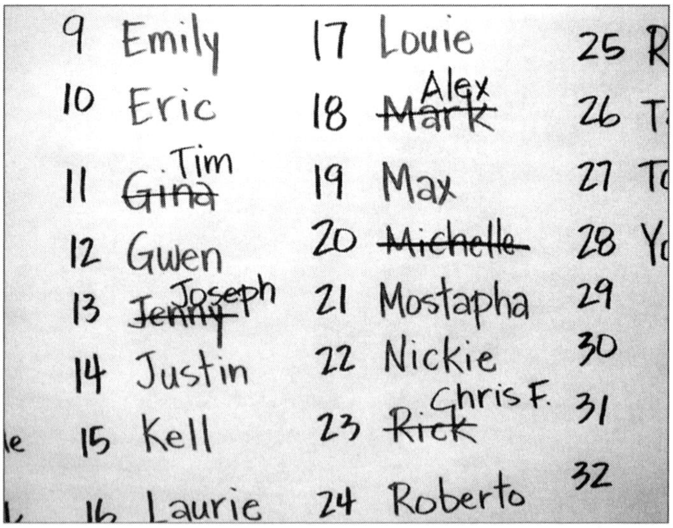

FIG. 6-3
A butcher paper Class Chart after five students have transferred out and four have transferred in.

Reality: I mentioned it earlier in the book but thought that I should mention it again: Alphabetical order by first name—if that's what you used for assigning student numbers—is just a starting point. Accept the fact that names are going to get out of order as students come and go. And since it's really not that big of a deal, try not to worry about it. Just let it go.

---

†   Students, by nature, are both more observant and less observant than we expect. While they almost always can tell when you've redone your hair, they never seem to notice the new bulletin board display over which you slaved for 4 hours. Go figure.

There are a number of ways to make a functional Class Chart. Here are a few suggestions.

Pocket Chart

You can buy a nice pocket chart from just about any school supply store. The one I use has a blue vinyl back and clear plastic pockets that run across the front of the chart.

1. Write numbers on small rectangles of construction paper and place them behind the clear plastic.

2. Write the students' names on large rectangles of construction paper and place them next to the numbers behind the clear plastic.

FIG. 6-4
A Class Chart created from a standard, blue vinyl pocket chart purchased from a school supply store or mail-order company.

There are two advantages to making a Class Chart that is changeable.

Advantage One

It's easy to adjust. Whenever a student transfers out, all you have to do is remove the name card. Reassign the number to the next student who transfers in, insert a new name card, and your chart is up-to-date.

Advantage Two

At the end of the year—which comes sooner than you can believe—you just remove all of the name cards. Without a bit of preparation, your Class Chart will be ready for next year's student names.

Star Chart

The example below was used in one of my classrooms during the seven years I occupied it. I first covered the white bulletin board material with grass cloth, a type of textured wall paper. The numbered stars—cut using an Ellison die cutter—were then glued to the grass cloth. The names were written on white construction paper and then cut out in the shape of clouds. These clouds were attached to the wallpaper with a couple of tape loops applied to the back. All in all, it made for an attractive display.

FIG. 6-5
A very functional Class Chart. The names are attached with tape loops so they're easy to remove.

Changing the student information on this type of chart is a snap. Since the "name clouds" are only held in place with tape loops, they're easy to remove. Figure 6-6 shows that Patricia, student number 30, is no longer with us.

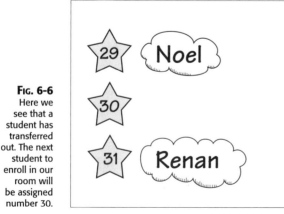

FIG. 6-6
Here we see that a student has transferred out. The next student to enroll in our room will be assigned number 30.

Sensitivity Training: Allow the student to leave before you rip his name off the chart.

Sweet Thought: You might want to present the name cloud to the departing student as a memento of his time in your classroom.

Photo Chart

Although this Class Chart might be too techno for you, I thought I'd share it with you anyway. Using a digital camera, I took photos of my students. The photos were then sent through Photoshop and imported into InDesign, the program I'm using to lay out this book. From there, I printed out the photo/name tags on card stock.

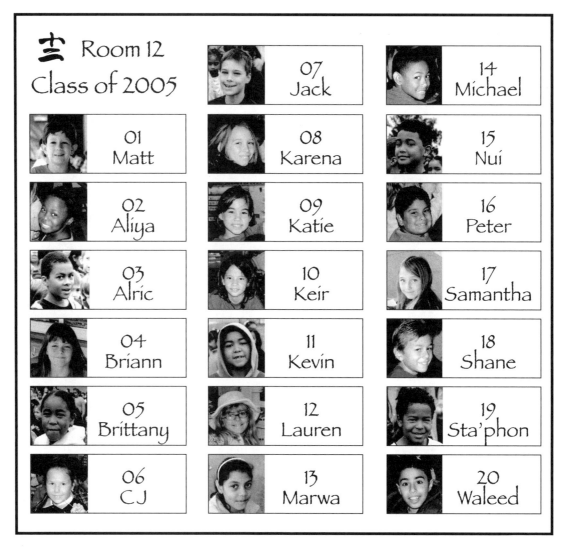

FIG. 6-7
A new Class Chart that uses digital photos as part of the name cards.

Room 12
Class of 2005

01 Matt	07 Jack	14 Michael
02 Aliya	08 Karena	15 Nui
03 Alric	09 Katie	16 Peter
04 Briann	10 Keir	17 Samantha
05 Brittany	11 Kevin	18 Shane
06 CJ	12 Lauren	19 Sta'phon
	13 Marwa	20 Waleed

power
love
fun
freedom
safety

Similar to the Star Chart, these cards were attached to the bulletin board with tape loops. Although they are easy to remove, making a new one requires that I take a digital photo of the new student and then create a new name card. It's a labor of love, I know, but worth it.

You could, of course, make the same kind of chart using a regular camera. The color photos will actually look nicer than the black and whites I print out.

29
Tools & Toys

Note: I use xerox copies of the photos—**PHOTO TAGS**—to post on bulletin boards next to their assignments and activities.

Your Own Chart

Although I couldn't possibly include all of the Class Charts I've seen in my travels around the country, I'm hoping that the examples I've just provided will stimulate your creative energy.

You should realize, of course, that you don't have to do it alone. You could put on a Class Chart Design Contest and see what your students come up with. You can never tell when one of your underachievers will come up with a killer idea and end up being a hero.

General rule: Don't make a deluxe Class Chart at first unless you happen to be that kind of person. Just make a rough draft and live with it for a month. By giving yourself some time to experience student numbers, you just might come up with a new, more effective way to create your chart.

Extending Your Basic Chart

Since you are using up an entire bulletin board for your chart, you might want to maximize the space. There are a number of ways you could do this.

Awards

Why not post awards on your Class Chart? You could make small badges and place them on or near the names. An example of this would be a spelling award for everyone who scored 100% on the final test. This award would stay on the chart until your next test.

Native Language Information

I saw a Class Chart in a bilingual room in which the teacher color-coded the name tags. The names of Spanish speaking students were written in green ink; the names of English speaking students was written in blue. This kind of information might be helpful to someone coming into your room for the first time.

Student Grouping

You could color-code the name tags so that they show which group a student belongs to. (I've used the team colors—red, orange, yellow, green, and blue—for this. The names of the students were written on colored paper that matched their team color.)

Attendance Taking

A first grade teacher told me that her Class Chart is a simple pocket chart with the names of the students written on tag board (See Figure 6-8.)

When the students arrive in the morning, they get their name cards out of the pocket chart (obviously, it's accessible and within reach) and take them to the teacher. Any cards left in the chart would indicate an absent student.

Tip: To help remind students that they need to bring up their name tags, I would use the name cards that had already been brought to me.

> MR. MORRIS
> Slowly shuffling the name cards:
> *Let's see who's going to be chosen to lead the Pledge of Allegiance.*

power
love
fun
freedom
safety

You've got to figure that anyone who hadn't yet brought up his card would scoot to the back of the room to go get it. This would eliminate the need for a verbal reminder which, for some students, can be a real source of embarrassment.

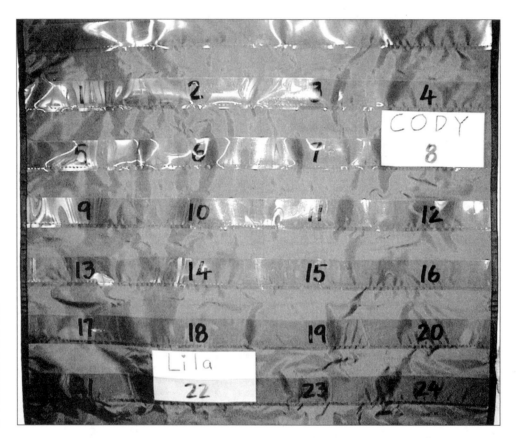

FIG. 6-8
Since their cards are still in this attendance-taking Class Chart, we can see that Cody and Lila are absent today.

No matter how you decide to make your Class Chart, bear in mind that your hard work will pay off. As I mentioned earlier, because of the fact that your chart is based on numbers, you'll be able to use it year after year. All you'll need to do is to place the names of your new students behind their numbers, and you'll be good to go.

Now that's a comforting thought.

So, enough about Class Charts. I'm pretty sure you've got it figured out by now. But before I close this lesson, let me offer a couple more samples and then some suggestions for the secondary teachers.

Sample Class Charts

Here are two more samples of Class Charts that other teachers have created. Don't get crazy, though, until you've done your rough draft.

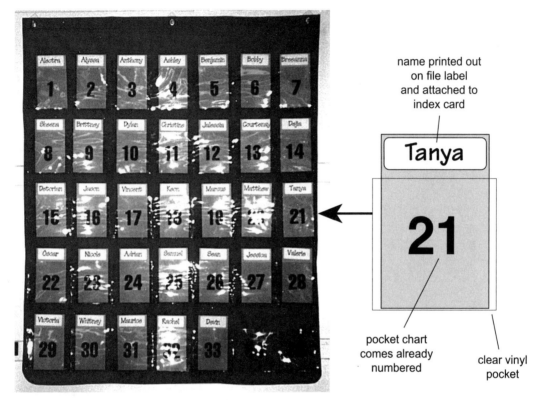

name printed out
on file label
and attached to
index card

pocket chart
comes already
numbered

clear vinyl
pocket

FIG. 6-9
This red vinyl pocket chart was actually designed to hold student calculators.

FIG. 6-10
Here's a Class Chart that also doubles as a place to showcase student work.

Secondary Teachers

Obviously, you're not going to create large Class Charts for each of your separate classes. However, the information is important enough that it should be posted in a convenient location.

If you're lucky enough to be in the same room throughout the day, here's how I'd do it.

Bulletin Board Display

1. **Choose a bulletin board for your Class Charts.**
   Pick a convenient, easy-to-get-to location.

2. **Create a roster for each class.**
   Using a computer, create a letter-sized roster of each of your different classes. The rosters should include each student's number and first and last name.

3. **Put 'em up.**
   Make a header for the bulletin board and a nice label for each roster. Staple everything to the bulletin board.

4. **Let 'em know.**
   Make sure your students are aware of the fact that the student number information they may need to complete a task can be found on your Class Charts bulletin board.

FIG. 6-11
Letter-sized printouts will work fine if you teach more than one group of students.

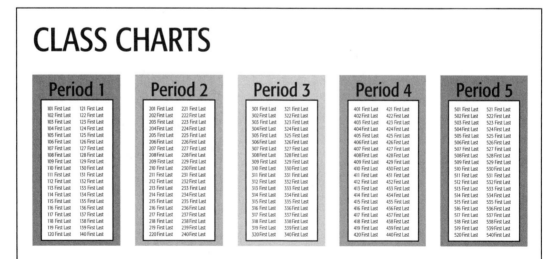

Helpful Tip: If you decided to go with the color-coded period idea (see page 1-13) you might want to think about framing the rosters with colored construction paper. It would not only make it more attractive but would also make it easier for your students to use.

If you are in the unenviable position of having to move around from one room to another, you have two options.

Charts for More Than One Classroom

Use the previous sample.

Pick a spot in each room and post a roster. I'm thinking that a printed roster stapled on top of a sheet of colored construction paper should do the trick.

Set up the rosters using Binder Stand.

Binder Stand is one of my inventions. It's a little piece of plastic that turns a 3-ring binder into a table-top display. (You can see it clipped to the bottom edge of the front cover of the binder shown below.)

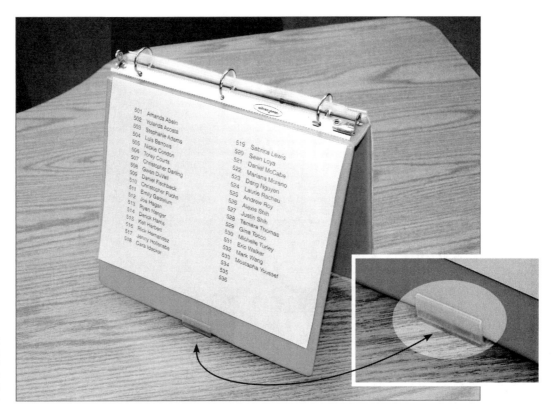

FIG. 6-12
You can order Binder Stands in our on-line store.

The beauty of doing it this way is that you could have all of your rosters in one handy binder. Students would then flip to the proper roster to find the name and number information they need.

An additional advantage is that your student helper could place the binder on his desk as he processes papers. As opposed to having to get near enough to the bulletin board to read the printed roster, your helper will have all of that info at his fingertips.

Lesson 7

Before We Begin

How It All Got Started

Numbering Your Students

Using Student Numbers

Timers & Sound Makers

Class Chart

Check Off List

Check Off Sheet

First Aid Kit

Grade Books

The truth is that I am enslaved...
in one vast love affair with thirty children.

—Sylvia Aston-Warner

Lesson 7
Check Off List

◆ ◆

Goals for this lesson:

☑ Have a better understanding of the power of using student numbers.

☑ Learn how to use a Check Off List to collect something from your students.

☑ Learn how a student can use a Check Off List to collect something for you.

☑ Learn how the entire class can use a Check Off List to turn in an assignment.

☑ Become acquainted with variations on the basic Check Off List technique.

◆ ◆

*W*ith the introduction of the Check Off List, the power of student numbers takes a major leap forward. The Check Off List was the first New Management tool that convinced me that student numbers was going to be *the* foundation upon which I was going to build a system of classroom organization and management.

Over the years, the Check Off List (COL) has proven itself to be a powerful tool for reinforcing the basic tenets of the New Management philosophy. Here's the action to back up my words. Here's the muscle behind my smile. It's both simple and efficient. It empowers me to stay calm, which does wonders for the overall sense of control I am able to maintain. And, as a direct result of these factors, my stress is reduced.

For the students, the Check Off List helps them in developing a sense of accountability and ownership. They end up spending more of their time completing assignments and activities and less time trying to figure out how to get out of them.

The Check Off List is Mr. Do Everything. If you need something taken care of, the COL is your guy. This wonderfully versatile tool will keep track of just about anything you *or your students* need to complete.

Among a host of other abilities, this little helper will:

- ✔ check off,
- ✔ chart,
- ✔ monitor,
- ✔ remind,
- ✔ enforce,
- ✔ organize,
- ✔ verify,
- ✔ confirm,
- ✔ record,
- ✔ update,
- ✔ prompt,
- ✔ cue,
- ✔ nudge,
- ✔ warn,
- ✔ alert, and
- ✔ advise.

Just about everything but slice and dice, eh?

The Check Off List is nothing less than a trusted attendant who possesses a perfect memory. How can this be, you ask? No mere slip of paper is worthy of such praise, you say? Well, bear with me as I demonstrate.

Up Close

If you take a close look at Fig. 7-1, you'll see that the COL is composed of four parts.

1. **Header**

   The area at the top has been left blank so that you can add your own artwork and personalize your copy.

2. **Assignment and Date**

   Below the header are spaces for you to write the assignment you're collecting and the date it's due.

3. **Student Numbers**

   The blackline masters in the appendix are set up for two class sizes: 20 or 36 students.

4. **Symbol Key**

   At the bottom of the COL is a key that explains the symbols which will be used during the check off procedure.

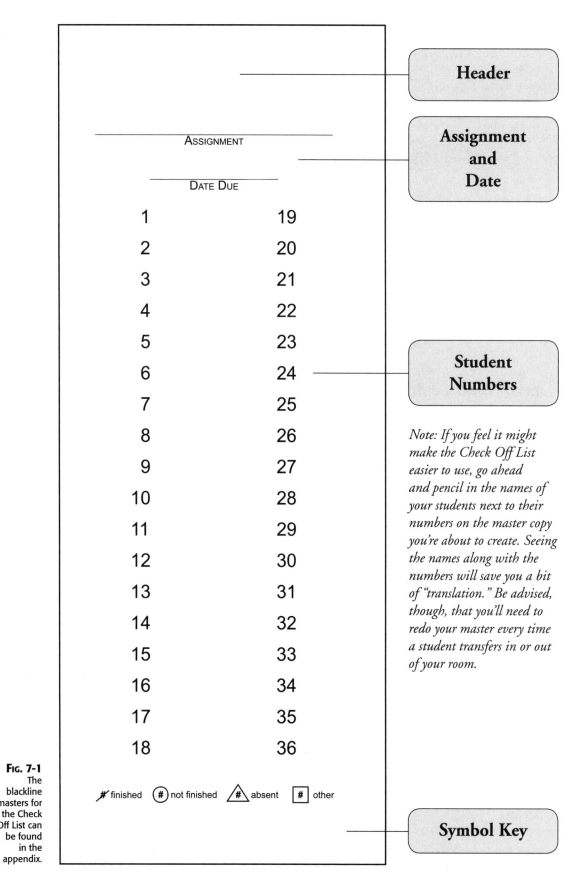

ASSIGNMENT

DATE DUE

1	19
2	20
3	21
4	22
5	23
6	24
7	25
8	26
9	27
10	28
11	29
12	30
13	31
14	32
15	33
16	34
17	35
18	36

finished not finished absent other

Header

Assignment and Date

Student Numbers

Note: If you feel it might make the Check Off List easier to use, go ahead and pencil in the names of your students next to their numbers on the master copy you're about to create. Seeing the names along with the numbers will save you a bit of "translation." Be advised, though, that you'll need to redo your master every time a student transfers in or out of your room.

Symbol Key

FIG. 7-1
The blackline masters for the Check Off List can be found in the appendix.

Header

Although the header has been left blank on the blackline master, I encourage you to fill the space with something appropriate. Here are a few examples to get you thinking.

(Xeroxed cartoon)   *(Class logo)*

FIG. 7-2
The possibilities for creating a header for your Check Off List are just about endless.

Sequoia Elementary School
Room Twelve
Third Grade
Mr. Morris

(Class Letterhead)   *(Student art)*

Assignment and Date

These are pretty self-explanatory.

Student Numbers

This is the area where you or your students will mark off numbers to indicate who has completed the assignment being collected.

Note: As I mentioned earlier in the book, if your class size does not match the blackline masters in the appendix, which are based on the maximum class size in the state of California—most primary grades have a max of 20; upper grades have a max of 36—don't panic. You can always go to the website and download a modified set of blacklines. I've got them set up for class sizes of 16, 18, 20, 24, 27, 30, 36, and 40.

Symbol Key

We use four different symbols on the Check Off List that mean four different things.

Line: the student has completed the task.

Circle: the student hasn't completed the task.

Triangle: the student is, or was, absent.

Square: the student is excused from this assignment.

Preparing the Check Off List for Use

Here are the six steps to get ready to use the COL.

1. **Make a xerox copy of the Check Off List found in the appendix.**

2. **Add a letterhead or design in the blank space at the top.**

    Don't worry about this step if you're not in the mood. Just leave it blank until you've got the time or energy to do something about that big, annoying empty space at the top.

    By the way, it doesn't have to be fancy.

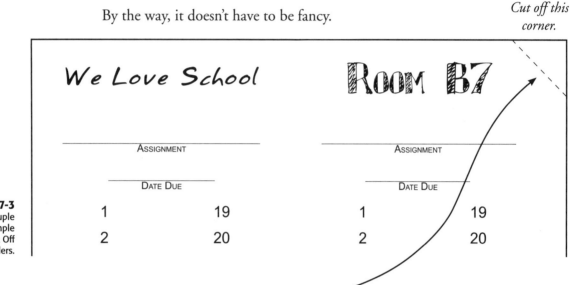

Cut off this corner.

FIG. 7-3
A couple of simple Check Off List headers.

3. **Mark your new blackline master.**

    When you are happy with the customized copy you've made, cut off a bit of the top right corner. This will alert you to the fact that this copy is your original. Otherwise, you might end up using it.

4. **Make a bunch of copies from your blackline.**

    You might want to run them on some kind of colorful paper. (Since I run off just about everything else on white, the colored COL's add a touch of brightness to the collection procedure.)

5. **Cut them down the middle.**

    Cut them in half, and then place your new Check Off Lists in a number of convenient, usable locations: your desk, your class secretary's desk, the parent volunteers' folder, etc.

6. **Create a "New Management" file folder for your blacklines.**

    Label a file folder "NM Masters" and place your COL blackline master inside the folder. Having all of your blacklines in one place will help to make them easier to find which will make them easier to use.

5

Putting Your Check Off List to Work

Now that we have a pile of Check Off Lists just waiting to go, we're ready to put one to work. Before we do that, though, let's take a quick look back to my early years of teaching—before I started using student numbers—and examine how I used to collect items from the students.

Seminar Note

If you've been to one of my seminars, you might remember that I told a story about how hard it was to collect things from my students. The difficulty resulted from the fact that I didn't have a system for taking care of business. In fact, for my first five years of teaching, I was lost and confused; didn't have a clue.

I went on to relate how I struggled to collect something as simple as Federal Survey Cards. These cards, which contained information about each of my students, were a high priority for the office staff. Among other items on the cards would be each student's emergency phone number. Here's how it went the first five years.

Year One

I got the cards from my office mailbox the second week of school. I passed them out to the students, gave them instructions about taking them home, having the folks fill them out, and then returning them to class as soon as possible. I then sat back and waited for them to come rolling in. I had high expectations because I remember bringing my card back right away when I was a student. Therefore, I thought, the students would all bring their cards back with no problem.[†] Wrong.

I gathered cards every day, but not at the rate I had hoped for. And, since I didn't have a system for monitoring the return of the cards, I didn't stay on top of the task. I just tossed the cards on my desk and kept reminding the students—when I remembered myself—to bring them in.

Well, Friday rolled around, and I had maybe half of the cards. I naively gave the cards I had collected to the head secretary whose trained eye immediately spotted the fact that I wasn't turning in all of them. Needless to say, she wasn't happy with me. I promised to have the students return the missing cards as soon as possible.

[†] Research shows that teachers project upon their students their own school experience. Thus, I was projecting my successful school career and my functional family onto my students. I just assumed that they would do things the same way I did them. This, as I now know, is not always the case. Unrealistic expectations can very often lead to feelings of frustration and failure when the teacher's expectations are not met by the students.

Two weeks later, I still didn't have them all collected and took to avoiding the office whenever possible.

Year Two:

The cards were waiting in my mailbox on Monday of the second week of school. I wasn't happy to see them but knew it was a part of my job. I cheered myself by thinking that my new students would certainly do a better job than the students from last year's class. Wrong again.

The students brought them back in dribs and drabs. Once again, by the end of the week, I didn't have them all. This time, though, I vented a bit of frustration on my students for their lack of diligence in returning the cards. Not terribly fair to blame them for my lack of organization, mind you, but that's human nature.

Year Three:

I did another sad job of collecting the Federal Survey Cards. My lack of control and organization were beginning to have an adverse effect upon my disposition. I was no longer the rather friendly guy I started out being in year one. Instead, as I briefly mentioned in Lesson 2, I started to come across like a pirate. This was especially true when things weren't going well. As you can imagine, the Federal Survey Cards waiting in my mailbox the second week of school would be just the kind of situation that would summon the pirate.

Year Four:

No system, no control, no clue. I started to anticipate my failure at taking care of what should have been simple tasks. As a consequence, I began to interact negatively with my students.

And even though I had students who would return their cards the first day, I wouldn't stop to celebrate their success. Instead, I would rage against the students who hadn't returned their cards. What was especially troubling was that the students who had complied with my wishes received the same verbal broadside that the other students did.

Let's take a closer look at how that Friday actually transpired:

In the morning, I counted the cards to see if I had them all and found out that three cards were missing. Without a way to identify who those three students were, I was stuck having to ask the students.

"WHO DIDN'T BRING BACK THE SURVEY CARD?" I wailed.

(Come on, Rick. Which student is going to be dumb enough to raise a hand and incur the wrath of Blackbeard? Answer: Not one of the three.)

> *And so, there I was, three cards short, not sure which students hadn't returned them. I sent the stack of returned cards to the office knowing that I'd be hearing from the office staff before too long.*
>
> *Sure enough, I found the cards back in my mailbox with a note that read, "You're still missing three cards. Please have Calvin, Monica, and Andrew return their cards as soon as possible."*
>
> *After lunch, I vented my frustration on my class. They got an earful of complaining. I moaned and groaned about how they had let me down. I whined about how embarrassed I was and how I couldn't show my face in the office. I grumbled about their lack of responsibility and how it was going to have to improve. They heard all of that and more. What they didn't hear, sadly, was anything positive about all of the students who had returned the cards. The pirate was more focused on what hadn't happened instead of what had.*

Before we leave this sad, sad story, let's ponder the effect that my lack of organization had on my students.

Think, for a moment, about Calvin: one of the three students who hadn't returned a card. As he heard Mr. Morris demand to know which students still hadn't brought back a card, he came to a stunning realization.

His first thought:

> ---*Whew. Mr. Morris doesn't know I'm one of the kids who didn't bring back a card. Hey, wait a second. Mr. Morris doesn't know who any of the three students are. He talks tough, but he doesn't really know what's going on in here.*

His second thought:

> ---*Gee, I wonder if he's going to know about math assignments and book reports?*

What a terrible message to send to my students at the beginning of the year. Nonetheless, that's what they were getting. My lack of a system was creating loopholes through which my underachievers were already planning an escape.

Isn't there a better way?

I'm here to tell you that, fortunately, there is a better way. Let me show you.

Federal Survey Cards, Take 2

Everything changed dramatically when I began to use a Check Off List to monitor the return of the cards.

In Control

From the very beginning of the card collection process, I felt my stress begin to ebb[†]. No longer did I anticipate failure. I knew that I now had a procedure that was going to put me in control.

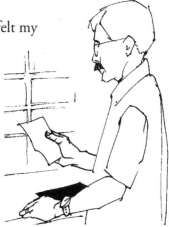

> MR. MORRIS
> > Picking up the stack of cards from his mailbox:
> > > *---This looks like a job for my trusty Check Off List.*

A Place for Everything

16
Tools & Toys

After cleaning out my mailbox, I headed to my classroom. Upon arrival, I located my *TODAY FOLDER*. My Today Folder is a distinctive, one-of-a-kind paper portfolio that holds items I need to share with my students. I would place the cards in the folder and then set it aside until our mid-morning "staff meeting." (Check the Class Glossary in the back of the book for a description.)

At 9:30, our normal time for our staff meeting, I pulled out the Today Folder and began to go through the items I had placed there earlier.

> MR. MORRIS
> > Pulling out the first piece of business:
> > > *Here's a reminder about the sixth grade bake sale this Friday. It will be held after school on the lawn near the office.*
> > Handing the note to one of his students:
> > > *Katrina, would you pin this to the bulletin board on our door? Thanks.*
> > Removing two envelopes from the Today Folder:
> > > *I've got two letters from the nurse. One's for Jessica and the other is for Brian. Here you go, guys.*
> > Handing them the letters, he turned his attention to the Federal Survey Cards:
> > > *Well, it's that time of the year again. The office staff would like each of you to take home this information card and have your parents fill it out.*

---

†   The latest studies on stress indicate that stress is not caused by how much pressure you are facing. The stress actually comes from feeling that you are not in control of the pressure. As teachers, we have a massive amount of pressure. The key concept is: Are you in control of it? One easy way to control pressure is to have procedures in place for taking care of business which takes care of some of the pressure.

I then rang the hotel bell as a signal to the teams to send up a student to receive a set of cards. I gave each team representative the proper number of cards. As the cards were being disseminated, I grabbed a Check Off List from the top right drawer of my desk where I had placed a bunch of them. I wrote "Federal Survey Card" on the ASSIGNMENT line. I then wrote the date these cards were to be returned to the office on the DATE DUE line.

FIG. 7-4
The Check Off List I'll use to collect the Federal Survey Cards.

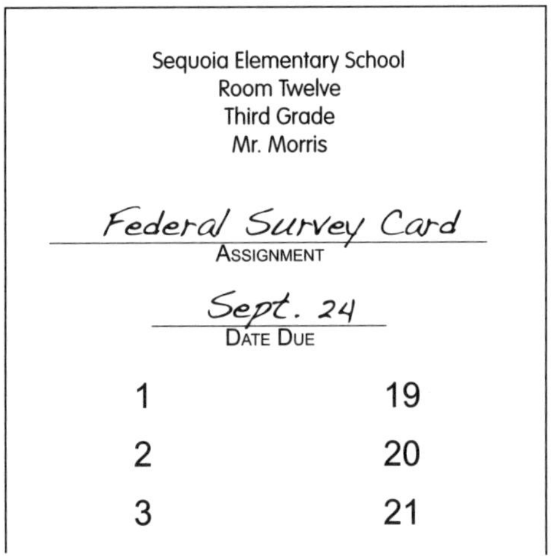

Sequoia Elementary School
Room Twelve
Third Grade
Mr. Morris

Federal Survey Card
ASSIGNMENT

Sept. 24
DATE DUE

1	19
2	20
3	21

By the time I was done labeling the COL, I discovered that we had three "extra" cards. These cards were actually for three absent students, but the team reps knew to bring them back to me. I'd rather not leave the cards on the desks of the absent students. They might get misplaced before the absent students returned. So, I clipped the cards to the COL and drew a triangle around the student numbers of the absentees.

Helpful: The triangles will remind me to give them their cards when they do finally return to class. After all, it is my responsibility to make sure everyone gets a card. The triangles, coupled with the fact that the extra cards are attached to the COL, will make it easier to do this.

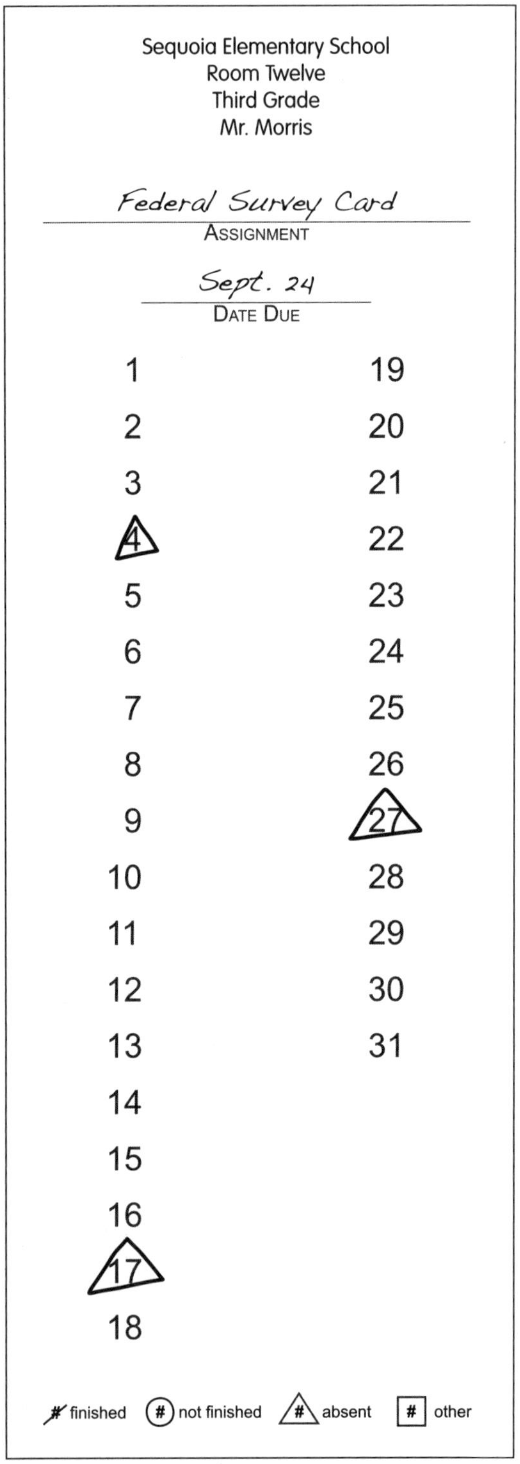

Students 4, 17, and 27 were absent when the cards were passed out. Numbers 32 to 36 were whited out since there are just 31 students in my class.

Sequoia Elementary School
Room Twelve
Third Grade
Mr. Morris

Federal Survey Card
ASSIGNMENT

Sept. 24
DATE DUE

1	19
2	20
3	21
△4	22
5	23
6	24
7	25
8	26
9	△27
10	28
11	29
12	30
13	31
14	
15	
16	
△17	
18	

✗ finished   (#) not finished   △# absent   [#] other

MR. MORRIS
Knowing that everyone present now has a Federal Survey Card:
Please take these home today and ask your parents to complete the information. You have until Friday to return it. Do yourself a favor, though, and try to bring it back as soon as possible.
Seeing that the Today Folder is now empty:
I'm all done. Anyone have any announcements to make?
Waiting for a response but hearing none:
Okay. Let's get ready for our next reading rotation.

And with that, I tossed the Check Off List and the three extra cards into my **RED BASKET.** This basket is specifically designated to hold all of the "business stuff" that needs my attention. Purchased at a stationery store, it's the only one of its kind in the room. It's not a tote tray or a cardboard box or an empty space on a bookshelf: nothing school issue or ambiguous. It's red. It's made of wire. It's right there next to my desk. You can't miss it.

The Red Basket makes my life easier. For one, it keeps important tasks in one place. I don't find myself rummaging through my room looking for some item my principal has asked me to take care of.

For another, the Red Basket is a convenient spot for my students to place papers they want me to have. I'm not talking about assignments. I'm talking about the stuff that wears you out: the notes from home, the book club orders, the volunteers slips the PTA asked you to collect, etc.

If you don't have a place for these papers, you'll leave your students no choice but to bring them to you. (And you can bet that they'll bring them to you at the worst time.) However, with the Red Basket, you'll quickly develop the habit of telling your students to "Put that in the Red Basket, please.† "

With the Federal Survey Card Check Off List—and three extra cards—resting securely in the Red Basket, we transitioned into our next reading rotation.

At the end of the day I offered a brief reminder about returning their cards as soon as possible.

MR. MORRIS
Holding up the COL for all to see:
*Tell you what I'm going to do, I'm going to give a **COUPON** to everyone who returns a completed Federal Survey Card. If you bring it tomorrow, you'll get a coupon tomorrow. If you bring the card on Friday, you'll get a coupon on Friday. However, we're going to have our first drawing tomorrow. Something to think about, eh?*

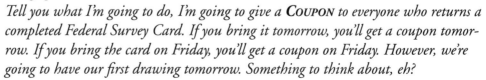

---

† Within a month, Calvin will have learned not to interrupt your guided reading group so that he can give you a note from his mom explaining why he didn't do his homework assignment last night. He'll know to put the note in the Red Basket where you'll be sure to see it later.

The Next Day

During our staff meeting on Tuesday morning, I asked my students to bring me their completed survey cards. As they brought them to me, I collected the cards, thanked each one, and drew a line through their numbers. (This is the time I begin to work on learning names and numbers. As each student brought up a card, I asked for the student number. As mentioned earlier, it takes anywhere from two weeks to a month to learn everyone's number.) Before returning to their seats, the seven students who had returned a card were given a coupon.

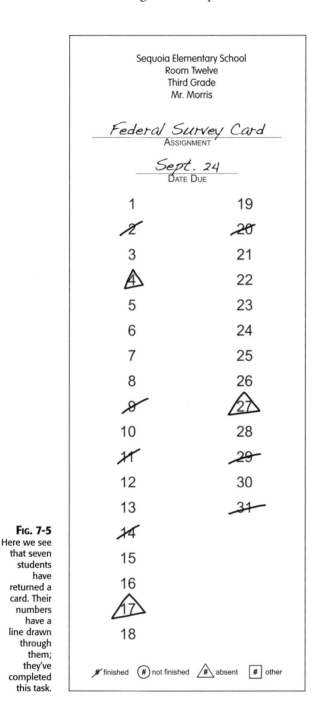

FIG. 7-5
Here we see that seven students have returned a card. Their numbers have a line drawn through them; they've completed this task.

Each student knows to tear the coupon in half: one end is dropped into a container and the other end is held by the student. We'll have drawings once or twice a day. The prize can be something as simple as being the first student to go to lunch.

Note: I used to give out coupons on Tuesday only. After all, that was the American way. Be first.

Unfortunately, any student who had forgotten the card the first day no longer had the coupon to look forward to and, as a result, may have been less than motivated to return it.

I've since learned to give out coupons on each of the days I'm collecting cards. In other words, bring your card on Tuesday, you get a coupon. Bring your card in on Wednesday, you still get a coupon.

I tell the students, though, that we're going to start having drawings on Tuesday and that we'll pull coupons for the rest of the week. They'll eventually figure out this fact of life: The sooner I get my coupon in the container, the better my chances are of winning.

After collecting all of the cards that had been completed and brought back, I clipped the cards to the Check Off List. I then checked to see if any of the three students who had been absent on Monday were present. One of them, Brandon, student #4, was back so I gave him a card. At the same time, I drew a circle over the triangle. This lets me know that this student now has a card and needs to bring it back.

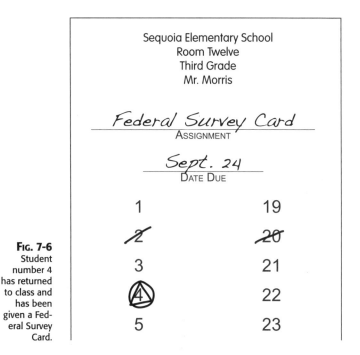

FIG. 7-6
Student number 4 has returned to class and has been given a Federal Survey Card.

Sequoia Elementary School
Room Twelve
Third Grade
Mr. Morris

Federal Survey Card
ASSIGNMENT

Sept. 24
DATE DUE

1	19
2	20
3	21
④	22
5	23

The Federal Survey Card packet—the COL and the cards that were clipped to it—were tossed into the Red Basket, and we moved on to the next order of staff meeting business.

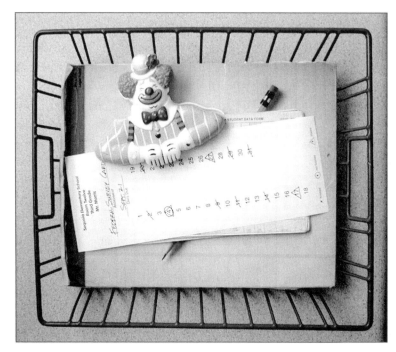

FIG. 7-7
My Red Basket of "Things To Take Care Of." The clown clip, sold as a chip bag clip in a 99¢ store, is more playful that an ordinary paper clip.

You can see my Today Folder sitting under the clown clip and Check Off List. (The red basket is by far the best place to keep it.)

The folder looks like a legal pad with a pencil sitting on top. It's a very realistic photo. I can't tell you how many times I've actually reached for that pencil before I realized that it's just the photographic image of a pencil, not the pencil itself.

Recess Reminder

One minute before Tuesday's morning recess, I decided to apply a little pressure: gentle, loving, and sensitive, to be sure, but pressure nonetheless.

> MR. MORRIS
> Checking outside to make sure that the playground supervisors were on the playground:
>> *Clear desks, please.*
> Momentary pause as he waited for them to comply. While waiting, he's looking over the Federal Survey Card COL.
>> *I'm going to read some numbers. If I read your number, please stand up.*

I then proceeded to call out the numbers of everyone who was marked off. (You could stop and translate the numbers into names if you wish; however, experience has shown that students don't mind if you call out their numbers. They get very attached to them.)

>> *Students 2, 9, 11, 14, 20, 29, and 31.*
> Pausing to make sure that they are all standing:
>> *The seven students standing have returned a Federal Survey Card. You are free to go to recess. See ya'.*
> Watching them leave with a smile on his face:
>> *What's that? P.E. equipment? Sure, go ahead. Take it all.*

Out the door they went.

And guess who's waiting for me? That's right. Just the students who hadn't returned their cards.

The beauty of the Check Off List, as you can now see, is that it enables me to separate the wheat from the chaff. By dismissing the students who had returned their cards, I was able to speak to just the students who were in need of a reminder. This helps me to stay calm and focused. I don't have to raise my voice to reach those who should be listening to my admonitions. Neither do I have to worry about speaking needlessly to anyone. If you had returned your card, you didn't need to hear this talk. You should be at recess enjoying yourself. If you hadn't returned your card yet, stick around. I've got something I'd like to share.

The Truth: To a student, action is the only reality. It's not what I'm about to say that speaks to them. The actual message is what I had just done. I had dismissed the card returners yet held back the cardless. That was one strong, but safe, message.

> MR. MORRIS
> Holding the Federal Survey Card packet for all to see:
>> *Don't forget, your card needs to be returned by Friday. Do yourself a favor and return it tomorrow. You may go to recess now.*

power
love
fun
freedom
safety

No pirate talk. No threats. Just a calm but pointed reminder about the importance of returning things to school in a timely manner, and they were then free to leave.

What some of them were leaving with, though, was a brand new awareness. Some of my students were walking out the door thinking:

> *Wow. Mr. Morris was really on top of*
> *that Federal Survey Card thing.*

> *He knew the first day who hadn't brought*
> *back the card. I'd better bring mine in.*

I had sent an unmistakable message that I was aware of what's going on in our classroom. In a nonthreatening fashion, my students had been reminded that: 1) they still needed to bring back their cards; and, *more importantly,* 2) Mr. Morris knew they hadn't returned their cards.

CALVIN
Heading to recess:
---*Man, this isn't going to be like last year. This guy knows.*

The Check Off List, with completed cards clipped to it, was returned to the Red Basket to await Wednesday's collection efforts.

Card Collection, Day Three

Wednesday arrived, as Wednesday always does, and at our 9:30 staff meeting I asked if anyone had a card to hand in.

> *Benefit:* One of the advantages of having a scheduled "staff meeting" is that it helps me deal with the students who attempt to give me who knows what the minute they see me. Whenever that does happen—which is more often than I care to think about—I'm able to say, "Oh, your Federal Survey Card? Good job. I'll get those at our staff meeting this morning." The student will then retract the extended card and place it on his desk or in his post office box.

power
love
fun
freedom
safety

I repeated the procedure that was used on Tuesday; i.e., I collected each card, thanked each student, and drew a line through each student's number. To help move things along, I gave the roll of coupons to the first student who brought me his card. This student then handed a coupon to the other card returners.

It only took a minute or so to collect and process the ten cards which had been returned that day.

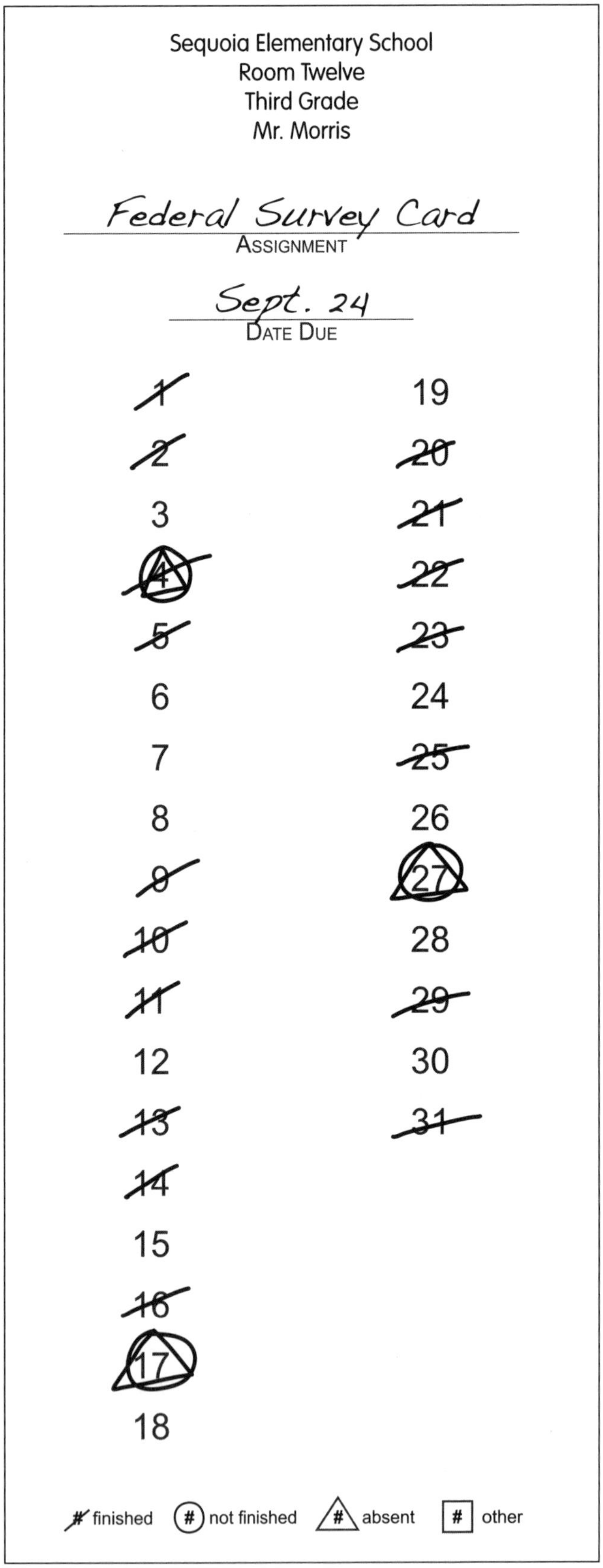

Sequoia Elementary School
Room Twelve
Third Grade
Mr. Morris

Federal Survey Card
ASSIGNMENT

Sept. 24
DATE DUE

~~1~~	19
~~2~~	~~20~~
3	~~21~~
④ (triangle)	~~22~~
~~5~~	~~23~~
6	24
7	~~25~~
8	26
~~9~~	㉗ (triangle)
~~10~~	28
~~11~~	~~29~~
12	30
~~13~~	~~31~~
~~14~~	
15	
~~16~~	
⑰ (triangle)	
18	

~~#~~ finished   (#) not finished   /#\ absent   [#] other

FIG. 7-8
Here's what the Check Off List looked like after two days of collecting cards.

A quick glance at the Federal Survey Card COL shows us making good progress in dealing with a somewhat tedious task. Also, notice how all three of the students who had been absent on Monday were now in possession of a card. Drawing a circle over the triangle takes a lot of the guesswork out of these kinds of situations.

Once again I clipped the package together, tossed it back into the Red Basket, and moved on to other business.

Wednesday afternoon, during social studies, one of my students finally showed up at school. She had been at the doctor's office all morning but was now present. She showed me her completed Federal Survey Card and asked if she should drop it in the Red Basket. What a sweet procedure. I thanked her and told her that I would mark off her number later.

Thursday Morning

Thursday's collection proceeded in the same fashion as Tuesday's and Wednesday's: collect the cards, thank the returners, draw a line through the numbers, and toss it all back into the basket.

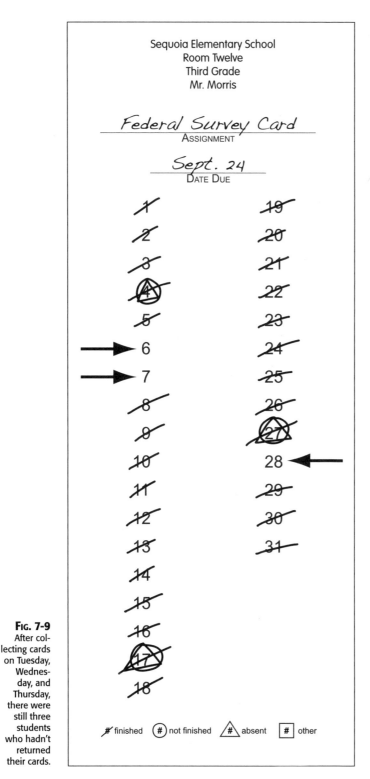

FIG. 7-9
After collecting cards on Tuesday, Wednesday, and Thursday, there were still three students who hadn't returned their cards.

Later on, during Thursday's morning recess, I hung out in the classroom to take care of a few things. (Normally I'm outside playing with the kids. On Thursdays, though, I like to work on the things in my Red Basket. It's a goal of mine to have everything processed by Friday.)

In no time at all, I came upon that lovely little Federal Survey Card package. A quick glance showed me that students 6, 7, and 28 had not yet returned a card.

Important factor: In a very short time, you'll find that numbers become very personal. Whenever you see a number, you'll see a face.

In the example to the left, numbers 6, 7, and 28 are not crossed out because I have yet to receive a Federal Survey Card from them. Instead of just seeing numbers, though, I see faces. I was actually "seeing" Calvin, Christa, and Steven.

Don't let anyone try to tell you that numbers rob students of their identities. It's just not true.

Alerted to the fact that Calvin, Christa, and Steven had not yet returned their cards, I decided to speak with them privately at the conclusion of recess. I didn't want to make a group announcement. Most of the students had already returned their cards, and I wanted to give them some respect. Calvin, Christa, and Steven, though, were in need of a reminder.

As I brought my students back to class and they returned to their seats to begin their ten minutes of independent reading, I called my three little buddies over to my desk.

As they drew near, I showed them the Check Off List and the previously collected Federal Survey Cards. I pointed out the fact that their numbers were not marked off. I even circled the numbers for emphasis.

Immediately I began to hear three separate tales of woe as to why they were late in returning their cards. Being well versed in the subtle art of reducing these kinds of dialogues to "yes" or "no," we quickly cut to the chase.

No, they hadn't returned them yet. *Yes*, they needed to.

However, I realized that an auditory reminder probably wasn't going to do much good. After all, they had received verbal reminders on Monday, Tuesday, and Wednesday but the cards had yet to be returned. Another auditory reminder was probably going to meet with the same lack of success. (This is another situation that would benefit from the wisdom of my grandfather's advice: "When the horse you're riding on dies, get off and walk." The auditory reminder was a dead horse. Time to walk and think of some other way to go.)

What I thought might work was some kind of visual reminder. Taking a washable felt-tip pen, I made a dot on my left thumb nail.

Mr. Morris
   Showing the three students his dotted thumb nail:
      *See this dot? I started doing this when I was in seventh
      grade. I figured out that I'm a visual person and that
      I need visual reminders. These dots really helped me
      to remember things. Whenever I would see one on my
      thumb nail, it made me stop and think. Because the dot
      reminded me to stop and think, I almost always remem-
      ber what it was I needed to do.*
   Taking their hands, one at a time:
      Okay. Here's your dot, and your dot, and your dot.
   Smiling at his handiwork:
      *Now tonight, when you're home, you're going to look down at your thumb, see this dot,
      and think about returning your Federal Survey Card.*

I then sent them back to their seats to engage in independent reading for the remainder of the time. The Check Off List and Federal Survey Cards were tossed back into the Red Basket. What a system.

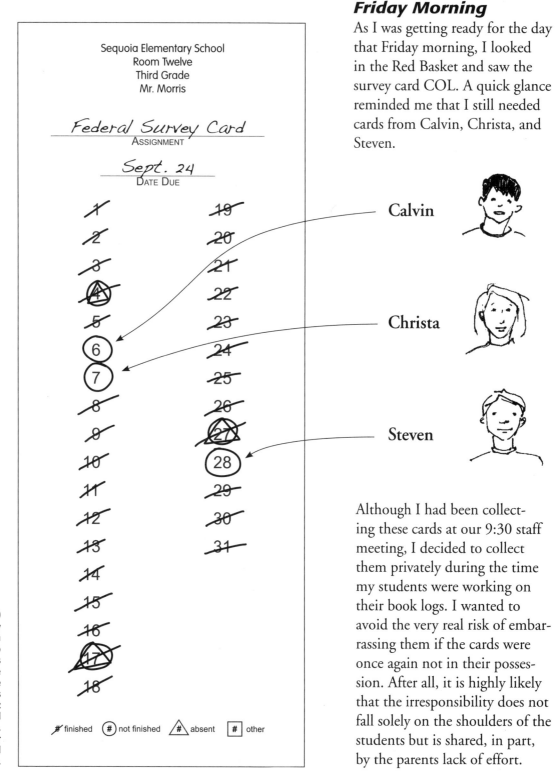

Sequoia Elementary School
Room Twelve
Third Grade
Mr. Morris

Federal Survey Card
ASSIGNMENT

Sept. 24
DATE DUE

~~1~~   ~~19~~
~~2~~   ~~20~~
~~3~~   ~~21~~
④(absent)   ~~22~~
~~5~~   ~~23~~
⑥   ~~24~~
⑦   ~~25~~
~~8~~   ~~26~~
~~9~~   ~~27~~(absent)
~~10~~   ㉘
~~11~~   ~~29~~
~~12~~   ~~30~~
~~13~~   ~~31~~
~~14~~
~~15~~
~~16~~
~~17~~(absent)
~~18~~

✗ finished   (#) not finished   /#\ absent   [#] other

FIG. 7-10
It will only take you about two seconds to realize that three students have not yet returned their cards. Just look for the circled numbers.

Friday Morning

As I was getting ready for the day that Friday morning, I looked in the Red Basket and saw the survey card COL. A quick glance reminded me that I still needed cards from Calvin, Christa, and Steven.

Calvin

Christa

Steven

Although I had been collecting these cards at our 9:30 staff meeting, I decided to collect them privately during the time my students were working on their book logs. I wanted to avoid the very real risk of embarrassing them if the cards were once again not in their possession. After all, it is highly likely that the irresponsibility does not fall solely on the shoulders of the students but is shared, in part, by the parents lack of effort.

Mr. Morris
> Approaching Christa with the Check Off List in hand:
> *Federal Survey Card?*

Christa
> Digging into her backpack with a big smile of relief:
> *Here it is, Mr. Morris. My mom filled it out last night.*

power
love
fun
freedom
safety

Mr. Morris
> Taking her card and marking off number 7:
> *Excellent. Here's your coupon.*

It took her all week, but you know what? That's okay. She had all week. How great, though, that she was able to experience the fact that I followed through on my request to return a Federal Survey Card. This type of consistent, predictable behavior on my part will lend strength to future requests.

The same thing happened with Steven. I got his card, marked off his number, and handed him a coupon. Just one more to go.

When I checked with Calvin, he told me that he didn't have his.

power
love
fun
freedom
safety

Mr. Morris
> *Did you forget your card? Well, that happens.*
> Taking the stack of collected cards and handing them to Calvin:
> *Would you take these to the office and tell them that you were the only one who did not bring back the card?*

You gotta love it.

34

Tools & Toys

The Check Off List, which had so faithfully served its purpose, was shown to the class at our staff meeting later that morning. I thanked them for doing such a good job on the Federal Survey Cards and then crumpled the COL and added it to our **REWARD TUBE**, an empty tennis ball container that holds completed Check Off Lists.

power
love
fun
freedom
safety

The students know that when the container is full—we only use COL's that have been generated from our staff meetings, not the ones from assignments and learning activities—they get an extra ten minutes of recess. It's just my way of saying "Thanks for being a responsible class."

powerr
love
fun
freedom
safety

General rule: Even though Calvin did not bring in his card, I would still add the COL to the Reward Tube. If you think about it, we got most of them. In fact, our completion rate was approximately 97%. That's an "A" in my book. Besides, I wouldn't want Calvin to be the recipient of hostile feelings from the other students who learned that the Federal Survey Card COL wasn't added to the Reward Tube because he hadn't returned his card.

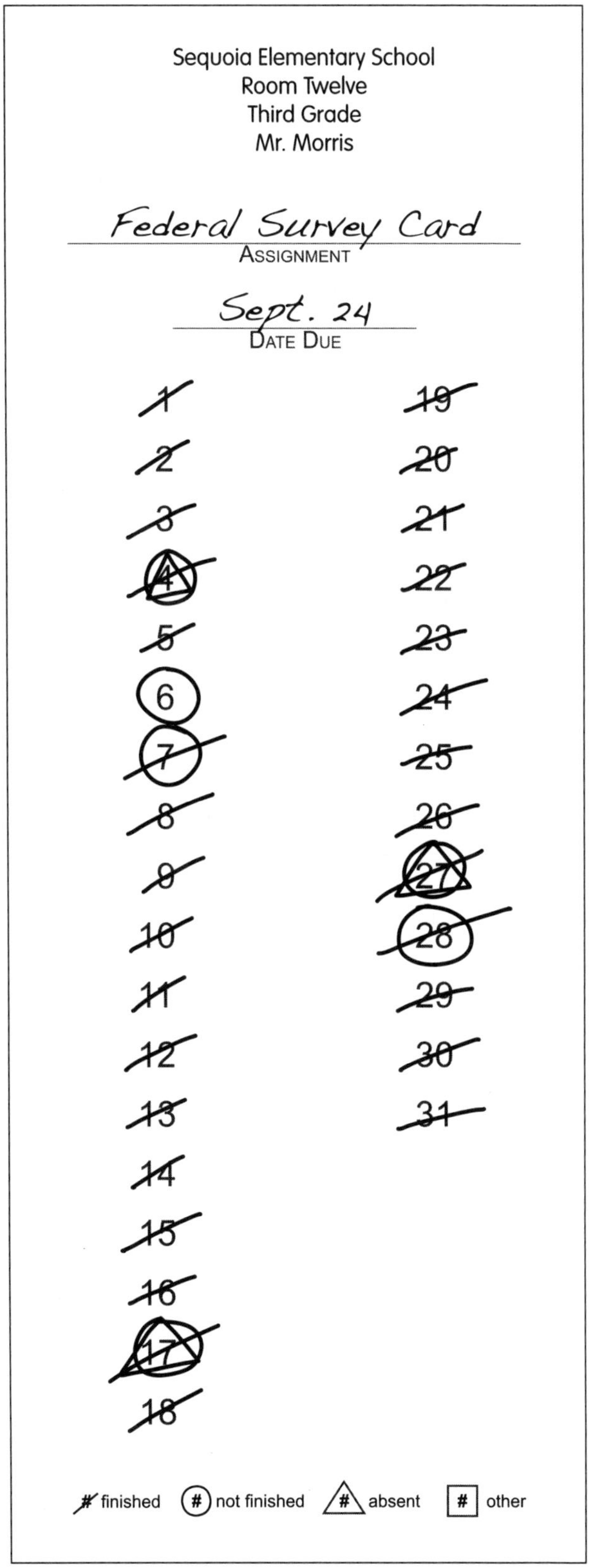

Sequoia Elementary School
Room Twelve
Third Grade
Mr. Morris

Federal Survey Card
ASSIGNMENT

Sept. 24
DATE DUE

~~1~~   ~~19~~
~~2~~   ~~20~~
~~3~~   ~~21~~
④   ~~22~~
~~5~~   ~~23~~
⑥   ~~24~~
⑦   ~~25~~
~~8~~   ~~26~~
~~9~~   27
~~10~~   28
~~11~~   ~~29~~
~~12~~   ~~30~~
~~13~~   ~~31~~
~~14~~
~~15~~
~~16~~
17
~~18~~

✗ finished   (#) not finished   △# absent   [#] other

FIG. 7-11
The Check Off List at the end of the week.

A Final Look

And here, one last time, is a view of the Check Off List that was used to collect the Federal Survey Cards. Notice how quickly your eye moves past the crossed out numbers and comes to rest upon #6? This kind of efficiency in paper handling really helps me maintain my focus as I manage my work load.

Throughout the week, as I dealt with the collection of Federal Survey Cards—not to mention the one hundred and one other things going on at the same time—I was always able to pick up the packet and know immediately where we stood. I didn't have to count the cards, lay them out, double-check them, or ask the students. The circled numbers on the Check Off List told me everything I needed to know. That is a major stress reducer.

Also, using a COL was a boost to student motivation. I could easily identify individuals who had taken care of business and recognize them for their efforts. The COL made sure that I knew who deserved praise and who needed a gentle reminder about being responsible.

On Your Own

Now that you've seen the basic teacher-managed Check Off List procedure, you should have no trouble doing it yourself. As you move through those first few weeks and collect those initial items, keep your eyes open to variations, improvements, and extensions. Your spin-offs may not arrive right away, but given time, you'll begin to adapt, adjust, and improve. Don't forget that part of the success of the New Management program has to do with making it *your* number system.

Right now, though, it's time to move on to another mode of Check Off List collection: the student-as-manager routine.

Student Collectors

Now that your students have experienced the basic Check Off List process and have seen how simple it was for you to use, it would be appropriate to turn over some of the collection proceedings to them. Worth mentioning again is the fact that student numbers creates a rich environment for actively involving your students in the running of your classroom. When Bill Glasser identified student involvement as a key ingredient of student achievement, he wasn't just talking about academics. Involvement has to do with ownership and participation; having an active, vital role in shaping the direction of the day.

Common error: Teachers sometimes fall into the habit of calling upon the same, small handful of overachieving, responsible students when they want someone to help take care of class business. Part of the reason this happens is that the teacher is reasonably certain that these students will do a good job.

It also has to do with the fact that, according to research, teachers hang out with overachievers more than underachievers. I can understand why. Overachievers are easy to be around. They love you, they nurture you, and they make you feel good. Underachievers, on the other hand, can suck you dry; and so we limit how much time we spend in their proximity.

Suggestion: Make a concerted effort to give each student in your class an opportunity to collect something with a Check Off List. Use these student jobs to "get close to" your underachievers, your fringe kids, your resistant learners. Show any and all disenfranchised students that you care about them and that you really need their help to run the classroom. By establishing this kind of personal connection, you'll be laying the foundation for an academic connection.

Sad reality: When I was teaching fifth grade, there were a number of times when, at the beginning of the year, I would go to my underachievers and ask them to help with a task. It was tragic to see, by the stunned expression on their faces, that some of them had never been asked before.

Collecting Permission Slips, Day 1

Having a student collect permission slips for a field trip would make an excellent example of putting a student in charge of a Check Off List to help you take care of things.[†]

MR. MORRIS
Ringing the hotel bell, giving the team reps copies of the permission slip, and then waiting until each student has one:
Here are your permission slips for the upcoming Math Field Day. After you get it signed by your mom or dad, please return it to class.
Turning to Vincent:
Would you like to be the one to collect them?

VINCENT
Not terribly thrilled at the prospect:
Uh, no thanks.

MR. MORRIS
Not a problem. Thanks anyway. Christina, how about you?

CHRISTINA
Sure, Mr. Morris.

power
love
fun
freedom
safety

Important factor: Always ask. Never assume that students want to help out. Some of them, especially the underachievers and the fringe kids, don't trust teachers. It's nothing you've done; it's just that you happen to represent another adult in what, for them, has been a whole world of untrustworthy adults. They might need to see how you deal with your student helpers before they feel safe enough to agree to help. The very act of asking—and accepting "no" for an answer—will go a long way to promote feelings of safety and trust.

Role reversal: I know I'd be much happier if, at a staff meeting, the principal allowed me to decide if I was going to participate in some project or join a new committee. Your students will feel the same way.

power
love
fun
freedom
safety

MR. MORRIS
Thanks, Christina.
Handing her a Check Off List and then addressing the class:
When you bring back your signed permission slip, you can give it to Christina. She'll be collecting them and marking off your numbers.

Now that I've enlisted Christina's support, I will need to make an arrangement with her

---

† You might not want to start with something as critical as signed legal forms. Although they'll eventually get to the point whereby they can collect just about anything you need collected, it might be less stressful for you if they started off collecting simple classroom assignments.

regarding the manner in which she is going to keep the permission slips organized. There are two basic ways we can go.

1. **Keep the returned permission slips clipped together in the Red Basket.**

   The Red Basket is convenient and accessible. It's also where I keep things that need to be taken care of, so it makes sense that Christina would keep the permission slips there. A paper clip will prevent them from getting separated.

2. **Keep the returned permission slips in a large envelope.**

   This is the option the students prefer. For some reason, they like to have an envelope for these collection jobs. And even though it's just a plain, manila envelope, there's something special about it. Christina would label the envelope "Field Trip Permission Slips" and keep it handy in her desk along with the Check Off List.

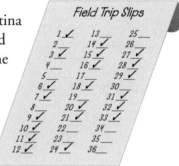

72

Tools & Toys

Tip o' the Hat: The "Christina" in this story is actually Christina Martinez, a member of Room Twelve's Class of '93. I handed her a manila envelope and a Check Off List. She returned the *unused* COL five minutes later and told me that she wasn't going to need it. She then showed me that she had made a Check Off List right on the envelope with her pencil. Sweet.

As an added step to help insure success, I'd asked Christina to write her name on the whiteboard in addition to the item she was collecting.

FIG. 7-12
A reminder to the other students is written on the whiteboard.

Collecting Permission Slips, Day 2

As the students return to class today, many of them will give their signed permission slips to Christina. One or two of them—and you know who I'm talking about—will try to give it to me. Even though the reminder is on the board for all to see, it's just how some of them think. (Or don't think, as the case may be.) Actually, it has more to do with conditioning than anything else. Students have been conditioned over the years that the teacher will take care of just about everything which is why they always want to give us just about everything.

CALVIN
  Trying to hand Mr. Morris his permission slip:
    Here.

MR. MORRIS
  Knowing exactly what it is but not touching it:
    What's this?

CALVIN
  Smiling because he's taken care of business:
    It's my permission slip.

MR. MORRIS
  Calmly:
    Oh. I'm not getting those.

CALVIN
  Slightly perplexed:
    Who is?

MR. MORRIS
  Patiently:
    Have you asked anyone else?
  Pausing for emphasis:
    What are you supposed to do when you're not sure about something? That's right, ask three, then me. Why don't you give that a try and see how it works?

> *Rule of thumb:* I don't mind helping, but I'm trying to break the Teacher Welfare mode whenever possible. With a bit of patience and practice, Calvin will eventually learn to ask his neighbors for guidance or direction before he asks me. This is just one more example of how I helped my students develop the ability to solve problems.

Sure enough, Calvin finds out that Christina is collecting them, and he takes his permission slip to her. Christina places it in the envelope, and draws a line through 6, Calvin's number.

Warning: Although the transaction between Calvin and Christina that I just described sounded like a simple procedure, I've learned that it's helpful to role play the entire process before the students actually bring back their slips.

How to give Christina your permission slip:

Mr. Morris
Addressing the class with a permission slip in hand:
Pick an appropriate time. Don't do it during a lesson or when someone is speaking to the class.

Before you try to give her your permission slip, ask her if she's busy. If she is, come back another time.

Tell her what you're trying to do. Although you know why you're at her desk—you want to give her your permission slip—she won't.

Give her a second to find the Check Off List and envelope. When she's ready, politely hand it to her.

Tell her your student number.

Stand there and watch her mark off your number.

Thank her for helping and get back on task.

At the conclusion of those instructions I would model each of the steps as I gave my own permission slip to Christina.

Without simple instructions and a clear model, students might be inclined to just toss their slips on Christina's desk and make her do all of the work.[†]

Collecting Permission Slips, Day 5

As the days pass, Christina continues to collect slips and mark off student numbers on her Check Off List. Since today is Friday, and our field trip is one week away, it would probably be a good idea to check with her to see how things are going.

Mr. Morris
Christina, how are we doing on those permission slips?

Christina
Finding the envelope and checking the numbers that aren't marked off:
I only need five more, Mr. Morris.

For the purposes of discussion, let's pretend for a moment that Christina is an under-achiever. To begin with, going to her to ask her help did wonders for her sense of positive

---

†   If you don't help to make the collection job a manageable one, no one is going to want to help in the future.

power
love
fun
freedom
safety

power, importance, and involvement in our classroom. And, since I know that she likes being the one to collect each student's permission slip, I can now begin to use the collection process as a motivator.

power
love
fun
freedom
safety

MR. MORRIS
Looking over the Check Off List and smiling at the good job she's doing:
Wow. Just five more? Nice job, Christina. Hey, if you finish your vocabulary assignment early, would you go ask those five students for their permission slips?

Being an underachiever, Christina rarely gets her vocabulary assignment finished on time. She's not one of those students. (Not yet, anyway. She soon will be.) The typical motivators she's seen in the past have just never seemed to click with her.

Christina's Thoughts About Our Motivators:

The Star Chart on which students are given a star to put next to their names to show that they've completed work on time.
---*The Star Chart. Big deal. One more star and I have four of them. Everyone else has twenty-four. I'm so embarrassed by my lack of stars that I don't even want my mom to visit our room.*

Candy or treats given for a job well done.
---*My mom says I'm not supposed to have sugar.*

Verbal praise given in front of the other students.
---*They'll just tease me later. Everyone already knows that I'm not a good student.*

power
love
fun
freedom
safety

However, by giving Christina an important job to do, by asking her to help out, by letting her experience the fact that she is a necessary part of our room, I'll see her respond. I'll see Christina finish her classroom assignments—the important stuff in my mind—so that she can collect permission slips—the fun stuff in her mind.

And it's so easy to do. (Core Principle #5: Make Things Manageable.) By comparing the circled numbers on the Check Off List to the Class Chart hanging on the wall, Christina, faithful little bloodhound that she is, will track down those five students and begin to gently remind them of their status.

CHRISTINA
Standing at Jennifer's desk with the Check Off List in hand:
Hey, Jennifer. Are you going on our field trip next Friday?

JENNIFER
Somewhat startled:
Yeah, why?

CHRISTINA
Well, I haven't gotten your permission slip yet.

JENNIFER
Oh! I'm glad you asked me. I put it in my backpack last night and forgot all about it.
Retrieving her permission slip and handing it to Christina.
Thanks for reminding me.

Not only are we getting another slip turned in, but Christina is getting her classroom self-esteem some badly needed strokes.

With a bit of diligence on Christina's part, she would eventually collect the last one. A quick count to verify that we had them all—I wouldn't want to overlook any that might have slipped out of her envelope—and they are on their way to the office.

Another task taken care of.

Another student involved.

To complete the entire process, I'd have Christina crumple up the Check Off List she used and add it to the ones already in our Reward Tube.

And think how great it would be if, for some strange twist of fate or clever planning on my part, the Check Off List that Christina added was the one that cleared the top and triggered the extra recess. There would be a burst of sincere applause, a hip-hip-hooray, and an outbreak of high fives all around the room. Christina would relive that moment for weeks.

power
love
fun
freedom
safety

As I am sure you have realized by now, the possibilities for using a Check Off List to monitor activities in your room are enormous. By having two or three students managing lists for you, it becomes infinitely more bearable to deal with all of the things that need your attention but not your direct involvement.

The Check Off List will take care of so many needs, you'll wonder how you ever got through a day without one. And since we need to get through this lesson, how about one more example of how you could use a Check Off List?

How about setting up a Check Off List somewhere in the room and allow the students to turn in an assignment on their own? This easy-to-use strategy, as explained in the next section, will be a major step away from Teacher Welfare and toward true student self-determination.

Reality: If I collect something with a COL, it's a form of Teacher Welfare. It's me taking care of my students, which is part of my job and something I enjoy doing. However, it's also part of my job to monitor how much welfare in which I engage. Too much can be counterproductive.

The same thing can occur if a student collects something with a COL. It's still a subtle form of welfare. As we saw in the previous example, Christina was the one who had to track down five students. I want my students to learn how to take care of themselves. All they need is some practice and encouragement.

Collecting a Book Report

In this third, and final, example, we're going to take a Check Off List, attach it to a folder, and have the students mark off their own numbers.

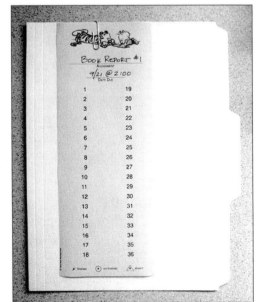

FIG. 7-13
A Check Off List clipped to a file folder will serve as a collection tool for book reports.

Set-Up

The set-up for this procedure is simple:

1.   **Label the Check Off List**

Get a copy of your COL and write the assignment to be collected on the AS-SIGNMENT line. Add the date and the time it's due on the DATE DUE line.

2.   **Attach it to a collection folder**

Using a paper clip, attach your labeled COL to the front of a manila file folder.

FIG. 7-15
Instead of the paper clip, you could staple the COL at the top and bottom. This would prevent it from getting accidentally detached.

3.   **Set it aside until you're ready to show your students**

I usually place mine in the Red Basket. (Life in the classroom will be so much easier when you adhere to the philosophy of "a place for everything and everything in its place." That's not to say that you need to be rigidly compulsive about the matter. It's just that the book report collection folder has got to be put *somewhere,* so why not use a consistent, dependable location?)

Ready to Go

Now that your book report COL has been prepared, we're ready to use it.

1. Show students the COL/file folder arrangement.

Pick an appropriate time. My normal routine is to show the folder during our 9:30 staff meeting. Obviously, though, you should pick the time that you feel would be best.

MR. MORRIS

Holding up the folder for all to see:

As you know, your book report is due today by 2:00. I'd like you to place your report in this folder and then mark off your number.

2. Provide a few guidelines.

They shouldn't have too much trouble with this procedure.

MR. MORRIS

Waiting for their attention:

Please pick an appropriate time to turn in your report. Doing it in the middle of a lesson or when someone is speaking would not be the best times. Also, if you see two or three students standing near the folder to turn in their reports, you might want to wait a bit instead of just standing in line with everyone else. There's no rush. You have most of the day.

power
love
fun
freedom
safety

3. Remind them to mark off their numbers.

Although most of the students will remember to mark off their numbers, a few of them won't. That's okay. They'll get better at it over time. Also, marking off the number is really a secondary skill. The primary skill, turning in the book report, is the one I'm more concerned about.

MR. MORRIS

Holding up the COL folder again and using his finger for emphasis:

Please remember to mark off your number when you turn in your book report. A simple line through your number will be fine.

It might help make the "mark off" step easier if you were to place a cup of pencils near the folder. I use the thick, blue primary ones with no eraser because they are somewhat immune to theft.

Tactic: If you have to, tie a pencil to the cup handle with a length of twine.

4. Put the folder in a convenient location.

Find a spot in the room where the folder can be placed so that it is easily accessible.

Open For Business

We're now set. The COL/file folder will quietly take care of the important task of collecting book reports. At the same time, since each student is responsible for turning in his own report and marking off his own student number, everyone will be getting practice at becoming self-reliant. They won't have to involve you or anyone else. They'll do the whole thing all by themselves.

As if that weren't enough, there are two other advantages to using a Check Off List in this fashion.

Advantage One

power
love
fun
freedom
safety

You will be providing your students with a wonderful opportunity for exercising freedom. It's the simple freedom to get up out of your seat and turn in an assignment. This is much better than the typical excuses students come up with for getting out of their seats. They'll either sharpen a pencil or get a drink of water they don't really need. The book report COL/file folder technique will allow students to get up on their own, turn in their book reports, and experience the immediate benefits of taking care of themselves.

Advantage Two

This type of assignment gathering is a model of what I've come to call *asynchronous* collection, or collecting an assignment from students at different times. Most of the collection techniques being used by teachers are synchronous ones. That is, we're gathering everyone's assignment at the same time.

Examples of synchronous methods:
> students place homework in a tote tray as they enter the room in the morning
> students pass their completed assignments to the end of the row
> team captains collect work from team members
> the teacher stands at the door and gathers papers as students leave

For the most part—80% of the time—this is the way you want to go. Synchronous methods are efficient and expedite the collection process. They enable you to quickly gather up assignments and then get everyone back on task.

power
love
fun
freedom
safety

For the other 20% of the assignments you collect—especially something like a book report which students complete at different times—the asynchronous method will be more effective. By allowing each student to determine the best time to turn in an assignment, the teacher provides an opportunity for the assignments to be processed in a more timely and rewarding fashion. Overachievers no longer have to wait for everyone else. They are free to turn in the assignment as soon as they've finished it and then move on to something else.

Let me show you the striking difference between the two methods. I'll start by showing how I used to do it during my first five years of teaching. It was an old-school model my own teachers had used. Although it's not a pretty example, it was the only method I knew at that time.

Book Report Collecting, Synchronous Model

MR. MORRIS
  9:30 on Thursday morning:
  As you know, book reports are due today at two o'clock. Since we've been working on them all week, I'll expect everyone to have a report ready to hand in when I ask for them later.

Tick-tock, tick-tock. An hour goes by.

JENNY
  Attempting to hand Mr. Morris a paper at 10:30:
  Here, Mr. Morris.

MR. MORRIS
  Puzzled:
  What's this?

JENNY
  Beaming with obvious pleasure and pride:
  It's my book report. I'm all done.

MR. MORRIS
  Not in a book-report-collecting frame of mind:
  HEY! I SAID THAT I'D GET THEM AT TWO O'CLOCK! WOULD YOU JUST WAIT!

And there I was, coming across like Blackbeard, getting upset because I wasn't prepared to deal with a finished book report at 10:30. Why I felt that I was such an indispensable part of the collection process, I'll never know. I just knew that I had said 2:00, and, gosh darn it, I meant 2:00. I'm sorry if I hurt your feelings, but you are just going to have to wait.

In other words, *don't be productive, don't be an overachiever, don't be so on-task that you're finishing ahead of schedule. It'll just mess up my plan to get all of the book reports when I said that I would.*

So, be a good little student, and wait until Mr. Morris is ready to collect the book report on which you've worked so hard. I know that you're done early, that you've demonstrated excellent work skills and study habits, and that you're proud of your efforts. Unfortunately, though, that's just not as important as my need to gather papers at one time.

Granted, I wasn't verbalizing those thoughts, but I'm sure they were coming through loud and clear.

The end results of using a synchronous collection technique for the book reports were that: 1) I sometimes felt besieged which led to frustration; and 2) some of my more productive students were being needlessly restrained.

With the asynchronous method in place, I can avoid this whole mess.

Book Report Collecting, Asynchronous Model

> Mr. Morris
> > Holding up the collection folder:
> > > *Don't forget, book reports are due today by two o'clock. Place your report in the folder and mark off your number on the Check Off List.*
> > Moving to the back of the room:
> > > *I'll put the folder on this shelf.*

Tick-tock, tick-tock. An hour goes by.

> Jenny
> > Attempting to hand Mr. Morris a paper at 10:30:
> > > *Here, Mr. Morris.*

> Mr. Morris
> > Puzzled:
> > > *What's this?*

> Jenny
> > Beaming with obvious pleasure and pride:
> > > *It's my book report. I'm all done.*

power
love
fun
freedom
safety

> Mr. Morris
> > Smiling back:
> > > *That's terrific! Just put it in the folder and mark off your number.*

(Now then, you tell me. Which way would you rather go? That's what I thought.)

> Mr. Morris
> > Encouraged by this little slice of organizational heaven:
> > > *Oh, by the way, after you've turned in your report, come back and see me. I've got a Neon Necklace for you.*

33

Tools & Toys

Neon Necklaces were made from neon-colored shoe laces that I purchased from the Oriental Trading Company. I bought 18 pairs and then tied the ends together to produce

36 necklaces and hung them from a hook in the room. The necklaces, worn by students w have finished an important assignment, are a visual indicator of who's done and who's not.

> MR. MORRIS
> Handing Jenny a necklace as she returns:
> *Here you go. Nice job, Jenny.*

Jenny, having turned in her completed book report, is now a member of what we call "Club Ed."

Suggestion: In the interests of physical safety, students are asked to remove their necklaces from around their necks and wrap it around their wrists before they leave for recess. Or, you might want to try what I've been doing lately. I've been using scrunchies. I found them at the dollar store, six for a buck. I bought a class set along with a little plastic tub in which to keep them. The beauty of the scrunchy is that you don't have to worry about anyone being gagged accidentally but they're still highly visible on a student's wrist. You could also use the kind of rubber bracelet popularized by the Lance Armstrong foundation.

**power
love
fun
freedom**
safety

The morning progressed and students, when it was appropriate to do so, turned in their reports, marked off their numbers, and came to see me for a Neon Necklace.

As morning recess drew near, I grabbed my dog squeak toy—*Stop, Look, Listen*—and made an announcement.

> Mr. Morris
> Slipping a Neon Necklace around his neck and holding it out:
> *If you're in the Club, you may go to recess right now.*

I'd pause as the students who have already turned in their book reports were dismissed to recess. I'd also be beaming at them in recognition of their hard work and effort.

> MR. MORRIS
> Turning to the students who are still in their seats:
> *Please don't forget: book reports are due by two o'clock today. You know, you might want to work on it during recess, but...*
> Giving them a knowing grin:
> *That's just a suggestion. See you later. Enjoy your recess.*

Similar to the message my students received earlier about their Federal Survey Cards, I was once again in the position to show them that I was aware of who still hadn't turned in a book report. This ability to focus my attention on just the students who need it does wonders for my need to back up my words with actions. *Mr. Morris wasn't just talking about the book reports. He actually held back the students who hadn't turned in a book report yet and gave them a reminder.*

As you can imagine, action that backs up your words has a very powerful impact upon student productivity.

A Quick Recap

Well, things are progressing nicely. So far this morning I was able to:

✓ **organize a Check Off List/file folder to collect book reports,**

✓ **show my students how the COL/file folder works,**

✓ **recognize students who turned in their book reports early,**

✓ **remind the students who weren't done yet to have it in by 2:00,**

✓ **take a break at morning recess, and**

✓ **sit back and marvel at how smoothly things were progressing.**

Little did I realize, though, that at that very moment Calvin was on the playground pondering his predicament. You see, Calvin doesn't have a book report to put in the folder. He never completed book reports last year. His teacher didn't really have a system for monitoring student accountability. When a book report *was* due, the teacher would have the students pass them to the end of the row. Calvin learned that it would take his teacher a day or two to realize that he hadn't passed his to the end of the row. Granted, he knew that he would eventually get caught and receive an earful of grief and a few empty threats. But he also knew that, if he were to drag his feet for a few days, it was very possible that his teacher would forget about his missing book report. The end result was that he decided it was easier to take the verbal punishment than it was to write a report.

However, in just three short weeks, he's already figured out that it's not going to be as easy to slip through the cracks with Mr. Morris.

> ---*Oh, man. What am I going to do? Mr. Morris has got that Check Off List thing and he's going to know I'm not done with my book report because my number won't be marked off.*

And then, in a moment of clarity, Calvin makes a startling discovery†.

> ---*Wait a second! I don't need a book report to mark off my number. I just need a pencil.*

And with that thought, he begins to relax. He sees a faint light at the end of what had been a very dark tunnel. (He doesn't yet realize that the light is actually a train bearing down on him. He just sees what he thinks is a clever way to solve his no-book-report problem.)

The realization that he could mark off his number and not turn in a book report is comforting to Calvin. This kind of behavior is right up his alley. After all, he's been making a living on deceit. Why should he stop now? Calvin's thinking: 1) if Mr. Morris is dumb enough to trust students to turn in book reports on their own; then 2) I'm smart enough to take advantage of him.

> ---*This is going to be a piece of cake.*

Back in the classroom after recess, Calvin plans his attack. When he's sure no one was watching, he weasels over to the COL/file folder, casually glances around to make sure he's not being observed, quickly marks off his number, and then saunters away.

> ---*I like this number system. It's not going to be as bad as I thought it was going to be.*

On his way back to his seat, he remembers that Mr. Morris has been giving out Neon Necklaces to students who had turned in their book reports.

> ---*Hmmmm. I'd better cover my tracks.*

CALVIN
> With a look of innocence about him:
> *Hey, Mr. Morris. I turned in my book report. Do I get a necklace?*

MR. MORRIS
> Smiling:
> *Did you remember to mark off your number?*

CALVIN:
> Relieved that he wasn't asked to show Mr. Morris his book report:
> *Sure did! Just like you said to.*

---

† For the record, Calvin does have a brain. Sadly, though, it's geared more toward the world of survival than the world of academics. If we can figure out a way to channel his survival smarts into school smarts, we'll see his test scores really jump.

MR. MORRIS
    Giving him a pat on the shoulder:
        That's excellent, Calvin. I knew you could do it. Here's your necklace.

Now before you question my sanity at giving Calvin a necklace on trust alone, let me point out something:

> *When he told me that he had turned in his report,*
> *I didn't know any better.*

I wasn't yet aware of the fact that I had just been ripped off by Calvin; that he had lied to me about turning in his book report.

For the moment, though, that's okay. I'll be able to deal with his deceit later when I become aware of his missing book report and he finally becomes aware of the power of numbers. Right now, as I interact with him, I want to begin to build a relationship of trust.

> *Important factor:* I think a great deal of my success with students is that I trust them. However, it's not a blind trust. It's not some weak, myopic "I hope you guys are all doing the right thing" kind of trust. It's a trustworthiness we develop as we use this student number system.
>
> When students tell me that they've turned in an assignment, I accept it as the truth. No one has to prove it by showing me the actual paper. This is especially true for my students who don't seem very trustworthy.
>
> If Calvin tells me that he turned in his book report, I take him at his word. After all, any initial attempts at deceit will be quickly thwarted anyway because the student number system will provide the true picture of student accountability. So why not start from a position of trust?
>
> With the easy-to-use number tools I've created for verifying compliance, Calvin will not only learn to turn in assignments on time but develop a sense of honor and integrity as well.

Fast Forward to Two O'Clock

Just before 2:00, I'd pick up the COL/file folder, remove the stack of book reports, and hand them to one of my students.

MR. MORRIS
    With a reassuring smile:
        Amanda, would you collate† these?

---

†   As opposed to saying, "Would you put these papers in numerical order from 1 to 31?", it's actually easier to teach your students the proper term for this procedure. You can find the word **collate** in our Class Glossary.

AMANDA
Happy to help:
Sure, Mr. Morris.

Another student would be asked to gather up the necklaces and return them to the hook. I'd like to avoid embarrassing Calvin who is currently wearing one under false pretenses.

Putting Book Reports in Order

There are several methods students can employ when they collate assignments, most of which are ridiculously inept. I've seen students spread papers around the room and then scurry about trying to find #1. I've also witnessed students thumbing through the whole stack of papers looking for #1, extract it, and then thumb back through the whole stack looking for #2. Although the strategies these student helpers use do provide a bit of comic relief, their techniques don't do much for timely processing.

Here's the method I use myself and share with the students:

Step 1. Chunk.†
Sort the stack of papers into three piles.

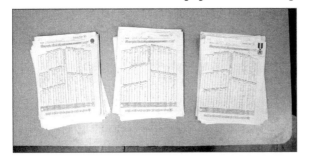

FIG. 7-16
The assignments are sorted into three separate piles: 1-10, 11-20, 21-31.

With 31 students, I would have piles for 1-10, 11-20, and 21-31.

Caution: As with most of the procedures I've described so far in this handbook for creating a happier, more productive classroom, this one seems rather simple. However, during my first year or two of using my new number system, I did encounter a few potholes on the road to success. With a bit of problem solving, though, I learned how to drive around them. Before you blow a tire, allow me to show you how to avoid the potholes and keep things moving along smoothly.

> **Pothole #1:** *Your helper is sorting papers into three piles and comes upon a paper that does not have a student number.*

No sweat. Remember Lesson 6 on the Class Chart? Your helper would look on the chart, find the name, and write the number on the paper for the stu-

---

†   "Chunking" is the management phrase for taking a large task and breaking it into small, manageable ones. This is a good skill to teach your underachievers, and one of the best ways to learn it is to do it.

dent. While he's at it, it would probably be best to somehow draw attention to the fact that the helper had to add the number. A circle around the now-written number would provide the neglectful student with a visual reminder when his paper is finally returned to him.

Pothole #2: *Your helper is sorting papers into three piles and comes upon a paper that does not have a name or number.*

This little nuisance used to cause problems until I developed a couple of procedures to remedy this situation.

First Procedure:
Don't tell Mr. Morris that one of the papers does not have a name on it. That just pushes all of his pirate buttons.

> STUDENT HELPER
>   Handing Mr. Morris a paper:
>   *This one doesn't have a name on it, Mr. Morris.*

> MR. MORRIS
>   Trying hard not to snatch the paper in disgust:
>   *Thank you.*
>   Turning his attention to the class:
>   *EXCUSE ME. WHO DIDN'T PUT HIS NAME ON THIS PAPER!*

Well, the student who didn't is also the student who's not listening to me right now. He's got that whole package of skills going for him: he doesn't listen, he doesn't put his name on his paper, he doesn't know what page we're on or what math problem we're doing.

Experience has shown me, though, that after my announcement, I'll be rushed by five or six neurotic overachievers who are worried that the paper with no name might be theirs.

> BOBBY BRIEFCASE
>   Running up:
>   *Let me see, let me see.*
>   Checking the paper:
>   *Hmmmmmm. Nope! It's not mine.*
>   Returning to his seat:
>   *Whew! I thought it was mine. I'm glad I checked.*

So basically, I'm going to see everyone I don't need to see. I won't see the one student I do need to see.

Second Procedure:

Just set aside the paper for right now. Maybe it's the only one we're missing. If that's the case, the process of elimination would determine the owner. The student could then add the name and number, circle them both, place it in the proper pile, and proceed to Step 2.

Third Procedure:

With upper grade students, you'll find helpers who can recognize each other's handwriting. If the helper thinks he knows, I'd want him to quietly check with the student to verify ownership. If the helper was correct, he could have the student write his name and number on the assignment and then head back to his desk to continue the collation process.

Bonus: You've got students working together to help make your classroom run smoothly.

Fourth Procedure:

7

Tools & Toys

If the helper can't figure out which student the paper belongs to, it's placed in our ***RETURN TO SENDER*** container. This empty Tootsie-Pop tub holds no-name papers so that they don't get lost or misplaced. Students know to check the tub if they can't find a missing assignment.

Step 2. Collate the papers in each stack.

Now that the papers have been chunked into three separate piles, it's an easy matter to collate each pile. It will take about thirty seconds for each stack.

power
love
fun
freedom
safety

Step 3. Put them all together and return them to Mr. Morris.[†]

Place the 1-10 pile on top of the 11-20 pile, and place both of them on top of the 21-31 pile. Give all of the papers to Mr. Morris and receive a big smile and a word of appreciation.

Although this may have seemed like a lot of steps, the whole thing will become automatic in a very short time. You'll have students—your underachievers, for example—collating papers quickly and efficiently. And the benefits are manyfold.

The process of placing book reports in numerical order will: 1) promote student involvement; 2) provide me with reliable information regarding missing assignments; and 3) streamline my grade keeping procedure like you can't believe. (See Lesson 10.)

Calvin Sees the Light

Now that I've got the book reports back, I'll get my students' attention and go through the stack of papers as they look on.

---

† Within a month or so, we add another step. Step 4: Put a Post-it on the top paper with the numbers of the missing assignments. This will alert me to the students I'll need to see privately.

MR. MORRIS
With a big smile and the best of expectations:
Let's see how you did turning in your book reports. After all, this was the first time you've turned in an assignment by yourselves.
Reading off student numbers as I thumb through the stack:
1…2…3…

Pan the camera over to Calvin.

CALVIN:
Stunned:
---Oh, man! That's why we use numbers. I thought I could mark off my number and look like I was done, but Mr. Morris put the papers in numerical order and mine's not going to be there.---

Cut back to Mr. Morris.

MR. MORRIS
Still thumbing through book reports:
4…5…7?
Looking up:
Calvin, your book report?

Now that Calvin's been caught, he'll most likely lie. It's how he's gotten through school so far. Even though the horse Calvin's riding on is now dead, he's not going to get off. He'll give it a kick or two in the ribs.

CALVIN
Righteously indignant:
I turned it in!

MR. MORRIS
Calm and under control:
I don't have it, son.

CALVIN
Never one to give up:
Ah, someone stole it.

Or "You lost it!" or "I know I put it in there!" or "It's not my fault!" or any number of things besides "I'm sorry. I didn't do one." Calvin is going to bluff and bluster in an attempt to escape reality.

My normal reaction to this situation—because this *is* a normal situation and occurs at the beginning of each school year as my students learn about the number system—is to remain calm and deal with it later. What I wouldn't want to do is the pirate thing and duke it out with Calvin in front of the class.[†]

power
love
fun
freedom
safety

MR. MORRIS
> Still smiling:
>> *Why don't we talk about it later?*
> Back to the paper chase:
>> *7...8...9...10...11...12...13...14...15...16...17...18.........20?*
> Translating student #19 into a name:
>> *Marshal? Oh, that's right. Marshal is absent today.*
> The shuffle continues:
>> *21...22...23...24...25...26...27......29?*
> Translating student #28 into a number:
>> *Troy? Your book report?*

Troy's book report is the one in Return to Sender because he didn't write his name or number on his paper. However, he clearly remembers turning in his report. If I ask him for his assignment, he's going to freak out.

TROY
> Shocked that Mr. Morris is asking him for his book report:
>> *I TURNED IT IN!*

MR. MORRIS
> Trying to be reassuring:
>> *Troy, calm down. It's not a late car payment; it's just a book report.*

TROY
> Earnestly:
>> *But I turned it in, Mr. Morris.*

Once again, it's time to move on. I don't want to take up class time with this issue. I also wouldn't want to vent my frustration because I think Troy's book report is sitting in Return to Sender.

What *Not* To Do:

MR. MORRIS
> Seeing a paper in the Return to Sender tub:
>> *WELL, DID YOU PUT YOUR NAME ON IT? I'VE TOLD YOU GUYS OVER AND OVER AGAIN. YOU NEED TO PUT YOUR NAME ON YOUR PAPER!*

No, no, no. Back off, Blackbeard. Allow Troy to figure out what's wrong with this picture. Usually, someone on Troy's team—who's thinking a little more clearly than Troy is

---

†   *Here's a tip from my discipline workshops:* Whenever I'm speaking to a student in what might be a confrontational situation, I visualize the student's parents standing right behind him. The mental image of his parents standing behind him reminds me not to be rude, sarcastic, or intimidating. Instead, I focus on displaying an appropriate amount of "professional concern."

right now—will spot a paper in Return to Sender and tell Troy about it.

TROY'S TEAMMATE
Leaning over to Troy:
Pssst. Troy. Check Return to Sender. I see a paper inside the tub.

TROY
Hurrying over, removing the paper, recognizing it as his, and clasping it to his chest:
Oh, here it is, Mr. Morris. I forgot to put my name on it.

Troy wrote his name and number on his book report, handed it to me, and then returned to his seat.

MR. MORRIS
Placing Troy's paper between 27 and 29:
Thanks, Troy.
Getting back to the stack:
30…31! Nice job, guys. I think that COL/file folder thing is going to work out great.

Meanwhile, Back at the Reality Ranch

Later on, at some convenient moment before dismissal, I'd want to have a brief conference with my little buddy, Calvin.

power
love
fun
freedom
safety

MR. MORRIS
At Calvin's desk, speaking quietly:
Calvin, I need to speak with you privately.
Moving to the back of the room with Calvin:
Let's talk about your book report. I know that you told me that you turned in a report, but it wasn't in the folder. I also don't think that it was misplaced or stolen. What I think happened is that you didn't have a book report and were too embarrassed to say so in front of the class.

CALVIN
Smart enough to know he's out of options:
Yeah. I didn't do one, Mr. Morris.

MR. MORRIS
Trying to make the best of it:
Doing book reports is going to be a part of your life in this room, and I want you to learn how to write them. I know it's not an easy assignment to complete, but I'll help you this year. I'm going to circle your number on this Check Off List and leave it in the Red Basket as a reminder.
Circling #6 with his pencil and showing Calvin the COL:
I'd like you to write a book report this weekend and have it ready to hand in Monday morning. Do you understand?

CALVIN
Still trying to escape the inevitable:
But I don't know what to write.

MR. MORRIS
Feeling empathetic:
You're right. It's a tough assignment. But don't worry. You'll get better at writing them as the year goes on. By the time you've done your tenth report, you'll be a pro.
Realizing that Calvin's going to need help to produce this first report:
If you'd like, I can make xerox copies of some of the other reports that were turned in so that you can see what other students have written. Would that help?

power
love
fun
freedom
safety

CALVIN
Thinking he'll just copy someone else's report:
Sure. That would help a lot. Thanks, Mr. Morris.

MR. MORRIS
Who's been around the block a few times:
Now, you realize that you won't be able to copy these reports. They're just to be used to give you some ideas. I'll expect you to use your own words and share you own thoughts and feelings.

CALVIN
Beginning to figure out that Mr. Morris really is on his side:
I won't, Mr. Morris. I'll write my own report and bring it in on Monday.

MR. MORRIS
Big smile, pat on the back:
Atta boy. See me after school, and we'll go to the office to copy some of the reports.

And with that, I'd drop the COL/file folder in my Red Basket as a reminder that Calvin will be turning in a book report on Monday. This will help me to hold Calvin accountable.

> *Reality:* If I ask him to write a book report over the weekend and then don't follow up on Monday to see if he wrote one, my actions aren't matching my words. When your actions don't back up your words, you're actually teaching your students that they can ignore what you say. Not a good way to go.

At the same time, I'll need to bear in mind that this might be the first time in Calvin's academic career that a teacher has done this for him. He's been able to wear out every other teacher with his manipulative bag of tricks. Consequently, it might take him months to accept the fact that he needs to complete assignments in a timely fashion. Granted, my overachievers can get with the program within six days, Calvin's going to need *six months*. But that's okay. I've got him all year long. The important thing is to have him walking the straight and narrow by the end of the year so that when I pass him along to his next teacher, he's heading in the right direction. Otherwise, he just ends up skating through another year and falling farther and farther behind.

The COL/file folder technique will be a significant part of Calvin's reeducation. All of the ambiguity and guess work will be gone. He won't waste any time pondering the possibility of his teacher overlooking him. He'll learn from the first experience that there's no messing with the number system.

However, he's going to need some guidance, assistance, and support in his journey to responsibility. This next section will show you how easy it is to modify the basic book report procedure and, in so doing, make life in the classroom more successful for Calvin.

Teaching Calvin How to Chunk

One of Calvin's biggest problems with the book report assignment is that he doesn't know how to chunk. He hasn't yet experienced how much easier it is to complete an assignment when you break it up into manageable pieces. He just sees the end product as one overwhelmingly complex task that should be avoided at all costs. However, we're going to be doing book reports all year, and it would be in everyone's best interests to get Calvin on board as soon as possible.

Here's our basic book report schedule:

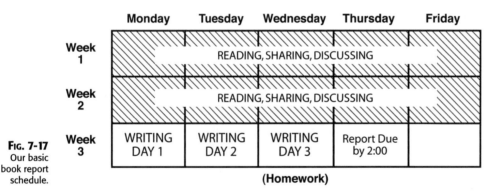

Fig. 7-17
Our basic book report schedule.

As you can see, we spend two weeks reading the same book—usually a core lit supplemental reader—and then spend the last week producing a book report.

Here's a small part of what contributed to Calvin's lack of effort: the announcement I made to my students at the beginning of Week 3.

MR. MORRIS
Holding up a copy of the book the students have just finished reading:
As you know, we're starting our new book reports this week. They will be due on Thursday at 2:00.

CALVIN
> Who has yet to meet a responsibility he hasn't tried to duck:
>> *---Thursday? It's only Monday.*

And with that comforting thought in mind, he makes little use of the time he is given on Monday to work on his book report. The same thing happens on Tuesday and Wednesday. Before he knows it, Thursday has arrived and he has just about nothing done.

It's time for a change.

Book Reports, Take Two

MR. MORRIS
> Holding up a copy of the book the students have just finished reading:
>> *As you know, we're starting our new book reports this week. They will be due on Thursday at 2:00. This week, though, we're going to change things just a bit. Instead of waiting to collect your finished book reports on Thursday, I'm going to collect a part of your report each day.*
>
> A brief but pointed pause for that thought to sink in.
>
>> *In just a bit, I'm going to give you some time for writing. Here's what I'd like you to do: I'd like you to write a paragraph about your feelings regarding the book we just finished. Tell me whether you liked it or not. Tell me why you liked or didn't like it. If you didn't like it, maybe you could identify an audience that might like the book. Maybe you could compare it to another book you've read recently. Give it two thumbs up, two thumbs down, five stars, call it a dog…whatever. This paragraph will then be used as the closing paragraph of your book report.*
>
> Holding up the COL/file folder:
>> *This paragraph is due today by 2:00.*
>
> Another pointed pause as the folder is placed on a countertop.
>
>> *Please place it in this folder and mark off your number.*

A paragraph about his own feelings is something Calvin can attempt. It's not the whole report; it's just a small, manageable part of the report. And if I can get Calvin to write part of his report on Monday, part of it on Tuesday, and another part on Wednesday, he'll have the basic components of a book report. It's not going to be a Pulitzer Prize winner but, for Calvin, it's going to be a huge accomplishment.

Conversely, if I can't get the paragraph from Calvin on Monday, I'll know to intervene. And Monday is a much better time to intervene than Thursday is when it's too late.

Variations on a COL Theme

So far in this lesson we've used a Check Off List in four different ways.

1. **Teacher use**

   I used one to collect Federal Survey Cards.

2. **Student use**

   A student used one to collect permission slips for a field trip.

3. **Class use (basic method)**

   Students turned in their book reports on their own.

4. **Class use (chunking method)**

   Students turned in separate parts of their book reports on their own.

These are the main ways I use a Check Off List in my room. There are, however, a number of other methods I have employed in my efforts to collect assignments. Let me show you just a few of them.

Around the World

Staple a COL to a file folder and fill in the assignment and date information. Announce to your students that the folder is going to "travel around the world" and gather assignments.

> YOU, THE TEACHER
> Holding the Around the World folder aloft:
> > *When you receive the folder, insert your assignment and mark off your number. If, for some strange reason, you don't have your assignment finished, please circle your number. I'll talk to the students who aren't finished later on.*

You could do the same thing with a large manila envelope instead of a file folder. The advantages to using an envelope is that the papers won't slip out the way they might with a file folder. The other advantage is that you could have a student make a COL on the front of the envelope and eliminate the need to staple one on. The disadvantage is that it's harder to insert an assignment in the envelope than it is to insert it in the file folder.

A Bulletin Board, a Bookcase, and Some Baskets

power
love
fun
freedom
safety

When I was teaching second grade, I used to have my students complete a number of independent activities each morning. When they had finished their assignments—seat work, if you will—they were free to use one of our many centers. To make the collection process easier, I created a collection center.

I placed a bookcase against the wall near one of our bulletin boards. On the bookcase I set four wire baskets. Above the baskets, stapled to the bulletin board, were four Check Off Lists. Also attached to the bulletin board, hanging from a length of twine, was a pencil for marking off numbers.

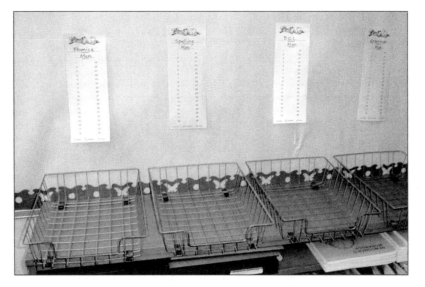

FIG. 7-18
Having all four independent activites collected in one place made it easier for me to check on the progress of my students.

It was a simple matter for the students to place completed assignments in the proper basket and then mark off their numbers.

Benefit: I was able to stand in one spot and check to see who was done and who wasn't. If, for example, I saw Calvin over at the listening center, and I had any doubts about whether he should be there, all I had to do was take a look at the Check Off Lists. If #6 was marked off on all four COL's, I left him alone.

As much as I want to be able to trust Calvin to do the right thing, his past failings can influence my present expectations. If, for example, I grilled him about whether he was done or not, it subconsciously reinforced that he couldn't be trusted. However, by using the collection center—and the easy-to-read record of his compliance with today's assignments—he'll be treated more fairly.

power
love
fun
freedom
safety

Laminated Check Off List

Think about making an oversized COL on tag board and then laminating it. Similar to the four COL's stapled to the bulletin board in the last example, you could attach it to a bulletin board. Add a dry erase marker or grease pencil for marking off numbers, a basket or box lid for collecting the assignments, and you've got a reusable Check Off List for handling the homework the students bring in each morning.

Opportunity: Have a student or two be in charge of the homework COL. At some predetermined time, they can collate the papers and erase all of the marks.

Advantage: Unlike the previous example with the four COL's stapled to the bulletin board, the laminated Check Off List won't need to be replaced each day. After the student managers have erased the marks, it'll be ready to go.

Team Check Off Lists

It's sometimes helpful to have students gather up assignments by teams. To help make the process work smoothly, I've had the teams make their own mini-COL's.

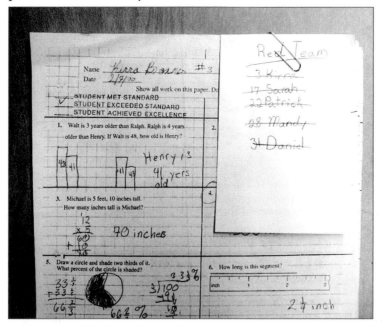

FIG. 7-19
Math papers collected by a team with the help of a team Check Off List.

These mini-lists, written on small pieces of note paper, are used just like a regular Check Off List. Students mark off their numbers, collate their papers, and clip their team COL to the top of the stack.

Enough Already

70; 74
Tools & Toys

We could go on and on and on. (Speaking of which, check out Chapter 4 of the *Tools & Toys* book for a couple of tools that can be used in lieu of a Check Off List. One is called **CLIP 'EM, DANNO** and the other is called the **CLOTHESPIN CHECK OFF LIST.**) Nonetheless, I think that's enough for right now. You're going to have to play around with the Check Off List anyway before you can accurately determine which variations are going to work for you and your students.

So, start with the basic collection techniques described in this lesson and see what happens. If you're like most teachers, you'll find that—before too long—you won't even need a COL for collecting assignments. You'll be able to gather them yourself, collate them in thirty seconds, and know immediately who's finished and who's not.

That's some pretty powerful stuff.

Lesson 8

Before We Begin

How It All Got Started

Numbering Your Students

Using Student Numbers

Timers & Sound Makers

Class Chart

Check Off List

Check Off Sheet

First Aid Kit

Grade Books

The best teacher is not the one who knows most,
but the one who is most capable of reducing knowledge
to that simple compound of the obvious and wonderful
which slips into infantile comprehension.
A person of high intelligence, perhaps, may accomplish
the thing by a conscious intellectual feat.
But it is vastly easier for the man or woman
whose habits of mind are naturally on the plane of a child's.

The best teacher of children, in brief,
is the one who is essentially childlike.

—H. L. Mencken

Lesson 8
Check Off Sheet

◆ ◆

Goals for this lesson:

☑ Discover the advantage of the Check Off Sheet over the Check Off List.

☑ Learn how to use a Check Off Sheet.

☑ Understand why there are two different Check Off Sheets.

☑ Learn how to build an "Island."

☑ Be able to determine which sheet you should use for which assignments.

◆ ◆

We're on a roll now.

So far, in just seven easy lessons, you have:

✓ **learned why students numbers are important,**

✓ **numbered your students,**

✓ **begun to use a digital timer and some sound making toys,**

✓ **made a Class Chart which is now hanging prominently in your room, and**

✓ **learned how to use Check Off Lists.**

Now what?

Well, if you feel like it, you could take a break. You've been working hard and deserve one. Go ahead. Put your feet up and relax. There, doesn't that feel better? I'll be waitin' over on the next page whenever you're ready to get back to work.

Soothing musical interlude plays here.

Okay, time to get back to work because, believe it or not, I've got another great student number tool to show you. It's called the Check Off Sheet, and it was designed to correct a minor defect in the Check Off List.

Actually, it's not really a defect; it's more of a slight nuisance.

Now, don't get me wrong. I love the Check Off List. We use them in class every single day. Either I'm collecting something or one of my students is. Also, as was demonstrated in the last lesson, COL's are attached to folders so that students are able to turn in their own assignments and mark off their own numbers. And that's where the nuisance factor first appeared.

The situation:
You see, we had begun to use the Daily Oral Language program (DOL). For those of you not familiar with DOL, it's a simple proofreading exercise in which the students are shown two sentences that contain errors. The students copy down the sentences, fix the mistakes, and then rewrite them correctly. We do this activity every morning; hence, the "Daily" in Daily Oral Language.

The nuisance:
I found myself having to set out a new COL every morning so that it was ready for the students to turn in their Daily Oral Language papers.

Monday: Set out COL; label it; check it before lunch; clip it to papers.
Tuesday: Set out COL; label it; check it before lunch; clip it to papers.
Wednesday: Set out COL; label it; check it before lunch; clip it to papers.
Thursday: Set out COL; label it; check it before lunch; clip it to papers.
Friday: Set out COL; label it; check it before lunch; clip it to papers.

I'll admit that in the world of hardships, this wasn't a major one. It was just somewhat tedious.

Wouldn't it make sense, I pondered one day, if I had a new Check Off tool that would collect the assignments for a whole week. I could set out this new collector on Monday and be all set for Tuesday, Wednesday, Thursday, and Friday. Man, we'd be livin' large.

 Suitably inspired by my yearning to make life in the classroom even easier, I created the Check Off Sheet (COS).

The Check Off Sheet

If you're a right-brained kind of person, you'll quickly realize that the Check Off Sheet is nothing more than five Check Off Lists turned sideways and compressed onto one piece of paper.

The Check Off Sheet

The blackline master can be found in the appendix.

ASSIGNMENT:

MONDAY _____   DUE BY _____

1	2	3	4	5	6	7	8	9	10	11	12
13	14	15	16	17	18	19	20	21	22	23	24
25	26	27	28	29	30	31	32	33	34	35	36

ASSIGNMENT:

TUESDAY _____   DUE BY _____

1	2	3	4	5	6	7	8	9	10	11	12
13	14	15	16	17	18	19	20	21	22	23	24
25	26	27	28	29	30	31	32	33	34	35	36

ASSIGNMENT:

WEDNESDAY _____   DUE BY _____

1	2	3	4	5	6	7	8	9	10	11	12
13	14	15	16	17	18	19	20	21	22	23	24
25	26	27	28	29	30	31	32	33	34	35	36

ASSIGNMENT:

THURSDAY _____   DUE BY _____

1	2	3	4	5	6	7	8	9	10	11	12
13	14	15	16	17	18	19	20	21	22	23	24
25	26	27	28	29	30	31	32	33	34	35	36

ASSIGNMENT:

FRIDAY _____   DUE BY _____

1	2	3	4	5	6	7	8	9	10	11	12
13	14	15	16	17	18	19	20	21	22	23	24
25	26	27	28	29	30	31	32	33	34	35	36

© 2007 New Management

FIG. 8-1
The Check Off Sheet: a simple variation of the venerable Check Off List. Notice how the COS is good for an entire week, not just one assignment.

Like his older brother, the Check Off List, this tool has a place to write the assignment being collected and the date it's due. Below those spaces are the student numbers to be marked off. In addition to these items, the COS also has a specific place to write the time that the assignment is due.

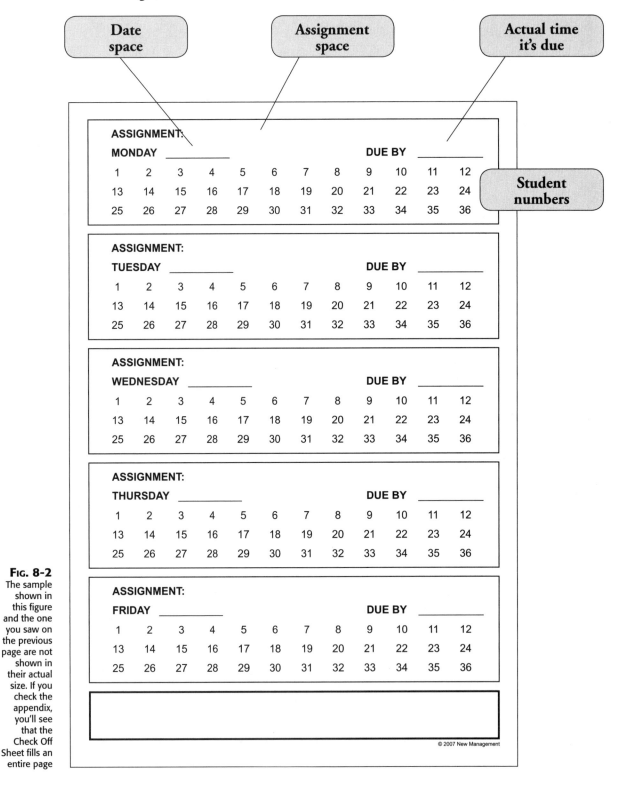

© 2007 New Management

FIG. 8-2
The sample shown in this figure and the one you saw on the previous page are not shown in their actual size. If you check the appendix, you'll see that the Check Off Sheet fills an entire page

Preparing the Check Off Sheet for Use

Here are the six steps for preparing your COS for use.

1. Make a xerox copy of the Check Off Sheet found in the appendix.

> *Before I forget:* You should probably take the time and make an additional set of blackline masters. Copy every page in the appendix and then place these backup sheets in a file folder labeled "New Management Back-Ups." Now, put them some place safe. Not so safe that you won't be able to find them again, but somewhere out of the way. (While you're at it, you might as well make two sets—it's just as easy to hit the "2" button on the xerox machine as it is to leave it on "1 copy"—and keep the second set at home.) You never know when you're going to lose/consume/destroy one of your blackline masters and then not be able to find your copy of the book because you loaned it to someone and you can't remember who it was. Sounds farfetched, I know, but sometimes it pays to be prepared. After all, aren't you glad you set aside all of that bottled water for Y2K?

2. Write the subject or activity in the title box at the bottom.

The Check Off Sheet is specifically designed to track student progress in one particular subject. Since we're going to use Daily Oral Language as our example, I'm going to write that as the title.

Fig. 8-3
Since a Check Off Sheet is normally used to handle one particular subject, the title box at the bottom will help to keep the different subjects from getting mixed up.

ASSIGNMENT:											
FRIDAY _____							DUE BY _____				
1	2	3	4	5	6	7	8	9	10	11	12
13	14	15	16	17	18	19	20	21	22	23	24
25	26	27	28	29	30	31	32	33	34	35	36

DAILY ORAL LANGUAGE

© 2007 New Management

3. Mark your new blackline master.

Cut off a bit of the top right corner. (See page 7-7 if you need a refresher.)

4. Make a bunch of copies from your blackline.

With the Check Off Sheet, you only need to make 5 or 6 of them. Since each one of them is good for a week, 9 copies would last an entire quarter.

5. 3-hole punch them and insert them into a report folder.

Although you could use a clipboard to hold the Check Off Sheets—a variation I'll get to in a bit—report folders, or portfolios, work great. You can get them at Staples or Office Depot. They come in a variety of colors which will enable you to color-code the subjects you're collecting thereby making it easier to keep them separate but easily recognizable. (See page 10-11.)

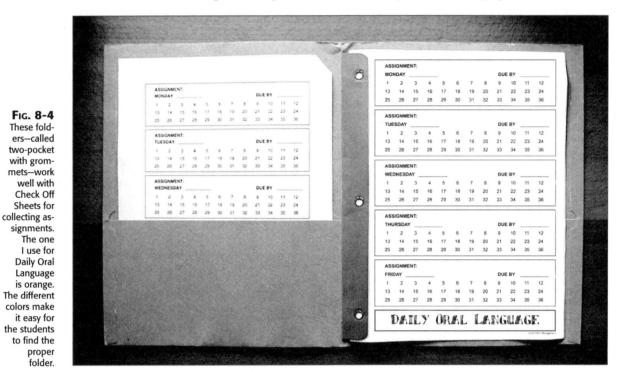

Fig. 8-4
These folders—called two-pocket with grommets—work well with Check Off Sheets for collecting assignments. The one I use for Daily Oral Language is orange. The different colors make it easy for the students to find the proper folder.

6. **Put away your blackline master.**

Place this master in the "NM Masters" folder you created in Lesson 7. (The info on the folder can be found on page 7-7.)

Ready to Go

The stage is now set to collect their papers. And once again, just as we did when we used a Check Off List to collect book reports, we will be providing students with the opportunity to improve their work skills and study habits while allowing them to exercise freedom. As if that's not enough, there are two *additional* advantages to be gained from using this new tool.

Advantage One

The immediate advantage, the necessity that gave birth to this invention, is the ease of operation. Unlike the Check Off List, which required that I use a new one for each assignment I wanted to collect, the Check Off Sheet has been designed to collect five of them. In other words, now that the Check Off Sheets are in the orange folder and the students understand to place their Daily Oral Language papers in the folder when they finish, we'll be good for the rest of the week. All I'll have to do is write the new assignment in Tuesday's section. Sweet.

Advantage Two

By its very nature, the report folder we're using to hold the Check Off Sheets and collect the papers will keep everything organized. It makes for one tidy, self-contained package. I mean, how nice that the Daily Oral Language papers, once collected, aren't going to get mixed up with science papers or phonics sheets or spelling lists. They'll just sit in the orange folder until I'm ready to process them.

Speaking of processing, let's take a look and see how the whole thing would work.

The Check Off Sheet in Action

We're going to use the same basic procedure we used when a Check Off List and a file folder was set out to collect book reports.

1. **Fill in the assignment information in the section reserved for Monday.**
   Assignment = Sentences 41 and 42.
   Monday = November 6
   Due by = 11:40

ASSIGNMENT:	*Sentences 41 and 42*										
MONDAY 11/6								**DUE BY** 11:40			
1	2	3	4	5	6	7	8	9	10	11	12
13	14	15	16	17	18	19	20	21	22	23	24

2. **Show students the COS/folder arrangement.**
   It would probably make the most sense to introduce this new collection folder during the Daily Oral Language lesson.

MR. MORRIS
   Holding up the folder for all to see:
   When you finish with your Daily Oral Language assignment this morning, please put it in this orange folder. Just lay it on the left side. After you've done that, mark off your number on the right side.

3. **Provide a few guidelines.**
   Since they've already experienced turning in a book report with the Check Off List, they shouldn't have too much trouble with this one.

MR. MORRIS
   Showing them the actual Check Off Sheet:
   As you can see, there are five different places for marking off your number. There's one

for Monday, one for Tuesday, one for Wednesday, one for Thursday, and, as you can probably guess by now, there is one for Friday. Please take a moment to make sure you are marking off your number in the Monday section†. If you're uncertain, just ask someone for help.

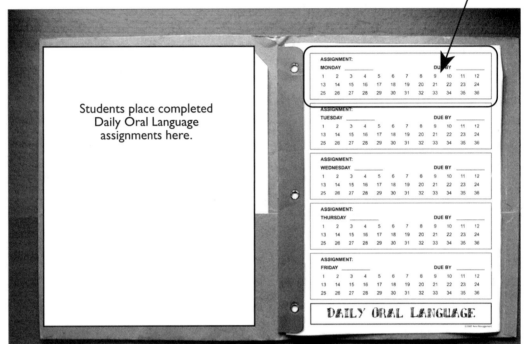

Students mark off numbers here.

Students place completed Daily Oral Language assignments here.

FIG. 8-6
Papers go on the left; numbers are marked off on the right. It doesn't get much easier than that.

4. **Put the folder in a convenient location.**

   Find a spot in the room where the folder can be placed so that it is easily accessible.

MR. MORRIS
   Standing near the spot where the folder has been placed:
   Don't forget: your Daily Oral Language assignment is due before lunch. In fact, I'll take the folder with me when we leave for the cafeteria.

As the Morning Continues

As you can imagine, the students will place their finished DOL paper on the left side of the folder and then mark off their numbers on the Check Off Sheet. Nothing to it.

For my part, the COS/folder enables me to intervene as I see necessary.

If I had a bit of spare time, I could check the orange folder and scan for numbers that have not yet been marked off. These students might get a quick visit or a word of encouragement.

---

†   If you work with young children, you might want to think about using something to draw their attention to the proper section of the COS. A clothespin clipped to the side of the folder or one of those "Sign here" Post-its that they use for legal documents could be the difference maker for some of your less-than-careful students.

Tools & Toys

I could ask a student to give a **COUPON** *to everyone who had already turned in a DOL paper. The coupons would then be placed in a special container for a drawing later on.*

Just before recess, I could read off the numbers of students who are finished with DOL and dismiss them before the others leave.

The possibilities fairly boggle the mind.

E.T. (11:30 to 11:40)

power
love
fun
freedom
safety

Every morning, from 11:30 until 11:40 when we leave for lunch, we have E.T., or educational time. It's a time when students are allowed to choose what they wish to do. They can finish assignments, read a book, use the computers, work on special projects, or any number of choices.

One thing I like to do during this time is to check up on the Daily Oral Language papers.

1. I take the Daily Oral Language collection folder and give it to one of my students. Let's use Jerome this time.

2. Jerome will collate the papers and place them back inside the folder.

3. On a Post-it note, he will write the numbers of the students who have not yet turned in a paper.

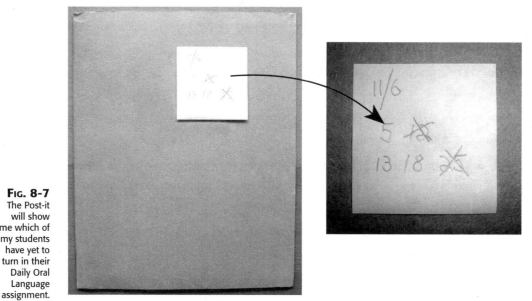

FIG. 8-7
The Post-it will show me which of my students have yet to turn in their Daily Oral Language assignment.

4. With the Post-it as a guide, Jerome will check with these students to find out if the assignment is finished or not.

> > If the assignment is finished, it's collected, added to the papers inside the folder, and the number is marked off on the Post-it.

> > If the assignment isn't finished, Jerome will ask the student to work on it during E.T.

5. The folder, with Post-it attached, is then returned to me.

At 11:40, when we head to lunch, I take the folder with me. We walk all the way to the cafeteria. Guess who walks back with me? That's right. The three students whose numbers are on the Post-it. They then finish their assignment and head to lunch.[†]

FIG. 8-8
Jerome has indicated on a Post-it that students 5, 13, and 18 did not finish the Daily Oral Language assignment. That sure makes it easy for me to intervene.

It doesn't take my students long to learn this fact of life: If you want to go to lunch, *and stay at lunch*, you need to have your Daily Oral Language paper in the folder by 11:40.

The Check Off Sheet Gets Better

In its basic form, the COS quickly proved to be an effective tool. It cut down on paper shuffling and enabled me to keep completed assignments organized. It was working so well, I started to use one to collect math assignments.

Now math, as I'm sure you know, is not a collect-something-everyday kind of subject. Some days I collect an assignment, while on other days we're engaged in group activities or some type of informal assessment. Consequently, the original COS with its five boxes specifically designated Monday through Friday didn't work well for math. I found myself skipping a lot of sections. Time to do some more noodling.

[†] Man, can students work quickly when they're working on their own time. What would normally take them 10 minutes during class time only takes them 5 minutes when it's lunch time.

After a bit of thought, and some work on my faithful Macintosh computer, I came up with this simple, yet effective, variation.

As you can see, the change I made was to eliminate the "day specific" labels and replace them with a label that would allow some flexibility.

ASSIGNMENT:

Mon	Tue	Wed	Thur	Fri	_____	DUE BY	_____
1	2	3	4	5	6	7	8	9	10	11	12
13	14	15	16	17	18	19	20	21	22	23	24
25	26	27	28	29	30	31	32	33	34	35	36

ASSIGNMENT:

Mon	Tue	Wed	Thur	Fri	_____	DUE BY	_____
1	2	3	4	5	6	7	8	9	10	11	12
13	14	15	16	17	18	19	20	21	22	23	24
25	26	27	28	29	30	31	32	33	34	35	36

ASSIGNMENT:

Mon	Tue	Wed	Thur	Fri	_____	DUE BY	_____
1	2	3	4	5	6	7	8	9	10	11	12
13	14	15	16	17	18	19	20	21	22	23	24
25	26	27	28	29	30	31	32	33	34	35	36

ASSIGNMENT:

Mon	Tue	Wed	Thur	Fri	_____	DUE BY	_____
1	2	3	4	5	6	7	8	9	10	11	12
13	14	15	16	17	18	19	20	21	22	23	24
25	26	27	28	29	30	31	32	33	34	35	36

ASSIGNMENT:

Mon	Tue	Wed	Thur	Fri	_____	DUE BY	_____
1	2	3	4	5	6	7	8	9	10	11	12
13	14	15	16	17	18	19	20	21	22	23	24
25	26	27	28	29	30	31	32	33	34	35	36

FIG. 8-9
This modification of the basic Check Off Sheet provides a bit more flexibility. The new COS can now be used at any time during the week. All you have to do is circle the day you're using it.

The Check Off Sheet: Generic Version

In the example shown below, you can see that, although I used the first section on Monday and the second section on Tuesday, the third section wasn't used until Friday. A circle around the actual day will alert the students as to which section they should be using.

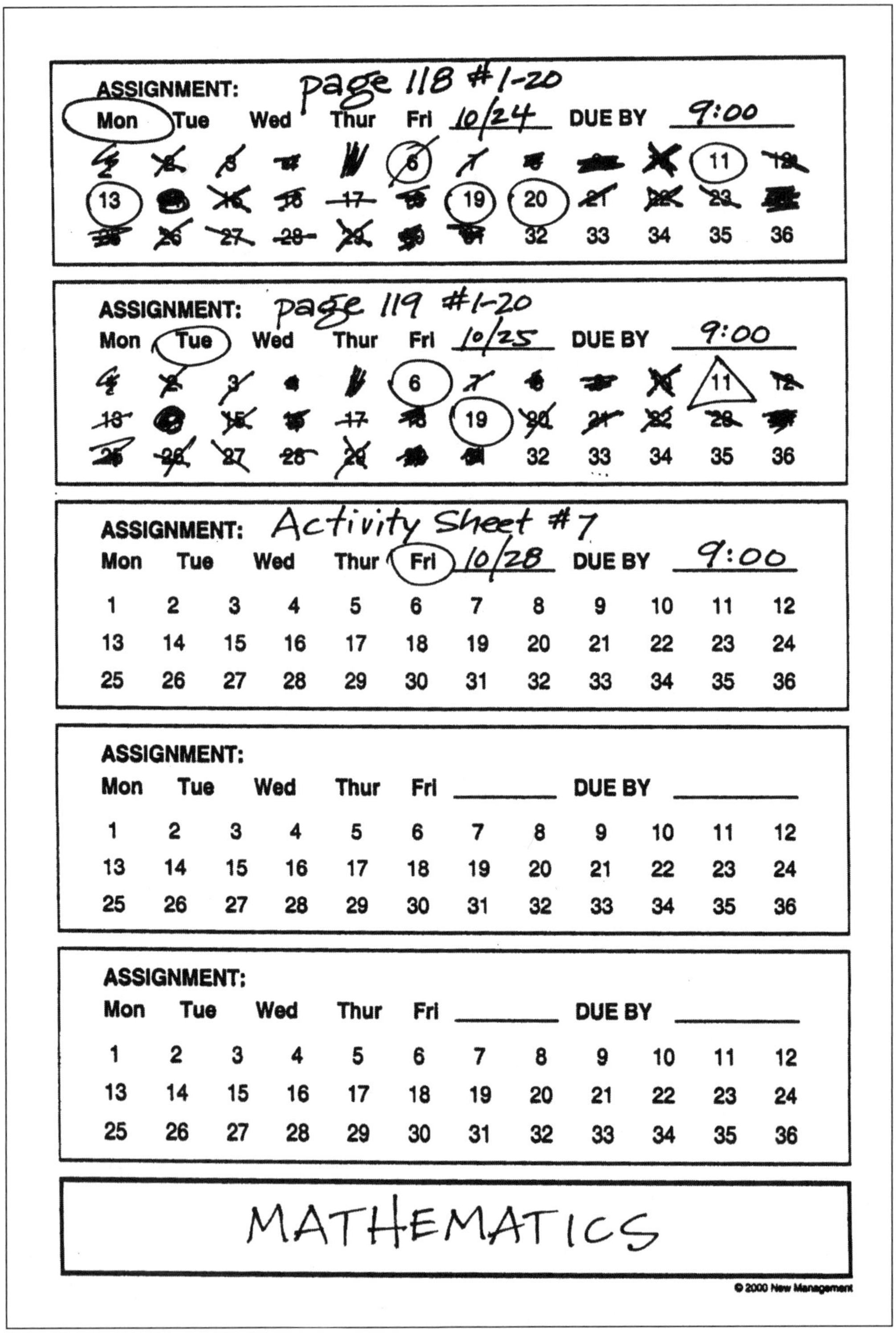

ASSIGNMENT: page 118 #1-20

(Mon) Tue Wed Thur Fri 10/24 DUE BY 9:00

ASSIGNMENT: page 119 #1-20

Mon (Tue) Wed Thur Fri 10/25 DUE BY 9:00

ASSIGNMENT: Activity Sheet #7

Mon Tue Wed Thur (Fri) 10/28 DUE BY 9:00

1	2	3	4	5	6	7	8	9	10	11	12
13	14	15	16	17	18	19	20	21	22	23	24
25	26	27	28	29	30	31	32	33	34	35	36

ASSIGNMENT:

Mon Tue Wed Thur Fri _____ DUE BY _____

1	2	3	4	5	6	7	8	9	10	11	12
13	14	15	16	17	18	19	20	21	22	23	24
25	26	27	28	29	30	31	32	33	34	35	36

ASSIGNMENT:

Mon Tue Wed Thur Fri _____ DUE BY _____

1	2	3	4	5	6	7	8	9	10	11	12
13	14	15	16	17	18	19	20	21	22	23	24
25	26	27	28	29	30	31	32	33	34	35	36

MATHEMATICS

© 2000 New Management

FIG. 8-10
With the first COS, shown in Fig. 8-1, I sometimes found myself skipping sections. With this one, I'll use every section before I begin another sheet.

Before I continue, allow me to share a rather embarrassing glimpse back to my first year of using the Check Off Sheet. At that time, the COS actually looked like this:

Fig. 8-11
Sometimes, things that should be obvious aren't. (It's very possible that we're confronted with these kinds of situations because they're part of a divine effort to keep us humble. Who knows.)

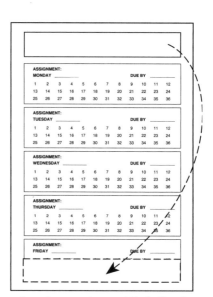

It took me quite a while before I figured out that I should move the title box to the bottom of the sheet.

Notice how the title box was at the top of the form. That's because in America, that's where you put the title of something. It goes at the top. It always has, and it always will. Well, as a result of the conventional placement of the title box, I was prevented from using a regular clipboard for holding these sheets. The clip at the top of the clipboard covered the words in the title box.

So, get this, I used to *tape* these sheets to a 9 X 12 inch piece of chipboard. (This was before I discovered folders.) Tape the top, tape the bottom, all set. *I did this for a month or two.* And then one day, as I was sitting at my Mac playing around with some of the forms I had created, I had an odd thought.

> *---You know…if I moved the title box to the bottom of the Check Off*
> *Sheet…can I do that? Sure I can. Yeah, if I moved it to the bottom,*
> *I COULD USE REGULAR CLIPBOARDS FROM NOW ON!*

> Running downstairs to find my wife with the new COS in hand:
> *Honey! Look at this! You won't believe it!*

A day in the life of Rick Morris, management guru. Pretty sad, huh?

Anyway, with the change in the section labels and the ability to now use clipboards to hold the Check Off Sheets, things really began to move along.

Clipboards are great because they're so easy to use. Unlike the folders, which require that you had to: 1) 3-hole punch the sheets; and 2) mess around with the metal tabs in order to insert the sheets, clipboards are a breeze. Basically, it's: 1) squeeze clip; and 2) slip in the sheets. Done.

73
Tools & Toys

The downside to using clipboards was that they didn't hold all of the papers in the same convenient way that the folders did. (It's always something, isn't it?) Well, I cleared that hurdle by placing the clipboard in a tote tray. We call this combination of Check Off Sheets, clipboard, and tote tray an *ISLAND.*[†]

Building an Island

Island building is a very simple, yet satisfying task.

1. **Make a copy of the modified Check Off Sheet.**

2. **In the white box at the bottom of the page, write "MATH."**
   Xerox a supply of these math Check Off Sheets from your new master, five or six should be sufficient, and attach them to a letter-sized clipboard.

   > *Benefit:* Using a clipboard to hold these Check Off Sheets will make them incredibly more usable. For one, it will be much easier to keep track of them all. For another, it will provide a convenient writing surface for your students as they turn in their assignments and mark off their numbers. And last, the weight of the clipboard will add substance to the Check Off Sheet as you wave it in front of the students when demonstrating, reinforcing, or merely reminding them about using the Check Off Sheet to monitor completed assignments.

3. **Place the loaded clipboard inside the tote tray.**

4. **With a thought toward traffic patterns, decide upon a workable location for this newly formed Island.**
   Although it would make sense to place it in the room, you might want to spice things up a bit and maybe place it outside. Maybe the librarian would allow you to put it in the library. Turn in your assignment; stay and read.

5. **Now play some Hawaiian music.**
   Just kidding; you're all done.

[†]   I started calling them Islands for two reasons. The first, as you can imagine, is that when the tote tray is sitting on top of a bookcase, shelf, or table, it rather looks like an island. The second has to do with motivation. "Island" just seems to be more intriguing than "tote tray."

The Math Collection Center

This Island will now serve as our math collection center. The tote tray will hold the finished papers while the clipboard and Check Off Sheets will take care of the monitoring. By having the math assignment processed in the same way and in the same place each day, you will be strengthening your management consistency. Also, with everything together in a single container, it will become easier for you to keep things organized as you take the assignments home—or to the staff meeting!—for correction, grading, and recording.

Just for the sake of demonstration, let's use these new Check Off Sheets to collect a couple of days worth of math assignments.

Monday Morning

Just as you would with a Check Off List, write the assignment information in the first available check off section. Circle the day, write the date, and enter the time when this assignment is due.

ASSIGNMENT: *page 118 #1-20*											
(Mon) Tue		Wed	Thur	Fri *10-24*		DUE BY		*9:00*			
1	2	3	4	5	6	7	8	9	10	11	12
13	14	15	16	17	18	19	20	21	22	23	24
25	26	27	28	29	30	31	32	33	34	35	36

FIG. 8-12
It's easy to create a new collection section.

Return the clipboard to the tote tray. Make sure your Island is in its proper location. Your consistency in this regard will help your students take care of their part.

Students' Part

First, they'll complete the math assignment—page 118, #1-20—and take it to the Island. After picking up the clipboard and placing their finished assignments in the tote tray, they'll mark off their numbers on the Check Off Sheet. The clipboard will be placed back inside the tote tray. Students who have now completed their math assignment will then move on to the next task at hand.

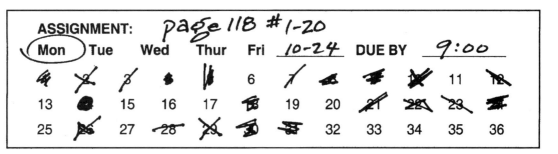

FIG. 8-13
Each student will develop a unique method of marking off his number, almost like a signature.

Teacher's Part

At 9:00, when math is over, pick up the COS and see if anyone's number is not marked off.

FIG. 8-14
A quick look
tells you that
students 6,
11, 13, 19,
and 20 are
not marked
off.

> **ASSIGNMENT:** page 118 #1-20
>
> (Mon) Tue   Wed   Thur   Fri 10-24 DUE BY 9:00
>
> ~~4~~ ~~2~~ ~~3~~ ~~4~~ ~~5~~ 6   ~~7~~ ~~8~~ ~~9~~ ~~10~~ 11 ~~12~~
>
> 13 ~~14~~ ~~15~~ ~~16~~ —17— ~~18~~ 19 20 ~~21~~ ~~22~~ ~~23~~ ~~24~~
>
> ~~25~~ ~~26~~ ~~27~~ —28— ~~29~~ ~~30~~ ~~31~~ 32 33 34 35 36

MR. MORRIS
> With the math COS in hand:
> *Calvin, your math assignment?*

CALVIN
> Somewhat surprised:
> *I turned it in.*

MR. MORRIS
> Circling his number as a reminder that he had forgotten to mark it off:
> *Your number is not marked off.*

Note: I could either have Calvin walk up and mark off the number—which I prefer—or I could do it for him. The choice is yours.

MR. MORRIS
> Looking at the next number not marked off:
> *Fabian, your math assignment?*

FABIAN
> *I'm not finished yet.*

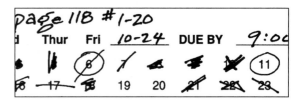

MR. MORRIS
> Circling #11 on the Check Off Sheet:
> *Put it in the First Aid Kit, please.*

Note: The First Aid Kit, which you'll learn about in the next lesson, is a technique for effectively dealing with unfinished assignments. One part of the First Aid Kit is a container for holding these papers until they can be processed. So, picture Fabian walking to the back of the room and dropping his unfinished math assignment in the First Aid Kit container and then returning to his seat. (Again, it's all explained in the next lesson.) For right now, let's get back to the three other students whose numbers are not marked off.

As you can imagine, I asked Heather (#13), Marshal (#19), and Meagan (#20) for their assignments. All three of them announced that it wasn't finished, and so all three of them put their papers in the First Aid Kit.

While they were doing this, I circled their numbers on the Check Off Sheet. The clipboard was then returned to the math island, and we moved on to our next activity.

Tuesday Morning

We used the next section for Tuesday's assignment.[†]

When I went to check the results, this is what I saw:

FIG. 8-15
Your trained eye is beginning to zero in on the numbers that aren't marked off. Very cool.

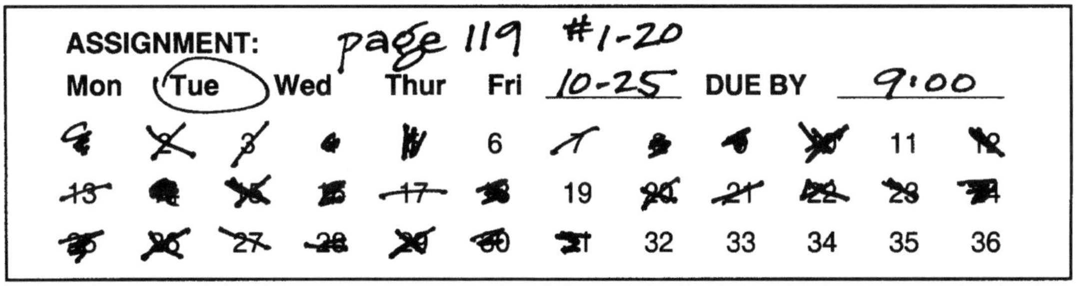

MR. MORRIS
As gently as possible:
Calvin, your math assignment?

CALVIN
It's not done, Mr. Morris.

MR. MORRIS
Circling his number:
First Aid Kit, please. Fabian? Oh, that's right. He's absent today.
Putting a triangle around #11:
Let's see. Marshal, your math paper?

MARSHAL
It's not finished yet, Mr. Morris. I'll put it in the First Aid Kit.

And with that, I'd circle Marshal's number and return the clipboard to the tote tray.

Friday Morning

Since I did not collect a math assignment on either Wednesday or Thursday, I used the next section on the Check Off List for collecting Friday's assignment. I really like the fact

---

[†] When all five sections of the Check Off Sheet have been used, it gets moved to the bottom of the stack, and I begin using the second one. (Are you beginning to see the possibilities for tracking and documentation that your Check Off Sheets will provide? I figured you did.)

that I can use any section on the sheet by just circling the day. That kind of efficiency just speaks to me.

After handing out Friday's math activity sheet and conducting a brief review session, I set Max for 25 minutes and let the students begin to work independently. I then walked over to the math island and picked up the clipboard.

In the third section of the COS, I circled "Friday" and wrote the date on the line. I then wrote the assignment and the time due. Looking around the room, I was reminded that Fabian was absent (again), and so I drew a triangle around his number, 11. As I was about to put the clipboard back, I glanced at the sections we had used for Monday and Tuesday.

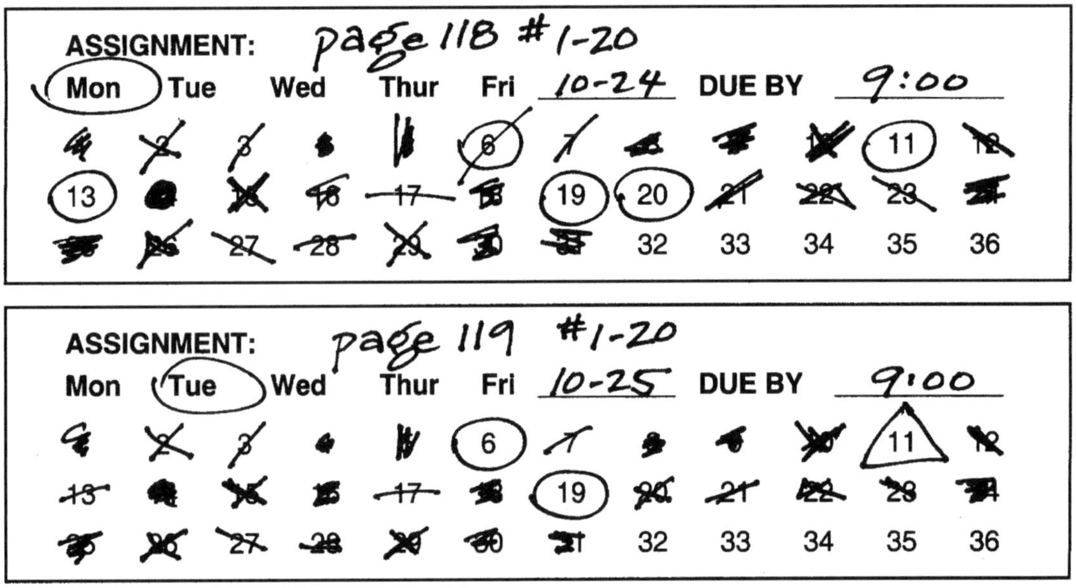

FIG. 8-16
By having Monday and Tuesday together on one sheet of paper, it became easier to see patterns (check out 19) beginning to emerge. You won't have to play "Where's Waldo?" with this tool. You'll find him right away.

MR. MORRIS
Looking at the circled numbers from Monday and Tuesday:
---*Well, well, well. Would you look at that. Marshal (#19) did not complete his assignment on either day. I wonder how he's going to do with today's assignment?*

Amazing. All along I had thought that the Check Off Sheet would enable me to cut down on the amount of Check Off Lists I had been using. Little did I realize that it would become a powerful document for tracking students.

Imagine, if you will, that I had been using Check Off Lists to collect those math assignments. I would have ended up with a COL for Monday, with 4 student numbers circled. That's good management. I know who's done and who isn't done. Then on Tuesday, I would have used a new COL and ended up with two numbers circled. Again, that's effective management. I can see who finished and who didn't.

What I probably *wouldn't have seen*, unless I happened to place the two Check Off Lists side-by-side, was that #19 was circled on both of them.

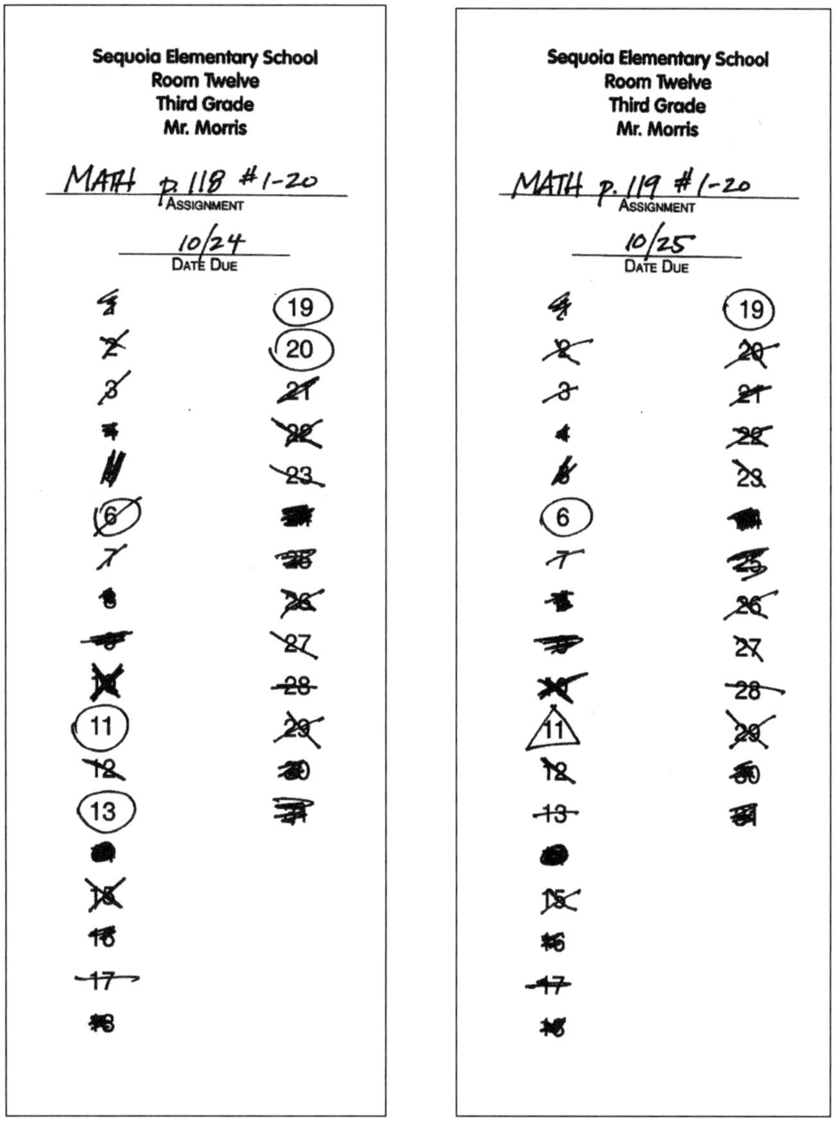

FIG. 8-17
Although you can see the pattern when the COL's are side-by-side, it wasn't very likely that I would have them sitting next to each other.

> *Major Advantage:* Because the Check Off Sheet: 1) is devoted to one specific subject; and 2) shows the completion results of five assignments in that particular subject, it becomes immediately evident when a student is demonstrating a lack of effort. And, by having this information so readily available, intervention strategies are that much easier to implement.

And so, having been made aware of his plight by the story contained on the Check Off Sheet, I'd plan to go see my needy little friend, Marshal.

Reality: Marshal doesn't like math. He's hoping that math is going to go away. Not likely, we know, but that's going to be his approach: denial and avoidance. And that's why I love the Check Off Sheet. It shows at a glance who needs intervention, whether they ask for it or not.

> Mr. Morris
>> After the math lesson but before the students began to work independently:
>>> *If you're still not sure how to do today's activity, please come see me. I'm happy to help.*

Not a peep from Marshal, which doesn't surprise me very much. For the most part, Marshal has made it through life by avoiding unpleasant situations. Based on the fact that math is just another unpleasant situation for him, he does not come see me for help.

And so, with the math Check Off Sheet in hand, *I'll* go see *him.*

> Mr. Morris
>> Approaching Marshal at the beginning of his time for completing Friday's math activity sheet:
>>> *Excuse me, son. Could I talk to you for a second?*
>> Showing him the math Check Off Sheet:
>>> *Nothing turned in on Monday, nothing turned in on Tuesday. How are you doing today? Would you like some help?*

power
love
fun
freedom
safety

Believe it or not, my experience has shown that the normal response to this question—and by normal I mean around 80% of the time—is, "Yeah."[†] Granted, it's not the kind of "Yeah!" you'd hear if you asked Marshal if he'd like to go to recess early. Nonetheless, he's responding in a positive way. Just another one of those many small steps on the journey to success.

> Mr. Morris
>> Smiling his appreciation at Marshal's acknowledgment of need:
>>> *Great! Let's go to the back table where we can work together.*

Bonus: I can almost guarantee that if Marshal and I go to the "study table" in the back of the room to work, there will be three or four other students who will join us.

Working one-on-one, I'll be able to help Marshal master this math skill.

---

†   *Attention new teachers:* If Marshal were to respond with "No" or some similar remark, it would be your job to intervene. The easiest way to go would be to ask Marshal to complete the next problem as you watched. This will give you the true picture of his ability to complete the task.

    If he couldn't complete the problem, you could let him know that, in your opinion, he could probably use a bit of help. On the other hand, if he *was* able to complete the problem you asked him to do, it would tell you that the unfinished assignments from Monday and Tuesday were more likely the result of a lack of effort than a lack of mastery.

    Either way, you'd be gaining information that you could use to help Marshal become more successful at completing his math assignments.

> *According to the research:* The way to help your students achieve mastery is through: 1) direct instruction; and 2) individual tutoring. The Check Off Sheet, among other things, points me in the direction of the students who need tutoring. And did you note how quickly I became aware of Marshal's need? It wasn't three weeks of math or three chapters of math or three months of math. It was the third math assignment. It's this kind of immediate intervention that produces results.

What usually happens is that, due to the extra attention he is going to be given during math, he will begin to improve. And when I do see progress—which might take a month or so—I've got to make an effort to get back and see him. I can't just be there for the bad news; I need to be able to share the fact that I am aware of the progress he has been making.[†]

Three weeks from now, when there has been improvement, I'll go back and see him.

MR. MORRIS
>> With the math Check Off Sheet in hand:
>>> *Excuse me, Marshal. May I show you something?*

MARSHAL
>> Not sure what's up:
>>> *Uh, sure.*

MR. MORRIS
>> Leafing back through the last several Check Off Sheets:
>>> *Do you remember how you were doing in math a couple of weeks ago? Look at this: not finished, not finished, not finished, finished, not finished. You completed one assignment out of five.*
>> Showing him the top sheet:
>>> *Look at you now. You've completed two out of the last three assignments and turned them in on time. Way to go, buddy.*

power
love
fun
freedom
safety

MARSHAL
>> Beaming:
>>> *Thanks, Mr. Morris.*

As you can see, the Check Off Sheet, which started life as an easier-to-use Check Off List, has taken on a much larger role. Its ability to provide you with student-by-student, subject-by-subject feedback makes it a very powerful tool. And although we only see marked out numbers and not grades or scores, the information it provides enables me to accurately assess a critical skill for success: completes work on time.

---

† It's important that I recognize Marshal's improvement. After all, it was not easy for him to achieve nor will it be easy to maintain. Unfortunately, if I'm not aware of his improvement and don't convey my awareness to him, there's a very good chance that he won't sustain his efforts. He'll go back to his old, underachieving ways. The Check Off Sheet, though, is an easy way to monitor a student's positive change in work skills and study habits so that you can verbally acknowledge it.

By keeping specific records, I can give Marshal the credit he deserves. Imagine, we had started a new Health unit. And imagine that Health is something Marshal really likes. Well, by using a set of Check Off Sheets to monitor the completion of Health activities, I will see Marshal's outstanding effort in this subject and reward him accordingly. The success he felt and the "A" he received for his effort might just encourage him to expend more energy in some of his other studies. You never know.

One More Idea

Whether you use Check Off Sheets in folders or on clipboards, the information you gather could be used as a student enrichment activity in data analysis.

Data Tally

power
love
fun
freedom
safety

1. Xerox several sets of the Check Off Sheets you used for a unit of study. For example, imagine you've just concluded the Health unit I mentioned at the top of the page. During the unit, you ended up collecting 14 activities. You would take the three Check Off Sheets you used to the office and make 4 or 5 xerox copies of each sheet. Collate the pages and staple them together so that you end up with 4 or 5 sets of the original, marked-off Check Off Sheets.

2. Find several students who want to do some extra credit work and give each student a xeroxed set of the Check Off Sheets.

3. Ask them to do a stick tally of how many times each number was marked out, circled, and triangled. (Is *triangled* a word?)

4. They would be creating something like this:

	Done	Not Done	Absent
1. Bill	⊔⊔⊤ ⊔⊔⊤ III		
2. Dan	⊔⊔⊤ ⊔⊤⊤	I	
3. Robin	⊔⊤⊤ ⊔⊤⊤ IIII	IIII	
4. Polly	⊔⊔⊤ ⊔⊔⊤ II		
5. Tim	⊔⊔⊤ ⊔⊤⊤ IIII	I	I

You can now use the information gathered by your helpers in your assessment procedure. After all, who would want to go through those three Check Off Sheets and tally the information for each and every student? (Nobody I ever worked with, I can tell you that.) Your student helpers, though, will see this extra credit assignment as something exciting and fun. They'll crunch the numbers for you, involve themselves in yet another class task, and end up providing you with some very usable information.

Man, I love this stuff.

Lesson 9

Before We Begin

How It All Got Started

Numbering Your Students

Using Student Numbers

Timers & Sound Makers

Class Chart

Check Off List

Check Off Sheet

First Aid Kit

Grade Books

*Fifty years ago teachers said their
top discipline problems were
talking, chewing gum, making noise,
and running in the halls.
The current list, by contrast,
sounds like a cross between
a police rap sheet and
the seven deadly sins.*

—Anna Quindlen

First Aid Kit

◆ ◆

Goals for this lesson:

☑ Learn how to create a powerful tool for handling unfinished assignments.

☑ Assemble the three components that comprise this tool.

☑ Learn how to recognize and avoid "bad choices."

☑ Understand the importance of maintaining a consistent program.

☑ Create an easy-to-maintain system for documenting underachieving students.

◆ ◆

*N*ow that you're using Check Off Lists and Check Off Sheets, you've found your-self circling the numbers of students who were not finished on time. Or maybe you've had students bring you a Check Off List with several numbers circled on it. Regardless of the technique or the manner in which it's being used, you've discovered that you need to do something about unfinished assignments.

Having struggled with this issue for more years than I care to ponder, I finally came to a conclusion. In order to be successful, I'm going to need a system that enables me to: 1) deal with an unfinished assignment as quickly as possible; 2) follow-up the next day to make sure the assignment was completed; and 3) in a simple, nonthreatening manner, keep the parents apprised of any unfinished work.

My solution was the First Aid Kit, a three-part program that does it all.

Right Now: a box where students can put unfinished assignments.
Follow-Up: a Log sheet on which I'll record unfinished assignments so that I'll remember to ask for them the next day.
Parent Notification: an "Unfinished Assignment" rubber stamp I can use on the paper which provides the parents with some information.

Here's a brief overview of how the First Aid Kit (FAK) in my room works.

1. **Unfinished assignments are placed in the First Aid Kit.**

   Any student not finished by the appointed time will walk to the First Aid Kit[†] with his assignment, place it inside, and return to his seat.

2. **I'll meet with the FAK students at the end of the day.**

   Just before class ends, I will meet in the back of the room with the students who had an unfinished assignment in the FAK. I'll record the student numbers and the title of the unfinished assignments in the FAK Log. (*Note:* When I introduce the First Aid Kit to my students, I only focus on one subject. This makes it manageable for me and the students. Thus, writing the names of the unfinished assignments is rather easy because there will only be a couple of assignments in the box.)

3. **The assignments are stamped and comments are circled.**

   All assignments pulled out of the box are stamped with the Unfinished Assignment stamp. The assignments are given back to the students, appropriate comments are then circled, and a return date is added.

4. **The students complete the assignments at home.**

   Before being sent back to their seats for dismissal, the students all acknowledge their need to complete the assignments at home and return them to class the next day.

5. **The following morning, I check with the First Aid kids to see that their assignments were completed and returned.**

   Using the FAK Log as a guide, I see each student and collect the assignment. As I gather each one, I draw a line through it on the Log sheet. If, for whatever reason, the student does not have the assignment in class and complete, I circle the assignment in the Log and repeat my request that the assignment be completed at home and returned to class.

As you can see, the First Aid Kit technique is a relatively simple procedure for dealing with unfinished assignments. Its simplicity and manageability are what make it work.

The simplicity part, which we'll deal with first, stems from the fact that for this puzzle, there are just three pieces. They are:

---

† Although basically the same, the technique for secondary teachers is a bit different. If you turn to page 9-51, you will find my recommendations for using this strategy at the secondary level.

Building Your Own First Aid Kit

Let's organize the three components of the First Aid Kit, and then we'll talk about how to use it.

The Collection Box

The first item you'll need for your First Aid Kit is a collection box. The one I use comes from Target. It's a white, plastic bin that has a sliding drawer built into it. I bought it for about $5, and I'm fairly certain it will last forever.

There are other boxes you could use that won't cost you a dime. The easiest one would be an empty xerox paper case. You know the kind of box I mean: it holds 10 reams of copy paper and has a cardboard lid that fits neatly over the top. Just about any school supply room will have one or two sitting around just waiting to be put to good use. You could also use one of those white storage boxes in which people put tax papers and such.

FIG. 9-1
An empty cardboard box or storage carton will make a great First Aid Kit collection box.

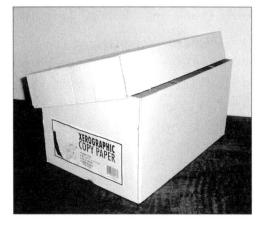
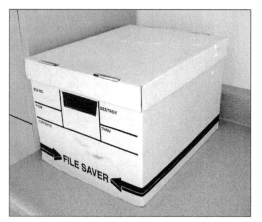

Whichever box you decide to use, take it to your room and decorate it. (The decoration will help it to be distinguishable from the other 40 cardboard boxes occupying your room's various nooks and crannies.) I put a large, red cross on mine. I used construction paper for the cross and then covered it with clear contact paper. Creating a FAK that is easy to find will make it easier to use.

FIG. 9-2
The collection box I use was purchased at Target. A red cross was attached to both sides so that the First Aid Kit will stand out clearly.

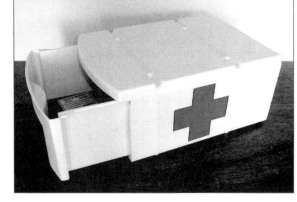

Going to the store to buy a plastic storage bin with a slide-out drawer may be a bit of overkill, but it's that kind of attention to detail that helps to produce a quality classroom.

If you look carefully at the drawer, you can see an Unfinished Assignment stamp hiding inside. You can also see the edge of the First Aid Kit folder I use for keeping track of assignments which have gone home to be completed.

The Assignment Log

In order to keep track of which assignments are being sent home to be completed, you'll need to maintain a Log. Don't worry, though; this part has already been done for you. You'll find the blackline master for the Log in the appendix. What you will need is a folder in which to keep the Log sheets you're going to reproduce and then use.

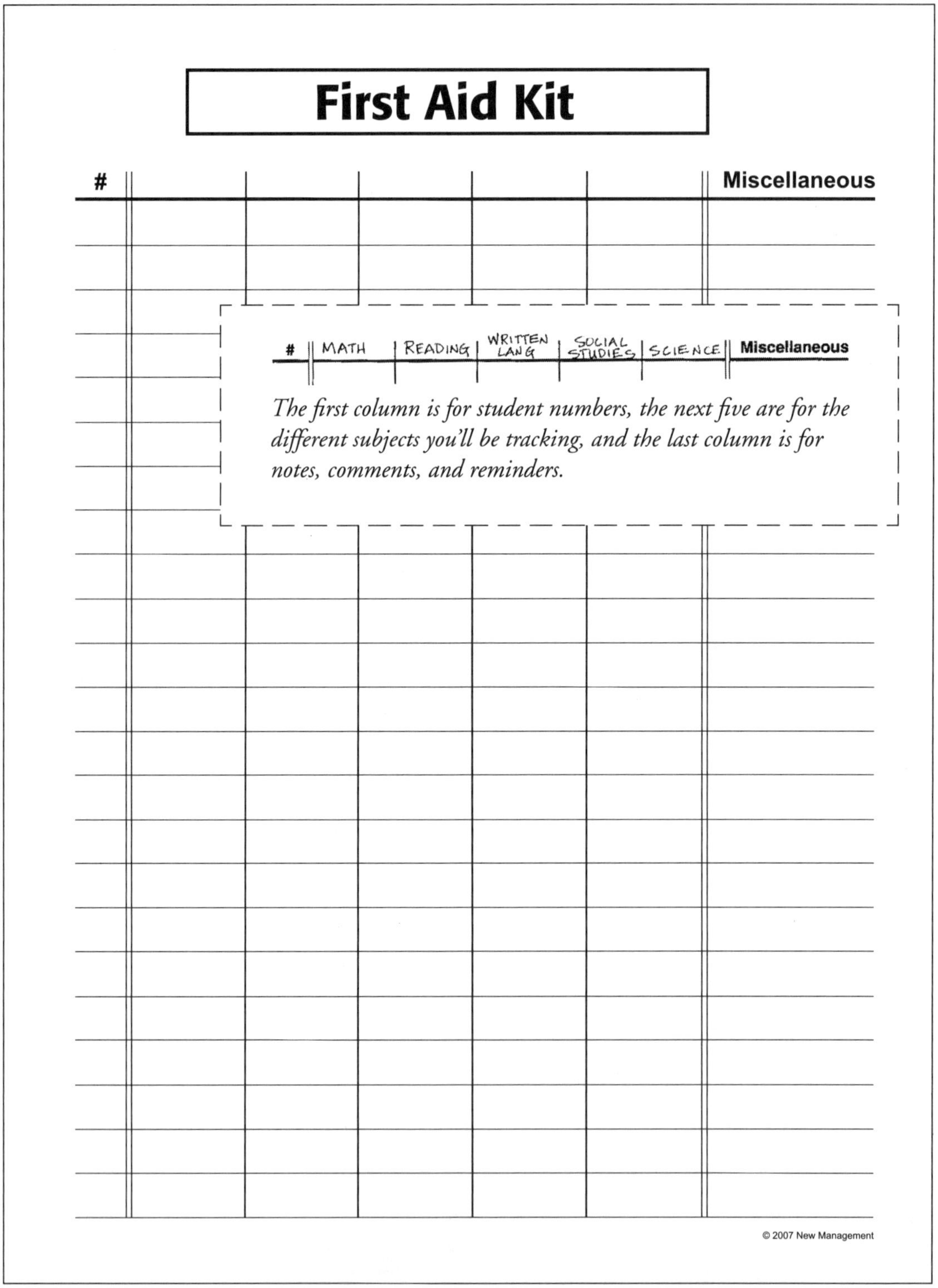

First Aid Kit

#						Miscellaneous

#	MATH	READING	WRITTEN LANG	SOCIAL STUDIES	SCIENCE	Miscellaneous

The first column is for student numbers, the next five are for the different subjects you'll be tracking, and the last column is for notes, comments, and reminders.

© 2007 New Management

FIG. 9-3
The blackline master for making First Aid Kit Log sheets can be found in the appendix.

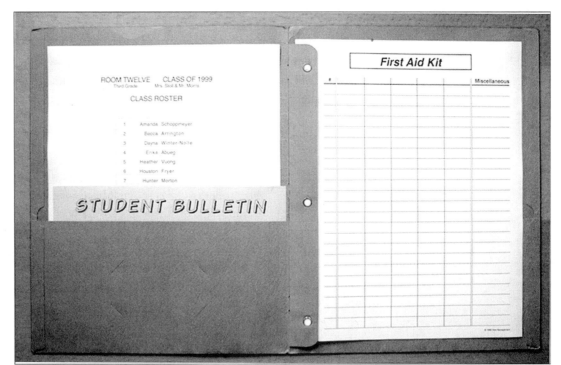

FIG. 9-4
Using a two-pocket folder with center fasteners will make the Log easier to maintain.

Directions for Making Your First Aid Kit Log

1. **Get a two-pocket folder.**
   Use the kind of folder that was described in Lesson 8: Check Off Sheet. (*Tip:* In addition to placing your FAK blackline in your "NM masters" folder, the back pocket of this folder is also a handy place to keep one. I also have a class roster—student number, first name, last name—and copies of the Student Bulletin in the front pocket.)

2. **Xerox ten copies of the blackline master.**
   You'll find the original in the Blackline Masters Appendix.

3. **3-hole punch the xerox copies, and insert them in the folder.**
   It may seem like some extra work, but having the forms securely attached will prove to be less of a hassle later on. This is especially true when your FAK folder has several student papers inside of it.

4. **Label your folder.**
   Use a felt marker and clearly mark this folder as being a part of the FAK package. "LATE LOG" or even a big red cross would be appropriate.

5. **Place your newly created Log in the First Aid Kit.**
   In keeping with the philosophy of "a place for everything and everything in its place," the best location for your Log is in the box.

The "Unfinished Assignment" Stamp

I use a nice pair of rubber stamps—an English version and an equivalent Spanish version—for marking assignments before they go home to be completed by the students. As you can see below, the stamp is perfect for not only highlighting the fact that the assignment should have been finished in class but also allows me to indicate the reasons why it wasn't done when it should have been.

> *Reality* It's important to keep in mind that **not all unfinished assignments represent inappropriate behavior**. If, for example, you have students who spend time tutoring other students, the tutors might not be able to finish on time. Although it's important for them to eventually complete the assignment, I feel that their contribution to the learning of our underachievers more than makes up for the fact that they weren't able to finish when everyone else did. With the Unfinished Assignment stamp, I'd be able to specifically state that the tardiness was due to tutoring and not a lack of effort. *(See suggestions on page 9-32.)*

The actual stamp—shown in Fig. 9-5 below—makes an impression as seen in Fig. 9-6.

FIG. 9-5
The Unfinished Assignment stamp is a high quality rubber stamp that will last for years.

FIG. 9-6
The stamp comes in two versions: English and Spanish.

These are actual size impressions.

UNFINISHED ASSIGNMENT
Understands   Does Not
Concept   Understand Concept
Needs More Time   Needs More Help
Did Not Use Class Time Well
Complete and return by: _____
_____   _____
Student Signature   Parent Signature

TRABAJO NO TERMINADO
Entiende   No Entiende
El Concepto   El Concepto
Necesita Mas Tiempo   Necesita Mas Ayuda
No Usa Su Tiempo En El Salón Bien
Complete y devuélvalo el: _____
_____   _____
Firma del Alumno   Firma del Padres

Making an Impression

As you can imagine, it's a rather simple procedure to stamp the assignment and then circle the comments that are appropriate for the occasion.

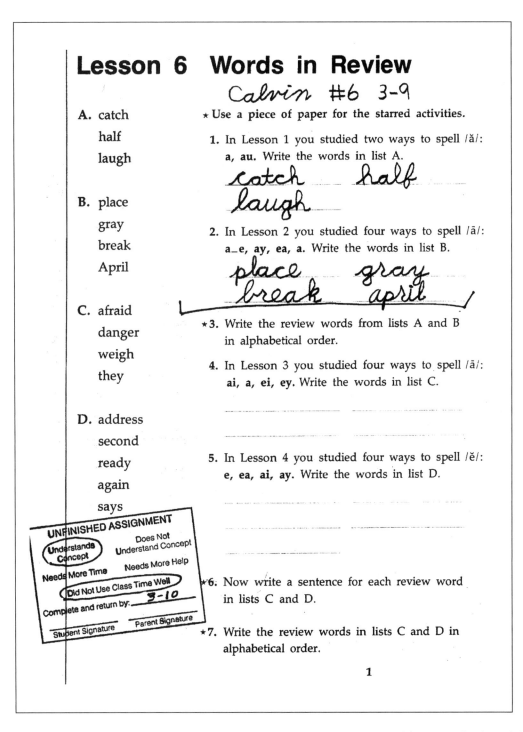

FIG. 9-7
The Unfinished Assignment stamp really stands out when used on unfinished assignments.

Helpful: To add impact to the Unfinished Assignment stamp, use a red stamp pad. Also, if there is no open space on the paper for the stamp, turn it over and stamp it on the back. The red ink will bleed through just a bit and draw attention to the back side.

Do I Really Need an "Unfinished Assignment" Stamp?

I'll tell you right now that you don't need a rubber stamp to make the First Aid Kit work. You could get by quite well using just the collection box and Log; nonetheless, having a rubber stamp for marking the late assignments has several distinct advantages.

ADVANTAGE ONE

By physically marking the assignments with a stamp, you'll be making a clear, unambiguous statement regarding late work. Everyone, from students to parents to administrators, responds to the written word. Writing implies dedication to the task and commitment to the objective. When your students receive a stamp on their unfinished assignments, the message is clear: you mean business.

ADVANTAGE TWO

The stamp will act as a simple reminder that the paper you are now looking at is one you had sent home because it had not been finished on time. This visual reminder is especially helpful for grade keeping or anecdotal records.

ADVANTAGE THREE

Stress management gurus teach their clients specific techniques for dealing with, or avoiding, stress. Taking deep breaths or thinking positive thoughts are but two of a handful of successful procedures. Consider the stress reduction value for you when you use a stamp. Instead of getting all worked up into some kind of raging, pirate lather, you can merely take the paper and, with a gentle yet firm flourish, stamp the offending assignment. By acting out your negative emotions in a safe, physical manner, you'll release those negative emotions instead of harboring them. Release, after all, is an effective stress reduction technique.

ADVANTAGE FOUR

Since it is imperative that you keep parents apprised of their children's needs, using an Unfinished Assignment stamp will provide immediate, yet non-threatening communication.

Fig. 9-8
There are many advantages to using a rubber stamp for marking unfinished assignments.

How Your First Aid Kit Will Help You

power
love
fun
freedom
safety

Now that you have assembled the parts you need, we can begin to put the First Aid Kit to work in the classroom. Without a workable procedure for handling unfinished assignments, your carefully woven tapestry of fairness, firmness, and consistency will soon begin to unravel. You'll find yourself responding emotionally which, depending upon your mood on any given day, can result in a variety of reactions. This unpredictability on your part is counterproductive to a child's essential need for safety.

By having a simple procedure you'll not only be able to avoid the emotional mess described above, but you'll be encouraged to stick to your assignment deadlines. Using the FAK will enable you to deal with the negative (unfinished assignments) so that you can focus on the positive (all of the students who were done on time.)

> *A Bit of History:*
> During my first five years of teaching, before I had created the First Aid Kit, I found myself facing the challenge of unfinished assignments and not handling it very well. Consequently, I made some bad choices. As embarrassing as these episodes are, I'm going to share two of them to illustrate how critical it is to have a systematic approach.

Bad Choice #1: Giving Students More Time

Imagine that Max, our digital timer, is beeping. I had set him for 20 minutes—the time allotted to my students to complete a summary paragraph about the social studies lesson we had just finished—and Max was now letting us know—"Time's up."

MAX
Beep-beep, beep-beep, beep-beep.

MR. MORRIS
Stopping Max and addressing the class:
I need to collect your paragraphs now.

I then heard that soft but unmistakable sound.

SEVERAL STUDENTS
Oh, no. Ohhhhhh.

For you new teachers out there, that sad little "Oh, no" is student language for: "We need more time, but I'm kind of afraid to ask for more time; so, I'll just make this pitiful little noise and hope that Mr. Morris figures out that I'm not done."

Having been made aware of the fact that some of my students weren't done with their paragraphs, I was thinking about the situation at hand.

MR. MORRIS
> ---*Oh, great. Some are done and some aren't. What a nightmare that is. It's so much easier to collect assignments all at once when everyone is finished.*

Addressing the class:
> *How many of you are not finished with your paragraph?*

Five or six hands were raised weakly into the air: the Mea Culpa High Five.

> ---*Just what I thought: some of them aren't done yet. Now what?*

After a bit of anguish and indecision on my part, I caved in and made a bad choice.

> ---*Well, I'd better give them more time to finish.*[†]

MR. MORRIS
Using his Pirate Voice to show that he's not happy with the decision he's announcing:
> *All right, I'll give you another five minutes to complete this assignment AND THEN I'M GOING TO COLLECT THEM ALL. Make sure you have it done this time.*

Coupla'-three things wrong here. By extending the deadline to accommodate the unfinished students, I wasn't fair to the students who were done, I wasn't firm with the ones who should have been done, and I wasn't consistent with my previously stated deadline for their summary paragraphs. So far I'm Oh-for-3. Pitiful.

Granted, the five or six students who weren't done will love me for the extra time I've just given them to finish. Unfortunately, the other twenty-five students, *the ones who were done on time,* are now asking themselves a number of questions.

> **Q:**   *Am I working too hard in here?*
> **Q:**   *Why did I bust my butt to get this assignment done in twenty minutes when I really had twenty-five minutes?*
> **Q:**   *What am I going to do with the extra five minutes?*

As long as we're contemplating the consequences of this easy-to-make Bad Choice, there's an even greater issue we should ponder: Trust.

Right now, some of my students are beginning to wonder if they can trust me. I had said earlier that they had 20 minutes to complete the paragraph, but it really turned out to

---

[†]   As mentioned in Lesson 5: Timers and Sound Makers, there are times when I've set Max for a certain amount of time only to realize later that I underestimated the time needed to complete an assignment. It's important to be aware of this and announce an extension before Max is beeping. Otherwise, my students will not take Max's guidelines as seriously as I would like them to.

be 25 minutes. What do you think might happen tomorrow when I tell them they have 20 minutes to complete an activity? That's right. Some of them will be thinking, "Yeah, maybe. Maybe not. He might give us more time like he did yesterday." This is one reason why inconsistency is such a killer.

By developing, and then using, a tool for processing unfinished assignments, you will no longer hesitate to say, "Time's up." And by using the First Aid Kit Log to follow up on these unfinished assignments, and the learning skills they reinforce, you will have more students attaining mastery of their grade level skills and objectives.

Bad Choice #1: The Solution

Let's revisit the situation that led to Bad Choice #1. This time, though, we'll use the First Aid Kit and avoid the "More Time Trap."

> MAX
> *Beep-beep, beep-beep, beep-beep.*

> MR. MORRIS
> Stopping Max and addressing the class:
> *I need to collect your paragraphs now.*

> STUDENTS
> *Oh, no. Ohhhhhh.*

> MR. MORRIS
> *How many of you are not finished?*

The same five or six hands are raised.

> MR. MORRIS
> Using his Mr. Rogers' Voice because he now has a new technique for dealing with the students who are not finished:
> *If you need more time, please put your unfinished paragraph in the First Aid Kit. You can finish it at home tonight. If you are done with your paragraph, I'd like you to bring it to me right now.*

Not only will the FAK handle the late assignments but, as you can see, this remarkable procedure will enable me to concentrate on the students who are successfully completing their activities. Too often, I've allowed the three or four unfinished students to overshadow the efforts of the twenty-seven or twenty-eight students who had completed this activity. Every time I'd stop to harangue Calvin for not being finished with math, I was denying myself the opportunity to express my satisfaction at the achievement of the finishers.

This same attention to the negative occurs in more areas than just assignment collection. Picking up my students at the end of morning recess, my eyes and energy are just naturally drawn to the three unruly children banging a ball off of some poor soul's head. As one of the guardian figures on campus, I sometimes feel compelled to don the sheriff's badge and dispense some frontier justice. Unfortunately, the remaining students in my line, the ones who were quietly taking care of business, are being overlooked.

I've actually had to condition myself so that I don't automatically look for the disruptions. This is not to say that I can ignore non-compliant behavior; it's just that I don't want the negative stuff to receive the lion's share of my attention. I feel it's critical to maintain the same outlook regarding assignments.

power
love
fun
freedom
safety

Let the students in your class who finish on time know and feel and see your pleasure. Don't let the shortcomings of the few detract from the achievement of the many. Build yourself a First Aid Kit, introduce it to your students, and start keeping things in their proper perspective.

Bad Choice #2: Getting Emotional

Here's another bad choice I used to make on a regular basis. It would usually occur in the morning right after our math lesson.

I was teaching fifth grade at the time, and one of our goals for that year was to have as many students as possible earn the California Physical Fitness Award. In order to qualify for the certificate and coveted jacket patch, fifth graders had to pass four physical fitness tests. The four tests were: the long run, sit-and-reach, sit-ups, and pull-ups. We called pull-ups The Eliminator because if you couldn't do a pull-up, you couldn't get a patch. The rather sad reality was that the average fifth grader couldn't do one; they just didn't have the innate upper-body strength. (I realize that we all have a small group of naturally gifted athletes in the room, the forty-pound ectomorphs, who can bang out about 12 pull-ups each. I'm talking about your basic 10-year-old TV-watching, video-game-playing sofa slug.) Out of thirty students attempting to earn the patch, maybe five or six would actually pass all four tests and receive one.

In an effort to help more kids qualify, we began to go outside every morning after our math lesson for a ten-minute upper body workout. In order to gather up the math papers quickly and ensure I had them all before going outside, I'd stand by the door and collect them in numerical order. I wouldn't use a Check Off List or a Check Off Sheet. I'd just use the power of student numbers.

Mr. Morris
   Standing by the door at the end of math:
      Okay, I need to collect your math assignments so that we can go outside for our upper body workout. Have them ready, please. 1, 2, 3, 4, 5.

Students 1 through 5 would bring me the math assignment. I would offer smiles and thanks as I received each one.

> *Thank you…thank you…nice job…beautiful…got it.*

The five students who had just brought me their assignments would then step outside and line up against the wall.

MR. MORRIS
6, 7, 8, 9, 10.

I was like the shepherd at the gate. No one was getting by without first handing me a finished math paper.

Here comes 6…"Thank you;" here comes 7…"Thanks;" here comes 8…"Nice job;" and here comes 9 with a rather sad look.

MR. MORRIS
Math paper, Eric?

ERIC, STUDENT 9
I'm not done.

Without a simple procedure for handling this unfinished assignment, I had a tendency to deal with it emotionally. And if, for whatever reason, I hadn't been having a good day so far, the response could get downright ugly.

MR. MORRIS
What, again?!?! What is this? Three days in a row? Not done, not done, not done? Hey, I'm getting tired of that. No, don't give me your paper. I want you to finish it. That's right. Finish it! Work on it outside while the rest of us are working out. Take your book, your paper, and your pencil and GET OUTSIDE AND GET THAT DONE NOW!

That was not a pretty scene, nor was it consistent. (Imagine if student Eric's mother had been a visitor in our classroom during this collection process. Do you think I would have flamed on her baby boy in the same fashion? Not likely. It would have probably been more along the lines of, "Not finished? Oh, don't you worry about that, you little dickens. You can finish that later.")

Sometimes, in the privacy of our classrooms, we allow ourselves to act out our frustrations instead of dealing with them in a more professional way.

Compounding this disaster was the treatment of student 10. Think about her for just a second. What did she get for being finished on time? Yes, that's correct. She not only had to stand there and listen to my Ode to the Unfinished Student, but she also missed out on getting a genuine thanks for her efforts. I had built up such a negative charge over student 9 that I wasn't able to calm down and recognize the fact that the next student *was* finished.

Bad Choice #2: The Solution

Let's try it again, with the First Aid Kit in place, and see if we can't keep away from the emotional booby traps.

> MR. MORRIS
>> Standing by the door at the end of math:
>> *Okay, I need to collect your math assignments so that we can go outside for our upper body workout. Have them ready, please. 1, 2, 3, 4, 5.*

Students 1 through 5 would bring me the math assignment. I would offer smiles and thanks as I received each one.

> *Thank you...thank you...nice job...beautiful...got it.*

As before, the five students who had just brought me their assignments would then step outside and line up against the wall.

> MR. MORRIS
>> *6, 7, 8, 9, 10.*
>> (After a while, it'll sound like one word. "Sixseveneightnineten.")

Here comes 6..."Thank you."
Here comes 7..."Thanks."
Here comes 8..."Nice job."

And here comes 9 with the patented I'm-not-done sad look.

> MR. MORRIS
>> *Math paper, Eric?*

> ERIC, STUDENT 9
>> *I'm not done.*

And instead of becoming Blackbeard, I can now handle this situation calmly.

> MR. MORRIS
>> *First Aid Kit, please.*

Watching Eric to make sure he was heading to the First Aid Kit; and then turning to Estella, student 10, take her finished math paper, give her a sincere smile, and share his simple, yet sincere appreciation:

Thank you.

power
love
fun
freedom
safety

Whenever I collect papers by the door, the students get a lot of smiles and a lot of thanks until I come upon someone who is not finished. These students receive a firm, yet polite, "Put it in the First Aid Kit, please." No lecture, no stress. I can discuss the finer points of accountability later on when I pass back the unfinished assignments.

When I'd received the last paper, I'd put them in my math grade book, and we'd all head outside for our upper body workout.

> *BTW:* If you're wondering about whether I'd allow the unfinished students to participate in the workout, you should try to figure out how you think it should be handled. Then, after you've reached a decision, you can turn to the back of this book—Frequently Asked Questions—to see how I would deal with it.

Now that you have seen how a procedure like the First Aid Kit can help you be fair, firm, and consistent—while increasing time-on-task behavior which boosts student achievement—let's get ready to introduce it to your students.

Decisions to Make Before You Begin

Before we actually bring the First Aid Kit into the classroom, we need to answer two important questions.

Q: *When is the best time of year to begin using the First Aid Kit?*

Q: *Should I use the First Aid Kit for every subject we do in class?*

When To Begin

Although it may seem logical that you would begin using your First Aid Kit the first week of school, experience has shown that it's a bit better to wait a month or so. Your students need time to adjust to you and your expectations. Then after you've gained their trust, you can begin to fine-tune their Completes Work On Time skills. With that in mind, I suggest you wait four to five weeks before introducing the First Aid Kit.[†]

---

†   If you are reading this book in the middle of the school year, you can begin the First Aid Kit as soon as you have it organized. Don't worry about this change in policy regarding unfinished assignments. Kids are amazingly flexible and can, with time and an opportunity for practice, adapt to new techniques.

During the first month of school, though, you can employ all of the traditional interventions teachers have used for accommodating late work.

FIG. 9-9
This classroom sign offers workable solutions for students who have unfinished assignments.

WHAT TO DO WITH AN UNFINISHED ASSIGNMENT

1. Keep it handy and work on it when you have a spare moment.
2. Take it home and finish it on your own.
3. Work on it during recess or lunch.†

These are fine ways of dealing with late assignments, but they're not going to work well beyond the first month or two. Within six to eight weeks of using these types of interventions, your students will begin to take advantage of your generosity in allowing them to complete assignments at a later time. Consequently, you'll see more and more of them not being finished on time.

By the fifth or sixth week of school, you can safely begin the transition to a more formal intervention for unfinished assignments that actually improves work skills and study habits. Nonetheless, the foundation of trust you were able to create with your students during their initial experience with you will add to the level of success you'll experience as you use this new technique.

Just One Subject

power
love
fun
freedom
safety

As long as you're going to wait a bit before you begin to use your First Aid Kit, you might as well modify one other aspect: the number of subjects you plan to send through your new system. Again, logic would seem to dictate that from the day you introduce this procedure to your students, every single unfinished assignment will be placed in the box, logged in, and shipped home.

Uh, no.

Having high expectations for success and an overachieving attitude are great; however, what I learned during the first couple of years of using this powerful technique taught me an important lesson: *Start with just one subject.*

---

† If you're going to require that your students work during their break time, it should probably be under your direct supervision. If you have them work outside, near the playground, they're resentful, easily distracted, and the finished product is usually at the low end of the quality scale. Try running a study hall during Thursday's recess. You can take care of bothersome administrative tasks as your students work at their desks.

As much as I'd like to shed immediate healing light on all of our dark problem areas, I've found it's usually more effective to illuminate one little corner.

Learning From Experience

I still remember the first year I tried the First Aid Kit. (It was called the Black Hole back then, a simple astronomy analogy, but that's another story.) Anyway, I brought it into the room and introduced the general concept to the students. I told them that, henceforth, all unfinished assignments would be placed in the First Aid Kit and would then be sent home at the end of the day to be completed.

As it turned out, there were so many papers to process that I would have been better off had I brought in the First Aid Dumpster. In just three days, I had become so overwhelmed with processing all of the unfinished assignments that I found myself backing out of the deal.

MR. MORRIS
Seeing yet another student about to place an unfinished assignment in the bulging First Aid Kit:
No, no, no! Don't put it in there!

STUDENT
Looking bewildered:
But I thought you said we're supposed to put unfinished papers in the First Aid Kit.

MR. MORRIS
HEY! I KNOW WE SAID WE WERE, BUT NOW WE'RE NOT! OKAY?

STUDENT
Thoroughly confused:
Then what should I do with my paper?

MR. MORRIS
Big sigh; slumping shoulders; a look of resignation on his face:
Just…take it home…and…oh…finish it on your own. I'll…see it…sometime.

In order for this technique to work, it must be manageable for you and your students. One guaranteed way of doing this is to target just one subject for the first two weeks. That is, choose just one of the many subjects you cover in the course of your day and use the First Aid Kit to process any unfinished assignments for that designated subject. (For right now, all other unfinished assignments will be handled with the interventions that were listed on the classroom sign in Fig. 9-9 on page 9-18.)

By starting with just one subject, you'll discover how simple it can be to use the First Aid Kit. Another advantage is that your underachieving students will have the opportunity to bear down a bit more on the activities related to that target subject. If they were forced to do that with every subject, they'd probably give up trying within a week and would merely revert to their old ways and bad habits.

Every two weeks you'll be able to add another subject to the one you've been collecting. By the third month, as you can imagine, every subject in the classroom will fall under the jurisdiction of the mighty First Aid Kit.

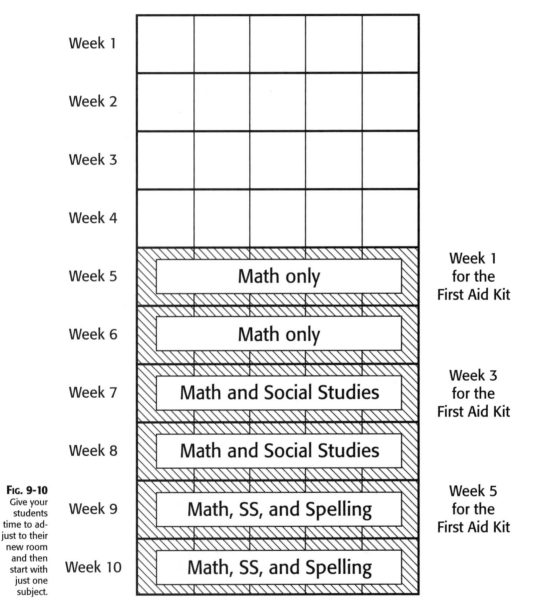

First Aid Kit Schedule

Week 1	
Week 2	
Week 3	
Week 4	
Week 5	Math only — Week 1 for the First Aid Kit
Week 6	Math only
Week 7	Math and Social Studies — Week 3 for the First Aid Kit
Week 8	Math and Social Studies
Week 9	Math, SS, and Spelling — Week 5 for the First Aid Kit
Week 10	Math, SS, and Spelling

FIG. 9-10 Give your students time to adjust to their new room and then start with just one subject.

As the weeks go by and you send more subjects through the First Aid Kit, it will continue to be a relatively manageable affair. Within two months, so many of your students will have improved their work skills that you'll find fewer and fewer assignments needing your attention. Won't that be nice.

So, pick a subject that you would like to take care of using your new First Aid Kit. Here are three suggestions:

1. You could start with the first thing you do each day and thereby establish a Completes Work On Time mind set for the remainder of the day.

2. You could choose the one subject that is giving you the most difficulty. By using your First Aid Kit for the unfinished assignments in this trouble area, you'll begin to see real improvement.

power
love
fun
freedom
safety

3. You might want to start with the one subject in which your students show a fair amount of success. The small number of unfinished papers you'll need to process for this normally successful area will encourage you to keep using your FAK.

Whatever you decide, for whatever reason, pick just one subject and commit yourself to tracking this subject's late, or unfinished, work for the next two weeks.

You are now ready to begin using the First Aid Kit.

Your Own First Aid Kit

A brief review of Lesson 9 to this point shows that we have:

✓ **Assembled the various parts of the First Aid Kit**
A box, a Log book, and a rubber stamp. (*Remember:* The stamp is an optional piece of the puzzle.)

✓ **Established a specific date to introduce the Kit to the students.**
It should be after you've spent a month or so with your students. If, however, you were applying this strategy in the middle of the year, you wouldn't need to wait. You would have already established a relationship with your students.

✓ **Identified the subject matter with which to begin.**
Although it's your call on this one, you might want to choose class work that is a bit more objective in nature. By that I mean this: it's somewhat easier to determine that the math activity sheet is not finished as opposed to a written assignment of some type. But, again, it's your choice and it's really hard to go wrong at this point.

power
love
fun
freedom
safety

It's now time to put Mr. FAK to work. Just be sure to keep your expectations realistic and your motivation for using this technique a nurturing, supportive one. Your First Aid Kit is designed to help, not hurt or humiliate.

Introducing the First Aid Kit to Your Students

You probably won't want to hit your students with your new First Aid Kit the first thing in the morning. As eager as you may be to begin using it, you might as well relax and wait a bit. After all, you're going to be able to use this all year long.[†]

For the sake of illustration, let's say that you've chosen Spelling as the *subject du jour*. It would make sense, then, to make the introduction of your First Aid Kit a part of the day's spelling lesson.

> YOU (AS THE TEACHER)
> Holding up the First Aid Kit collection box:
>> *Before we begin today's spelling lesson, I'd like to show you something new. It's an idea I think we should use in our room. It's a First Aid Kit. What are First Aid Kits used for, boys and girls?*

Take time to elicit responses.

> YOU
>> *That's correct. First Aid Kits are used to help people who have been hurt or injured in some way. What would you find if you opened up a First Aid Kit?*

Once more, pause for comments and pointless, rambling stories.

> YOU
>> *Well, our First Aid Kit doesn't have band-aids or boo-boo goo. It just has a folder and a rubber stamp. You see, our First Aid Kit isn't for people who have been hurt. Our First Aid Kit is designed to help students get better at finishing assignments on time.*

> STUDENTS
>> *Ooooh. Aaaaah.*

> YOU AGAIN
>> *Starting today, if your spelling assignment isn't finished on time, I'm going to have you put your paper in our First Aid Kit. At the end of the day, I'll give it back to you so that you can take it home and finish it.*

[†]   Experience has shown that I don't really need to use the FAK much beyond March. At that point in the year, I've been able to get the core group of non-finishers down to just two or three students. I then make separate folders for these students and run the procedure in a more individualized fashion.

And with that, you should wrap it up. Make your intro short and sweet. Although the tendency is to over-explain, it would probably be better to keep things simple and to-the-point. Besides, it's going to take living with the First Aid Kit before your students really understand how it all works anyway.

While you're at it, this would be an appropriate time for you to accept the fact that some of your students are going to think you're kidding about this Completes Work On Time thing. This would be especially true if you're trying the FAK in the middle of the school year and they've had a chance to experience how unfinished work has been handled in the past. Overcoming this previously established behavior with something new is going to require a great deal of patience on your part. If their prior experience was that you were more talk than action, they might see the First Aid Kit as a phase: something that will pass with time. However, if you consistently adhere to your goal of improving your students' work skills by using the FAK, you will eventually see progress. It's merely a matter of reconditioning your students to this new procedure. Consequently, you shouldn't expect overnight miracles with your resistant learners. Miracles are nice, but reality usually runs on a slightly slower time frame.

Speaking of reality, why don't we take a look at a couple of assignment collection scenarios that might play out in the classroom and see how the First Aid Kit could make the best of these situations.

Sending Unfinished Assignments to the FAK

Here are three ways in which an assignment can end up in the box.

Take 1: Collected by Teacher During Activity Time

power
love
fun
freedom
safety

I sometimes like to walk around the room and collect assignments as the students are working independently. I'll wander around, in some predetermined order so that I don't miss anyone, and pick up their papers. The students usually have them on top of their desks ready for collection. I like being able to look each one in the eye and give them a smile or wink or maybe offer a gentle pat on the shoulder to let them know their efforts are appreciated.

MR. MORRIS
As you work on page 2 of your spelling units, I'm going to come around and collect your independent spelling activity. The one in which you wrote the words in alphabetical order and then put in different word groups. Please have it out on your desk.
Starting with the first group of students:
Thank you, thank you, got it, this looks nice . . .

CALVIN
Trying to avoid eye contact but realizing it's hopeless:
I'm not done yet.

MR. MORRIS
First Aid Kit, please.
Continuing on with a smile and high expectations:
Thank you, thank you, thanks, Brian, thank you . . .

VERONICA
I can't find mine.

Uh-oh. Nothing for this student to put in the First Aid Kit. Now what?

First of all, don't panic. It should be obvious to you by now that you won't have an answer for every question. Likewise, you won't have a ready procedure for the multitude of situations you'll face on a daily basis. (That's why it's so tough being a new teacher. The same can be said for being a new cop or a new park ranger or a new nurse. Being new to a profession almost always means that you don't have a wealth of experience from which to draw inspiration. Nonetheless, before too long, you'll be wingin' it with the best of them.)

For the student who doesn't even have the assignment you're trying to collect, try this:

MR. MORRIS
Get a piece of paper and write your name, number, and today's date. Then write the heading, which was Spelling Practice. When you're done, place your paper in the First Aid Kit, please.

Nothing to it. No muss, no fuss. The student who tried to manipulate you by losing the assignment (Veronica) will actually be putting a paper in the First Aid Kit. That paper will act as a reminder at the end of the day that she did not hang on to the original assignment and will need to do it that night at home.

> *Note:* If the missing paper was an activity sheet you had passed out the day before, you'll want to have a procedure in place for dealing with students who need a replacement copy. An easy way to go is to have an **EXTRA PAPER TOTE TRAY** where you'll place extra copies of anything you've passed out to your students. (Always make extra copies. It's a guaranteed stress reducer.) By putting all of the extra activity sheets in one specific spot, your students will soon figure out that there's only one place where extra papers can be found. If you can't find it in the Extra Papers tray, we don't have any.

4
Tools & Toys

On to the next group of students who were successful, who do have the assignment, and who need my positive, supportive attention.

1

Thank you.
Thank you.
Thank you.

Take 2: Collected by a Student with a Check Off List

This next activity, spelling definitions, was being collected by a student using a Check Off List. It was a three-day assignment—assigned on Monday—and wasn't due until Wednesday just before morning recess. By having a student collect them, other students will be able to give it to the student collector as soon as they finish: another example of asynchronous collection. (See page 7-34 for the original explanation.)

As Wednesday's recess time drew near, I picked up the Check Off List and the finished assignments from the student who had been placed in charge of collection. By looking at the circled numbers on the Check Off List, I knew who was not finished.

> MR. MORRIS
> *The following students may stand up: 1, 2, 4, 5, 6, 7, 8, 9, 11, 12, 13, 14, 15, 16, 18, 19, 20, 21, 22, 24, 25, 26, 27, 29, 30, and 31. I have your spelling definitions. You may go out to recess.*

The thundering herd departs.

Rule of thumb:
If you're not comfortable identifying students by calling out numbers, just pencil in their names next to their numbers before you make a bunch of copies of the Check Off List.

For the most part, though, students don't have a problem with the teacher calling out their numbers, especially if it means they're done with an activity and are free to head out to recess.

Note:
Did you notice that the names above are not in alphabetical order by first names? Although I prefer it that way, I've used both methods in the examples throughout the book because either one of them will work quite well.

FIG. 9-11
Sending unfinished assignments to the First Aid Kit is easy. Just look for the circled student numbers.

MR. MORRIS
Talking to just the five students who are still in the room:
Let's see, Colleen? Spelling assignment?

COLLEEN
It's not finished.

MR. MORRIS
Put it in the First Aid Kit, please, and then have a seat. Kayla?

KAYLA
Not done.

Kayla follows Colleen to the First Aid Kit with her unfinished assignment.

MR. MORRIS
Have a seat when you're done. Mike?

MIKE
I can't find mine.

MR. MORRIS
Get a new sheet of paper. What's the heading going to be, Mike?

MIKE
Spelling definitions?

MR. MORRIS
That's correct. Let's see, who's next? Christa?

CHRISTA
It's finished, Mr. Morris.

MR. MORRIS
All done? I'll take it, thank you. Next time, please get it to the student who's collecting it.
Dismissing Christa for recess and looking at the next circled number:
Nicholas? Spelling definitions?

NICHOLAS
I'm not done.

MR. MORRIS
First Aid Kit, Nicholas.

Mike finally has his new paper prepped and heads over to the First Aid Kit along with Nicholas. Like Colleen and Kayla, they both return to their seats.

MR. MORRIS
Addressing the four students who weren't done on time:
You will all receive your assignment at the end of the day. You'll be able to do it at home. But guess what? There will be another spelling definition assignment due next Wednesday. What are you going to do next week when this assignment is given?

> *Recommendation:* Part of the success I'm able to achieve with the non-finishers can be attributed to the fact that I try to get them to focus on "next time." Spending unnecessary time bemoaning the fact that they should have been finished this time—the old shame-and-blame game—does little to alter subsequent behavior. So, instead of dwelling on things we can no longer change, we'll make plans for the future.

After eliciting appropriate responses, they are dismissed to recess.

Granted, I could have had them complete the spelling definition assignment during recess, but the quality of "recess work" is usually poor and there would be no communication with the home that the assignment had not been finished on time. Also, I don't want any of my students thinking they'll be able to trade recess to make up for a lack of effort during spelling. I want to consistently reinforce the concept that we have set times for completing assignments and activities. If you are not finished within our schedule, you'll have to use your own time outside of school.

Take 3: Turned In Using a Check Off Sheet

Tools & Toys

Every week we work on a four-page spelling unit. The activities come from our non-consumable spelling books. We do one page a day, Monday through Thursday. The students, after completing the activity, put their papers in the SPELLING ISLAND and mark off their numbers on the spelling Check Off Sheet. Spelling units are always due by the end of lunch recess. When we return to class after this break, it's the first thing I check.

MR. MORRIS
Looking at the Check Off Sheet and seeing three numbers have not been marked off:
Alberto? Your spelling unit?

ALBERTO
It's not done, Mr. Morris.

MR. MORRIS
First Aid Kit, please.
Slight pause as Alberto complies and it's back to the Check Off Sheet:
Travis?

TRAVIS
> *It's done. I put it in there earlier.*

MR. MORRIS
> *Well, your number's not marked off.*† *Would you please come mark off your number?*
> Another slight pause as Travis schleps over, makes his mark, and returns to his seat.
> *Thank you. Angelina? Your spelling unit, please.*

ANGELINA
> *Oh, it's not done yet.*

MR. MORRIS
> *First Aid Kit, if you will. Thanks.*

After putting the Check Off Sheet back inside the tote tray, I head to my desk, grab the oral reading book we are currently working our way through, and read to everyone for fifteen minutes.

In all three of these typical collection scenarios we saw how simple, yet effective, it can be to have a procedure for taking care of unfinished assignments.

The First Aid Kit will:
1. allow you to focus on the positive accomplishments of your students
2. keep you calm and in control
3. empower you to stay within your established time frames

Fair, firm, and consistent: It doesn't get much better than that.

Okay, we've learned how a handful of unfinished work can end up sitting in the First Aid Kit. What do we do with it now? Well, let's move on to the documentation portion of this procedure.

Using the First Aid Kit folder
This next phase involves five steps:

1. Set aside time at the end of the day before dismissal to deal with the unfinished assignments in the First Aid Kit.

2. Pull assignments out of the collection box and record them on the Log sheet in your folder.

---

†   As I mentioned in Lesson 7: The Check Off List, learning to mark off their numbers is a skill that takes some students longer to learn than others. The important part is that the assignment had been completed and was in the proper place.

3. Stamp the assignments with the Unfinished Assignment stamp, and then ask the First Aid kids to join you in the back of the room.

4. Give them their assignments and have them figure out which comments should be circled.

5. Have them verbally state that they will complete these assignments tonight and return them to class the next day. Send them back to their seats.

Let's take a closer look at each of the five steps

Monday Afternoon

1. **Set aside time at the end of the day before dismissal to deal with the unfinished assignments in the First Aid Kit.**

    Probably the best time for processing the First Aid Kit assignments is at the end of the day.[†] All I need is about five minutes of uninterrupted time. So, with about ten minutes left in our day, I have everyone begin working on the homework for that night. I've found that when my students are given a chance to start their homework in class before they leave, they are more inclined to complete it when they get home. Not only is this beneficial to their academic growth and development, but it also gives us an opportunity to clear up any misunderstandings they may have had regarding the assignment. Any confusion can be dealt with before dismissal. While the students are occupied with their homework, I use the time to meet with everyone who has a paper in the First Aid Kit.

MR. MORRIS
    With ten minutes left in the day and tonight's homework activity sheet in his hands:
    What is tonight's homework?

A STUDENT WHO IS AWARE AND PAYING ATTENTION
    It's a math activity sheet, Mr. Morris.

MR. MORRIS
    Right you are.

I then ring the hotel bell which signals to the class that I have materials to give them. Each team sends up a representative to request materials for the entire team. As soon as every student has the activity sheet, I give the directions.

---

†   If you've been wondering if it would be okay for a student to retrieve his unfinished assignment from the First Aid Kit and work on it during the day when he has a spare moment—a Frequently Asked Question at New Management workshops—you should check the FAQ Appendix for the response.

MR. MORRIS

Picking up Max, the digital timer, and setting him for five minutes:

I'm going to give you five minutes to complete five problems from tonight's activity sheet.

Writing on the whiteboard for all to see:

Let's do problem numbers 2, 6, 11, 18, and 20. You have five minutes, and then we'll check them. Any questions? All right, you may begin.[†]

2. **Pull assignments out of the collection box and record them on the Log sheet in your folder.**

    As the students begin work, I grab the First Aid Kit and head to a large table we have set up in the back of the room. Removing the folder from the box, I label a fresh form. I write the subject at the top of the first column and the day's date in the first row. Since I won't need to write in the rest of that row, I mark out the spaces.

FIG. 9-12
There are columns for the different subjects and a row for the date.

Next, I take the unfinished spelling assignments out of the First Aid Kit—there are four of them today—and log them onto the sheet. All I need to write are the student numbers and the name of the assignment.

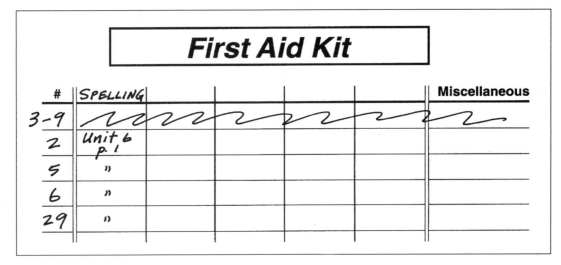

FIG. 9-13
Filling out the First Aid Kit Log takes less than a minute.

† When the timer goes off in five minutes, we'll still have a few minutes before dismissal. I'll spend this time discussing the five problems the students had just completed. This brief, interactive assessment let's me know which students are still having difficulty with the skill. It's best, of course, if I'm aware of this before they go home to work on their own.

3. **Stamp the assignments using the Unfinished Assignment stamp, and then ask the First Aid kids to join you in the back of the room.**

> *Reminder:* The use of the stamp is not necessary. Although it sends a clear message to the parents, it just adds another step to the process. As long as you can keep parents apprised of poor work skills you should be fine.
>
> And even if you do have the stamp, you might not want to use it immediately. (I always like to give my students an opportunity to resolve issues without the intervention of their parents.) If, however, you see the same students with assignments in the First Aid Kit day after day after day, you might want to crack out the stamp and take things to a whole different level. As always, the choice is yours. I just thought I'd offer alternatives before describing the standard operating procedure.

Each paper is stamped in a convenient, easy-to-see location. (Remember, if there isn't any easy-to-read spot on the front, you can always stamp on the back of the assignment.) After stamping all of the assignments, I invite the First Aid students to join me at the back table. Since I've already logged in the student numbers, it's an easy matter to identify the students I need to see.

MR. MORRIS
Reading from the Log sheet:

I need to see four students right now: Amanda, Brianna, Calvin, and Tony. Would you four come see me, please.

power
love
fun
freedom
safety

> *Caution:* Make sure your students know that the use of the FAK does not automatically mean that someone is "in trouble." I wouldn't want the four students whose names I just called to be teased by their classmates. If it *were* to happen, I would want to intervene and clarify the situation. "Maybe one of these four wants to make sure his answers are correct and just needs more time. There's nothing wrong with that, is there?" They'll get the point.

4. **Give them their unfinished assignments and have them figure out which comments should be circled.**

After stamping and logging, the papers are ready to give back to the students. As soon as they've all joined me, I return their assignments. Each student grabs a red ball-point pen for circling, and we discuss the comments. I then help each student decide which comments should be circled.[†]

Since we are able to circle a number of comment combinations, the stamp covers a multitude of situations.

---

† Although I could circle the comments, I feel it's better to involve my students in this process. Of course, if I were working with first graders, I would do the circling myself. As I'm sure you've already discovered, the manner in which you apply any idea in your classroom is shaped, in large part, by the ability level of your students.

Here are five possibilities:

FIG. 9-14
The Unfinished Assignment stamp is perfect for apprising parents of my concerns regarding their children.

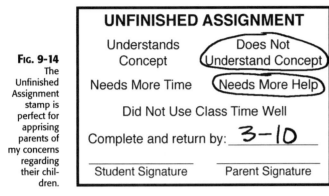

The circled comments in Fig. 9-14 indicate a student who needs help in mastering a new skill. Although the lesson was taught in class, this student still needs assistance. As I met with the student at the end of the day, we would determine how he is going to receive help. If there is no one at home who can do it, then the student and I would arrange a time to sit together for the necessary reteaching.

General rule: The primary purpose of this stamp is to help me stay on top of students who aren't mastering skills so that they don't "slip through the cracks."

FIG. 9-15
Students who can't finish because they're helping others still take the assignment home to be completed.

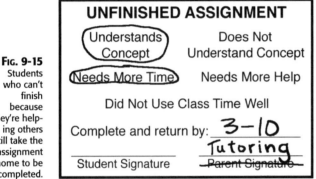

Sometimes you'll find that students were not able to complete an assignment even though they understand the concept. Tutoring other students, working in the office or cafeteria, missing lessons because of medical or dental appointments are but a few of the possible reasons.

This sample shows that the student was tutoring and, as a result, needs more time in order to complete the assignment. Since parent involvement was not really necessary, I drew a line through "Parent Signature."

FIG. 9-16
These comments would be used for your basic "goofin' off" situations.

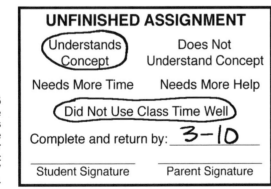

For those times when students did not complete an assignment in the allotted time due to poor work skills or self-control, we will indicate this to the parents. It is critical that I keep parents apprised of their children's progress, or lack thereof.

Reality: Although it's not always pleasant to share unfavorable information with parents, it's only fair I do so. I've found over the years that the more I communicate with parents, the more I want to. If, however, I hide from difficult situations at the beginning of the year, they just get worse. I end up wishing that I had done something sooner. This stamp provides me with the opportunity to open a dialogue in a timely, yet non-confrontative fashion.

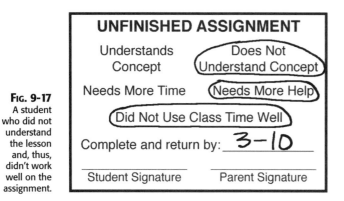

FIG. 9-17
A student who did not understand the lesson and, thus, didn't work well on the assignment.

Despite your best efforts, some students will make very little effort. They neither engage in your lessons nor work very hard to complete the assignment. The circles in Fig. 9-17 show that we need to address these two issues as soon as possible.

For the most part, I'll let this student know that the best time for learning is when I first teach the lesson. Then, I'll work at convincing this child that he needs to ask for help whenever he is not understanding the lesson.

FIG. 9-18
A student who didn't finish because he was working slowly in order to do quality work.

Again, having a paper stamped does not necessary indicate problems. Fig. 9-18 shows a student who was not working quickly enough to get his assignment in on time. Fortunately, this little guy didn't want to rush through it and turn in sloppy, inaccurate work.

This sample shows that this student just needs time because he wants to do a quality job. I'm more than happy to support and nurture this desire.

4. Circling comments (continued)

MR. MORRIS

Find the stamp on your paper. The top two comments have to do with whether you understand this lesson. If you know how to do this assignment and can finish it on your own, circle the words UNDERSTANDS CONCEPT. If you're not sure how to do it, circle the words DOES NOT UNDERSTAND CONCEPT.
Pause as they comply.

Now, figure out if you need more time or if you need more help. You may circle one of them or both of them. If you're not sure, ask me, and I can give you some suggestions.
Another slight pause as he watches them work.

Find the space for COMPLETE AND RETURN BY: and write "3-10." Everything circled the way you want? Good.

5. The last step is to have these students tell me they're going to complete the assignment and return it to class the next day.

This may seem like a step you could do without, but it's too important for you to skip. For the same reason that I had the students circle the comments and write the return date, I want to hear them state that they will complete this assignment and return it to class the next day. They need to stay involved in this First Aid Kit process, and these types of "I messages" help them develop a sense of ownership and commitment. Whenever a student tells me he is going to do something, I almost always respond with words of support while exuding a confident belief in the student's ability to follow through on his stated behavior.

MR. MORRIS
So, what are you guys going to do tonight?

AMANDA
I'm going to finish my spelling and bring it back.

BRIANNA
Me, too. I'm going to bring it back all done, Mr. Morris.

MR. MORRIS
That's a good choice, girls. Calvin?

CALVIN
Okay.

MR. MORRIS
I don't know what that means.

CALVIN
I meant I'm going to take this home and finish it tonight.

MR. MORRIS
What about bringing it back to class tomorrow?

CALVIN
Yeah.

MR. MORRIS
Calvin?

CALVIN
I'll bring it back tomorrow.

MR. MORRIS
I believe you. Tony, what about you?

TONY
I'm going to finish my spelling and bring it back tomorrow.

MR. MORRIS
Thanks, Tony.

Although this may seem like more talking than you'd care to do at the end of the day with four non-finishers, it's necessary to establish an attitude of self-discipline. Before long, you and your students will be able to have a sincere talk and wrap up the entire First Aid Kit meeting in less than three minutes.

At this stage in the game, the following things have occurred:

1. I set up the Log sheet for the day and recorded which students had assignments going home.
2. I stamped each assignment.
3. I called the First Aid kids to the back of the room for a brief meeting.
4. The students circled appropriate comments.
5. We heard each student say that the assignment would be completed and returned to class.

And that's it. I can now send them back to their seats for the last five minutes of our day.

Final Comments for Certain Students

If there is anyone I need to see privately, I wait until the others are leaving the table and then ask that student to remain for a moment. This is usually done for students who circled DOES NOT UNDERSTAND CONCEPT. We need to determine how they are going to get help.

MR. MORRIS
Tony, would you stick around for a second?
Waiting for the others to leave:
You're having a hard time with this lesson, huh?

TONY
Kinda.

MR. MORRIS
Would you like me to help you after school today?

TONY
No, that's okay. My big brother can help me. He likes to help.

MR. MORRIS
Wow, that's great that he wants to help you with your assignments. Tell your brother I said, "Thanks for helping."

Many times, though, the comments I make are positive ones designed to show students that I'm aware of the efforts they've been making to improve.

> MR. MORRIS
> Watching the students get up to return to their seats:
> *Amanda, would you stay here, please.*
> Giving her a reassuring smile as they wait for privacy:
> *I just wanted to say that I've noticed how much better you're doing on getting your spelling assignment finished on time. Today you only had three more words to do. That is so much better than two weeks ago when you didn't even have half of them done. Keep up the good work.*

power
love
fun
freedom
safety

> AMANDA
> *Thanks, Mr. Morris. I've really been trying to get my work done.*

> MR. MORRIS
> *I know you have, and I'm proud of you.*

Now it's just a matter of putting the folder back in the First Aid Kit and returning the First Aid Kit to its proper place.

28; 21

Tools & Toys

We then briefly review the five math problems the students had worked on, announce our *STUDENT OF THE DAY*, observe our *MINUTE OF SILENCE*, and then head on home.

> *Important factor:* By processing the unfinished assignments in the First Aid Kit before the day is over, you will allow the students receiving these papers to leave on the same positive note as the other students. After all, there was more to our day than just the unfinished spelling assignments, and it would be a bit of a bummer to have to stick around after school in order to get your paper.

Tuesday Morning

With the information recorded in the First Aid Kit folder, it's an easy matter to follow up (consistency) with each student who took home an unfinished assignment. I usually do this in the morning during our discretionary time and in such a way as to not draw attention to these students.

> MR. MORRIS
> Walking around the room with the First Aid Kit folder in hand:
> *Excuse me, Amanda. Do you have page 1 of your spelling unit done?*

She does. I take the assignment from her and check to see that it was signed by her parents. (You might want to save yourself the potential for frustration by not requiring a signature for the first few weeks of using your FAK. You can always resort to a required signature later on if events dictate the necessity.)

Then, in the Log sheet, I draw a line through her assignment.

FIG. 9-19
A simple line drawn through the assignment tells me that this one was completed and returned to class.

MR. MORRIS
Thanks for taking care of that, Amanda.

> *Opportunity:* Although her assignment wasn't done yesterday when it should have been, I want to make an effort to show my appreciation for its completion. This kind of closure can help turn a negative situation into a positive one.

I put Amanda's finished spelling assignment in the back of the folder, check the list, and move on to the next student.

MR. MORRIS
Brianna, your spelling assignment from yesterday, please.

BRIANNA
Page 1? I left it at home, Mr. Morris.

I draw a circle around the ditto marks—read: spelling unit 6, page 1—on the Log sheet. The fact that the assignment has been circled will be the reminder I'm going to need to check with her again tomorrow and thereby show her that I mean what I say.

FIG. 9-20
A circle around an assignment indicates that it was not completed and returned.

> MR. MORRIS
> *Bring it to class tomorrow?*

Brianna nods her head "yes."

> MR. MORRIS
> *Brianna, tell me you'll bring your spelling assignment to class tomorrow.*

> BRIANNA
> *I'll bring it back tomorrow, Mr. Morris.*

> MR. MORRIS
> *Thank you, dear.*

Again, it's an effective verbal technique to have students actually make an "I will" statement. It not only produces a heightened sense of involvement, but also makes them a bit more aware of their obligations.

> MR. MORRIS
> *Calvin, may I have the spelling assignment you took home yesterday?*

> CALVIN
> *I forgot to do it.*

> MR. MORRIS
> Circling the assignment next to number 6:
> *Will you bring it tomorrow?*

> CALVIN
> *Yeah. I'll finish it tonight and bring it tomorrow.*

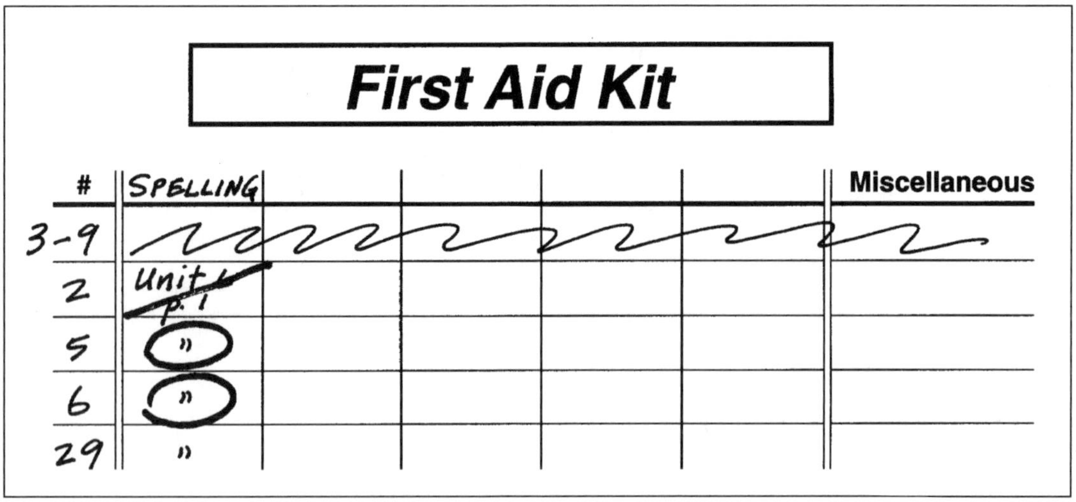

FIG. 9-21
Neither Brianna (5) nor Calvin (6) came to class with the assignment they should have finished at home.

One more student to check. Hey, this goes pretty fast.

> MR. MORRIS
> *Tony. I need to get page 1 of your spelling unit. Do you have it?*

> TONY
> *Yep. It's right here.*

> MR. MORRIS
> Drawing a line through the assignment next to Tony's number:
> *Nice work. Now, let's try to get today's spelling assignment in on time.*

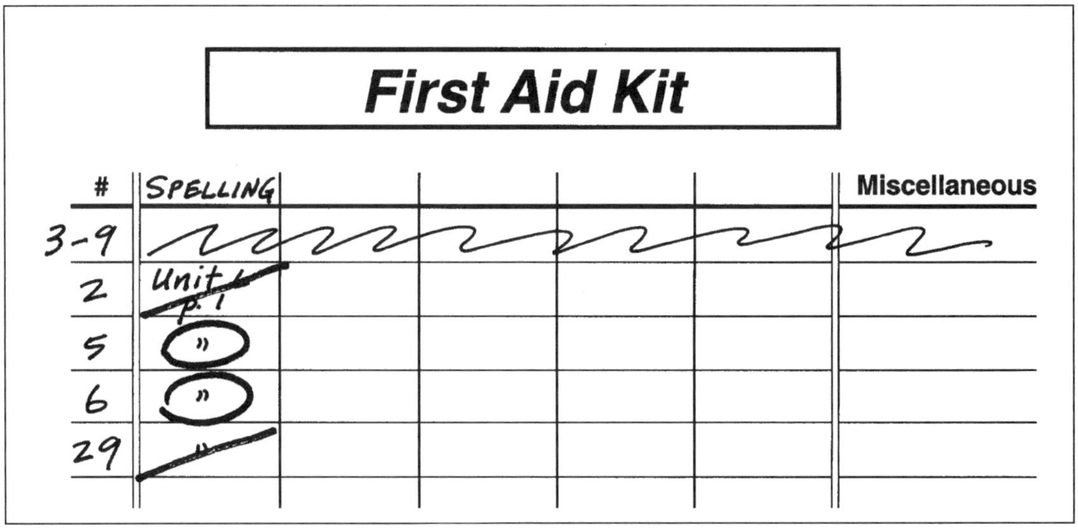

FIG. 9-22
After checking with all four students, two had completed their FAK assignments and two hadn't. I wish I could get this kind of return (50%) on my investments.

First Aid Kit

#	SPELLING				Miscellaneous
3-9					
2	Unit p.1				
5	"				
6	"				
29	"				

> *Reality:* I won't get too discouraged if I don't see great results for the first week or two. After all, this is a new group of students and some of them still think I'm kidding. Instead, I'll focus on the positive and patiently handle the negative. With that in mind, I put the two spelling assignments that were completed and given to me into my green spelling grade book (positive). The folder was returned to the First Aid Kit so that I would be sure to check tomorrow with Brianna and Calvin (negative).

So, other than eliciting a verbal agreement from Brianna and Calvin about being responsible and completing their unfinished assignments, that was it. There was no lecture; there were no threats. I don't need to bluff and bluster since I know I'll eventually wear them out with my bulldog-like tenacity. Instead of trying to verbally convince them that I am serious about this First Aid Kit, I'll show them I'm serious by my actions. This consistency on my part will speak much louder than anything I could say to the Briannas and Calvins in my room.

I've found that the Log sheet is so easy to use and produces such great results, I stick with it and keep checking with students for their FAK assignments. Before too long they discover that their misguided hope that maybe I was going to forget about these unfinished assignments just ain't gonna happen. Due to the repetitive nature of my daily requests, my students all learn this truth: Mr. Morris doesn't go away. He'll be back, day after day after day. He'll do it in a gentle, loving manner; but, he's not going away.[†]

Tuesday Mid-Morning

The First Aid Kit is now ready to collect more unfinished spelling assignments. Not only that, it is also ready to motivate the students to complete these same activities.

MR. MORRIS
After you finish page 2 of your spelling unit, don't forget to place it in the Spelling Island and mark off your number. Spelling units are due when?

GROUP RESPONSE
After lunch.

MR. MORRIS
Yes. Any page not finished by then will need to go into the First Aid Kit.
Holding aloft the FAK so that everyone receives the same message visually:
Please do yourself a favor and finish this assignment on time.

Tuesday After Lunch

As mentioned previously, the Check Off Sheet would be checked after lunch. Students who were not finished would put their papers in the First Aid Kit.

FIG. 9-23
Looking at the spelling unit Check Off Sheet after lunch showed me that students 3, 6, and 28 weren't done. Student 21 was absent.

> **ASSIGNMENT:** *Unit 6, p. 2*
>
> | Mon | (Tue) | Wed | Thur | Fri | 3-10 | DUE BY | 12:15 |
> |---|---|---|---|---|---|---|---|
>
> 4̶ ✗ ③ 4̶ ̶5̶ ⑥ 7̶ 8̶ 9̶ 1̶0̶ 1̶1̶ 1̶2̶
> 1̶3̶ 1̶4̶ 1̶5̶ 1̶6̶ 1̶7̶ 1̶8̶ 1̶9̶ 2̶0̶ △21 2̶2̶ 2̶3̶ 2̶4̶
> 2̶5̶ 2̶6̶ 2̶7̶ ㉘ 2̶9̶ 3̶0̶ 3̶1̶ 32 33 34 35 36

MR. MORRIS
Looking at the Check Off Sheet used for collecting spelling unit pages:
Beth, Calvin, and Steven. Do you have page 2 of your spelling unit finished? No? Please put it in the First Aid Kit.

[†]   I do have my limits. In fact, students know that they have just one week to clear the Log of an unfinished assignment. After that, it becomes an F in the grade book. By using the First Aid Kit, I feel that I've made an effort to help these students with their missing work. It's only fair that the students assume their share of the responsibility.

Tuesday Afternoon

Once again I set aside time at the end of our day to let my students get started on their homework. During this independent work time I record the information in the Log and stamp the assignments. Due to the fact that there were two different spelling assignments due today, I was seeing spelling unit papers and practice words.

FIG. 9-24
Day 2 of using the First Aid Kit found me having to deal with two different spelling assignments: page 2 from the spelling unit and practice words written 5 times each.

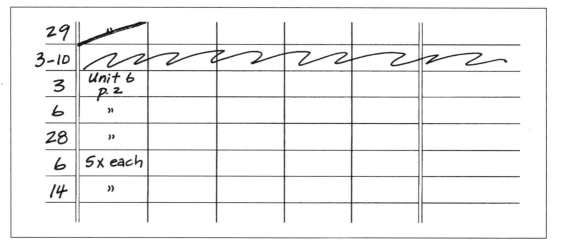

I then call the First Aid Kids to the back of the room, return their stamped assignments, and have them circle comments.† After a brief dialogue, they return to their seats and begin working on their homework. If there is a need to speak with one of them privately, I would do it at this time.

Wednesday Morning

Armed with my trusty First Aid Kit folder, I pay a visit to the First Aid kids. I not only see the students from yesterday, but I also check with Calvin and Brianna to see if they have Monday's assignment.

This may seem a bit overwhelming at first, but be of good cheer. You and your students will get the hang of it and, in no time at all, it will become a comfortable habit. And, let's face it: you've got to deal with unfinished assignments somehow. You can't just allow the days to go by without doing something.

> *Suggested Strategy:* Encourage your students to put their completed assignments back in the First Aid Kit when they return to class the next day. Not only will this put more of the responsibility on your students, it will also make things a bit easier on you. Think about the encouragement you'd experience at finding several of the FAK assignments already waiting for you as you retrieve your folder. These assignments can then be marked off in the Log sheet and put in your spelling grade book. To perpetuate this

---

† When it comes to our spelling program, the comments being circled are generally in the *Did Not Use Class Time Well* category as opposed to *Does Not Understand Concept.* For the most part, I'm the one who usually has to make this call. The students are inclined to deny the fact that they weren't using their time well.

behavior, merely acknowledge it. In fact, it would probably be a good idea to let each student know that: 1) you saw that the assignment had been completed and returned; and that 2) you appreciate the fact it was waiting for you in the FAK. An added bonus is that, by putting an assignment in the First Aid Kit for the *right reason*, your students might begin to see the First Aid Kit as the positive, supportive technique it's meant to be.

After making my rounds Wednesday morning to collect assignments and record my progress in the Log, it looked like this:

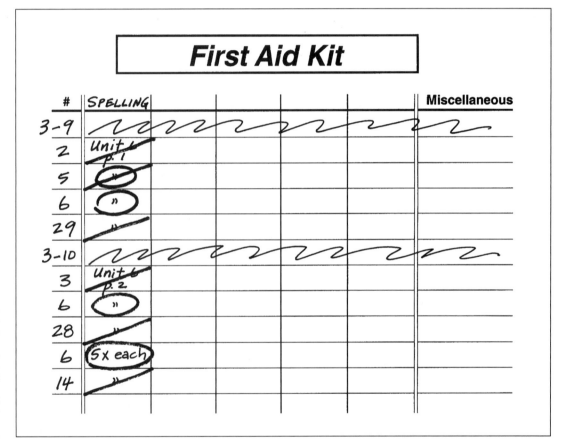

FIG. 9-25
By Wednesday, I was really starting to make progress. I was also beginning to document Calvin's (6) lack of effort in completing work on time.

Notice how I was able to collect all of the assignments except for Calvin's. Even Brianna had page 1 from Monday completed. They're already beginning to realize that I'm serious about this new technique of ours.

Wednesday Afternoon

The First Aid Kit meeting is starting to become routine. Recording and stamping assignments is quick and painless. Even the conversations I have with the First Aid kids are more natural, relaxed, and positive.[†]

---

† Be patient with any student who is attending the FAK meeting for the first time. Think back to how you ran the first meeting. It had an easy pace and was non-threatening. Make an effort to extend that same courtesy to your newest club members.

Nonetheless, after recording the unfinished assignment information in the First Aid Kit folder, the Log sheet looked like this:

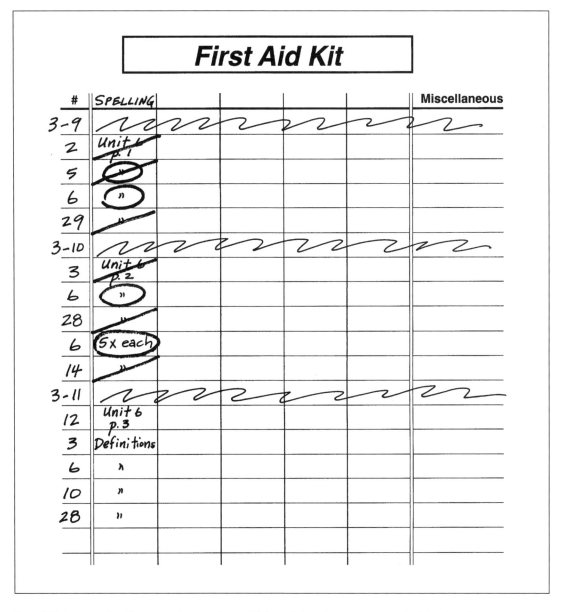

FIG. 9-26
As you look at this Log sheet, be aware of how much you've learned in this lesson. What was once foreign has now become familiar.

In addition to the four students who will be taking home one unfinished assignment today, Calvin will be taking home his fourth one this week. This may not be clear at first glance; but, with just a bit of practice on your part, you'll be able to spot these patterns quickly.

> *Suggestion:* Try to remain realistic about this new procedure. The fact that you might not see emerging patterns at this point in the game is not as important as the fact that *you are willing to try a new strategy to boost student work skills.* So don't expect to become an expert at this First Aid Kit thing right away. It's going to take you a bit of time to get the whole process flowing smoothly.

Check out this marked-up copy of the Log to more clearly see the pattern:

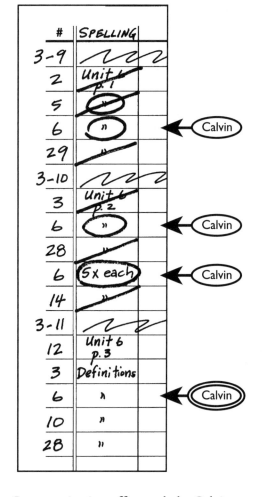

Documenting a Pattern

Calvin, student number 6, is beginning to display a disturbing, yet correctable, pattern of behavior. His spelling assignments that weren't finished in class were logged into the First Aid Kit folder and sent home to be completed. As you can see in the Log sheet to the left, the circles tell us that he has yet to complete and return any of these three assignments.

Acting on the Pattern

Since he'll be taking home Wednesday's spelling activity to finish, it would probably be a good idea to give him a note to take home to his parents.

In a continuing effort to help Calvin accept reality—in this classroom, we're serious about completing assignments on time—I will talk with him privately after meeting with the First Aid kids.

MR. MORRIS
   Dismissing the group, and then speaking to Calvin:
      Calvin, stick around for a second. I'd like to discuss something with you.
   Waiting for privacy and getting the FAK folder ready for Show and Tell:
      Take a look at our First Aid Kit folder.
   Pointing to the ubiquitous 6's:
      Spelling, page 1: not finished in class; not finished at home.
      Spelling, page 2: not finished in class; not finished at home.
      Spelling, practice words: not finished in class; not finished at home.
      And today's assignment, Spelling, definitions: not finished in class.
      You must think I'm kidding about finishing assignments on time.[†]

---

† Since I don't raise my voice to emphasize the fact that I'm serious—the way their parents might—it takes a bit of time for my students to realize that I *am* serious. That's okay. I'll eventually condition them to the fact that what I say—even if it's spoken softly—is what I mean.

CALVIN

No, I don't. I know you're serious.

MR. MORRIS

Well, I hear that you feel that way, but I don't see that you feel that way. Tell you what…why don't I send home a Student Bulletin.

And with that, I'd grab a copy of the Student Bulletin from the front pocket of the folder and record my observations.

Using a Student Bulletin

This versatile little communication tool can be extremely useful for times like this when I've got a student, such as Calvin, who has several assignments that are still past due. The bulletin, which can be found in the appendix, looks like this:

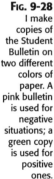

FIG. 9-28
I make copies of the Student Bulletin on two different colors of paper. A pink bulletin is used for negative situations; a green copy is used for positive ones.

STUDENT BULLETIN

Name _____　　　Date _____

BEHAVIOR

- ❑ Demonstrated leadership
- ❑ Set good example
- ❑ Strived to improve
- ❑ Sometimes forgot self-control
- ❑ Placed on restriction for one day

- ❑ Note on back of bulletin
- ❑ If checked here, please sign & return.

Teacher signature _____

WORK SKILLS

- ❑ Worked independently
- ❑ Showing improvement in work skills and study habits
- ❑ Needed some guidance to complete class assignments
- ❑ Needed constant guidance to complete class assignments
- ❑ Easily distracted
- ❑ Distracted others

Parent signature _____

EFFORT

- ❑ Excellent effort
- ❑ Very good effort
- ❑ Good effort
- ❑ Is improving
- ❑ Needs to improve

Conference requested
- ❑ by teacher
- ❑ by parent

Better: The Student Bulletin is actually more effective when I use it to communicate success. Recognizing positive behavior is one of the best ways to nurture and develop it. Unfortunately, it used to wear me out whenever I would use a bulletin to highlight a student's efforts. It took so long to do the rah-rah talk and then fill out all of the pertinent information that I found I wasn't giving out very many of them. Now, I give a student a bulletin and ask him to fill in his name and the date. I then ask him to write a brief note to his parents, on the back of the bulletin, describing why the bulletin was given. Later on, when he comes to see me to get my signature, I can verbally share my pleasure as I sign my name. Doing it this way gets more Student Bulletins into the hands of more students.

Let's use one of these bulletins to communicate with Calvin and his parents.

STUDENT BULLETIN

Name *Calvin Hobbes*   Date *3-11*

BEHAVIOR

- ❑ Demonstrated leadership
- ❑ Set good example
- ❑ Strived to improve
- ❑ Sometimes forgot self-control
- ❑ Placed on restriction
     for one day

- ☒ Note on back of bulletin
- ☒ If checked here,
     please sign & return.

WORK HABITS

- ❑ Worked independently
- ❑ Showing improvement in
     work skills and study habits
- ☒ Needed some guidance to
     complete class assignments
- ❑ Needed constant guidance to
     complete class assignments
- ❑ Easily distracted
- ❑ Distracted others

EFFORT

- ❑ Excellent effort
- ❑ Very good effort
- ❑ Good effort
- ❑ Is improving
- ☒ Needs to improve

Conference requested
- ❑ by teacher
- ❑ by parent

Teacher signature *Mr. Morris* Parent signature _____

FIG. 9-29
This bulletin, available in both English and Spanish, makes a handy communication tool for sharing your concerns with the folks.

While I'm at it, I'll write a brief note on the back. Written thoughts imply both determination and conviction.

Dear Mr. and Mrs. Hobbes,

Calvin has four spelling assignments that should have been completed this week in class.

–Unit 6, pages 1 and 2
–Practice words 5x each
–Spelling definitions

He needs to complete these at home and return them to class tomorrow.

Thanks for your help,
Mr. Morris

FIG. 9-30
This type of specific communication usually produces good results.

The Advantage of Documentation: Since the Log sheet—Fig. 9-27—is always handy, it's very easy to figure out which assignments have been taken home by Calvin but have not yet been completed and returned.

A simple entry in the Miscellaneous column will serve as a sufficient reminder.

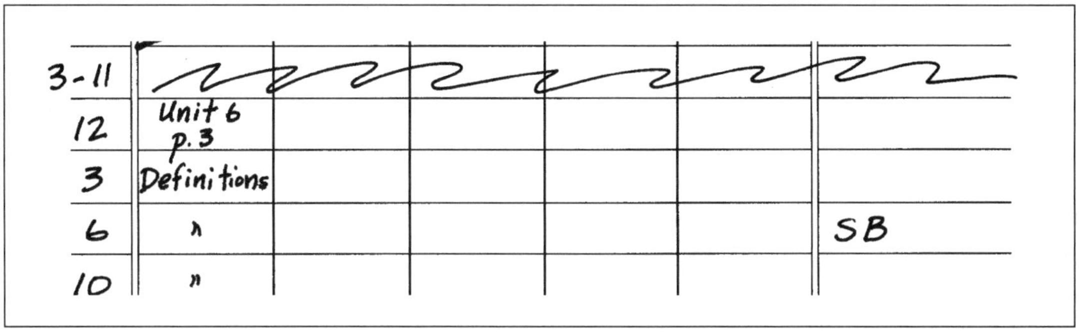

Fig. 9-31
The Miscellaneous column is a handy place for notes and comments.

Wednesday Afternoon Revisited

As I continue to meet with students at the end of each day, I sometimes see some anxiety on their part. This would be especially true for students who are once again at the FAK meeting. This is now the second time this week they've had to put an unfinished spelling assignment in the box and take it home.

MR. MORRIS
Meeting at the back table with the First Aid kids:
Okay, here are your spelling assignments. Help yourself to a red pen and figure out which comments should be circled.

We then hear some sad little sobbing noises.

MR. MORRIS
Beth, what's wrong?

Beth begins to sob louder now that she has my attention.

MR. MORRIS
Beth, why don't you stay here and we'll talk.
Addressing the others:
Everyone else okay? You all know what to do?

FIRST AID KIDS
Yes, Mr. Morris. We'll finish our spelling and bring it back tomorrow.

MR. MORRIS
I'm so glad to hear that.
Watching them all leave and laying a hand gently on Calvin's arm:
Calvin? It's time to get serious, son.

CALVIN
I know, Mr. Morris. I'll finish everything tonight.

MR. MORRIS

Thanks, buddy.

Waiting for Calvin to leave so that I can talk privately with Beth:

Now, what's the problem? Why are you so sad?

BETH

My mom (sob) said that if I take another paper home from the First Aid Kit (snuffle, gag) that (sob) I won't get to play (starting to cry) with my Barbies (voice rising to a wail) for a week.

MR. MORRIS

Hey, Beth, don't cry. It's all right. Settle down.

To Beth, this sounds like a reprieve is in the works and so she really lays it on.

BETH

Oh, but I really love my Barbies.

MR. MORRIS

I bet you do. But you know something, Beth? I don't remember you being this upset about your Barbies during spelling. In fact, I seem to recall that you were having a pretty good time during spelling. Now isn't the time to worry about your Barbies or having to take your spelling home or any of those things. The time to worry about all of that is during spelling.

Reprieve snatched away; she's back to crying:

Hang on, you'll be okay. You just need to take this assignment home and complete it tonight. And if your Barbies are gone for a week, they'll be back again. Maybe your Barbies will help you to be a better student. Who knows?

The next day in class, as I was wrapping up the spelling lesson, I used Beth's love for her Barbies to help energize her work skills.

MR. MORRIS

Remember to have page 4 of your spelling unit in by lunch.

I then held up the spelling Check Off Sheet for added emphasis.

Oh, and don't forget to mark off your Barbie, I mean, your number.

You should have seen her head snap around.

Better yet, you should have seen how much better she became at getting her spelling assignments turned in on time. And that's all I'm really looking for and the reason I use the First Aid Kit.

Thursday Morning and Beyond

This morning, when I make my rounds, I'll want to meet with Calvin at the table where we have our FAK meetings. He'll either have a number of activities to give me or nothing at all. Either way, we're going to want a minute or two of privacy. If he has his spelling assignments finished and returned, he'll get a sincere thanks and a congratulatory handshake. And if, as it sometimes turns out, he still doesn't have them finished, I'll calmly repeat my expectations.[†]

Here are a couple of things I try to keep in mind whenever I'm dealing with my Calvins:

1. **Change is sometimes slow to appear.**

    Calvin didn't develop his poor work skills and study habits overnight. Therefore, I shouldn't expect an overnight change. Nonetheless, an intervention that is consistently applied will often lead to improvement.

2. **Education is a process.**

    Although I would like each day to be as successful as possible, I've got to keep a year-long perspective in mind. This long-term vision helps me to recognize Calvin's progress when he does begin to improve. Sometimes, the progress he makes is so small, it's almost invisible. I need to continually remind myself that, as much as I'd like to see Calvin leaping tall buildings in a single bound, his first steps are probably going to be small ones. So, here's my challenge: celebrate the little changes. By doing that, I'll be laying the foundation for the bigger ones.

A Month From Now

I mentioned earlier that the First Aid Kit is actually designed to handle unfinished assignments in all of the subjects you teach. In this lesson, we were only collecting spelling assignments because it's really best to start in a manageable way. However, as you continue to use your FAK and refine your technique, you'll soon be ready to add another subject to your First Aid Kit Log. It shouldn't take you more than a week or two.

To add a new subject to the one you started with, merely write the title of the subject at the top of the next column. Then, as you meet with the First Aid Kit students, all you have to do is record the assignment in the proper column.

The example on the next page (Fig. 9-32) shows what a First Aid Kit Log might look like after a month or so. As you can see, this teacher is processing spelling, social studies, and math. The different columns help to keep the Log organized and the teacher focused. At

---

[†] As I mentioned in Lesson 7: Check Off List, one way to maintain my cool is to picture Calvin's parents sitting with us at the FAK table. This visual helps me converse with him in a manner that is professional and dignified. Instead of resorting to sarcasm or intimidation, I'll remain calm and stay focused on the issue. I'll want to be able to repeat what I said to Calvin, word-for-word and tone-for-tone, when I get together with his parents for a conference regarding his need to improve his work skills and study habits.

the same time, the experience that was gained during the first month eventually made the recording process a simple one.

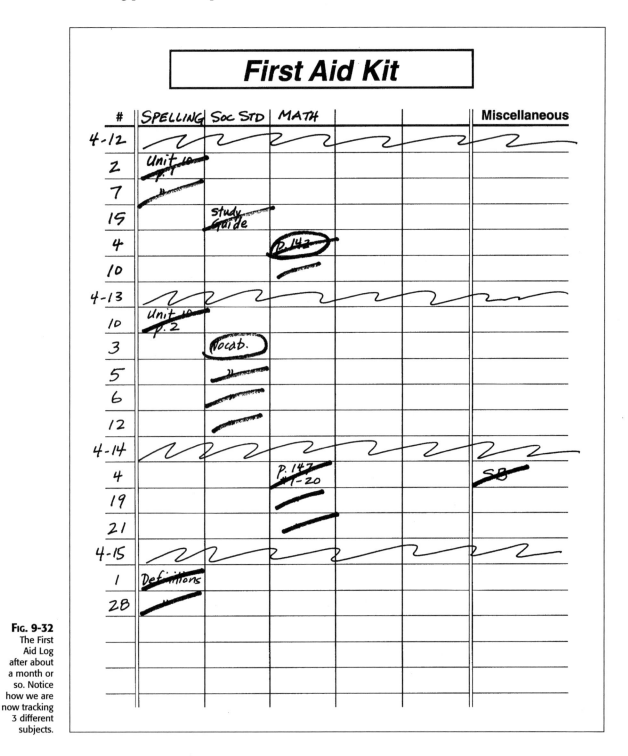

As with most things in life, you more you do something, the easier it gets. Before you know it, you'll be a First Aid Kit pro.

Secondary Teachers

Due to the nature of your situation, you should probably make some simple modifications of the basic First Aid Kit procedure. Here are a few suggestions.

Forget the Kit

You don't really need a box or plastic drawer to make it work. Just use colored folders, one for each period. Label each folder "Late Log" and use these colored folders to process the unfinished assignments for each class. (Check out the folders in the next lesson on grade keeping. They work great.)

Use a Different Blackline Master

The blackline master for the elementary teachers has multiple columns for handling the various types of activities done during the course of the day. For the most part, your class assignments will be more focused and, thus, you won't need to deal with such a wide range. I think you'll find that the Late Log, a blackline I designed specifically for you guys, will do a better job of keeping track of things than the standard First Aid Kit blackline.

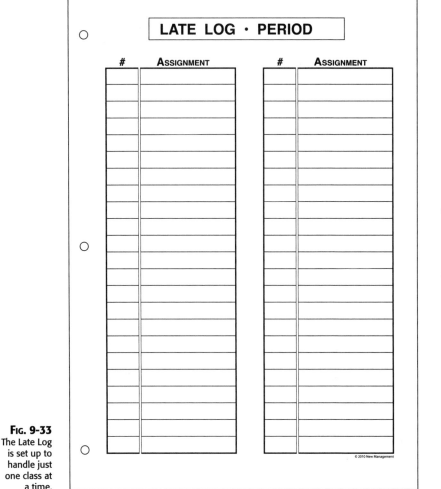

Print five copies, 3-hole punch them, and then insert the sheets into a two-pocket portfolio. (Check pages 10-10 and 10-11 for folder suggestions.)

Place a copy of the Late Log master in the back pocket of your portfolio for future xeroxing.

Place a copy of your class roster, complete with student numbers, in the front pocket of your Late Log portfolio as a reference tool.

FIG. 9-33
The Late Log is set up to handle just one class at a time.

Put a Student in Charge†

To make your life easier, I suggest that you find a student or two to handle your Late Log. As soon as you become aware of an unfinished assignment, turn it over to your helper for processing. Once it's been recorded, it can be returned to the student for completion.

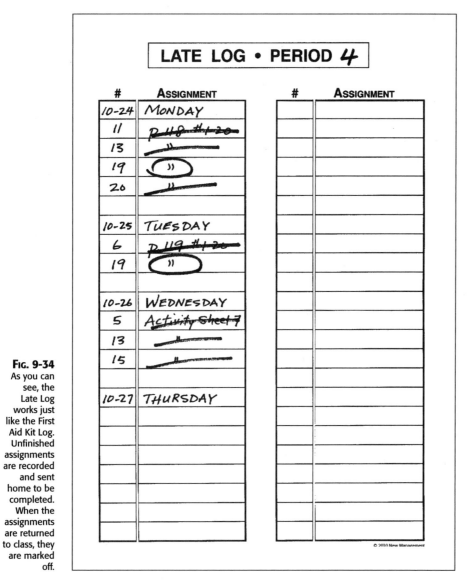

FIG. 9-34
As you can see, the Late Log works just like the First Aid Kit Log. Unfinished assignments are recorded and sent home to be completed. When the assignments are returned to class, they are marked off.

Additional Suggestions:

1. Encourage students who are returning late assignments to bring them up for processing so that you don't need to ask for them.

2. Instead of using one of the Unfinished Assignment stamps described in this lesson, a self-inking stamp (PAST DUE) from Staples or Office Depot might do the trick.

---

† Don't automatically think of using your overachievers. Think about giving Calvin a shot. It might help him to get a grip on his own assignment tardiness.

Other than those few changes, secondary people, I think the First Aid Kit will work for you as well as it works for those of us who teach at the elementary level.

Speaking of Which...

Here's a replay of what I have heard from more than one teacher:

TEACHER (USUALLY WITH LESS THAN FIVE YEARS OF EXPERIENCE)

I set up the First Aid Kit and introduced it to my students. They seemed to be okay with the idea.

On the first day, which was Monday, several students placed their unfinished math assignments in the box. (Wow, was that a nice change from the emotional back-and-forth it used to be!) Just before the end of the day, I recorded the info in the Log and then called the students to join me.

I returned their assignments and had them tell me that they would return the work to class the next day. (I didn't use the stamp because I wanted to see how they could do without it.) The students then returned to their seats and school ended soon after.

During the morning on Tuesday, I took my First Aid Kit folder and went to see the students who had taken home an assignment yesterday. Although I didn't get back all of them, most of them were returned and I felt good about that.

Later in the day, students deposited unfinished math assignments in the box. (I did it the way you recommended: I started with just one subject. That really helped me to keep things manageable.) Once again, before the class was dismissed for the day, I recorded the info in my Log, called back the students, returned their unfinished work, and received a verbal pledge that they would complete the assignment at home and return it the next day.

On Wednesday, I went around and gathered the now-finished work. I even got two of the assignments that had gone home on Monday. Wow!

At the end of math on Wednesday, several students put their unfinished work in the box. There wasn't as much unfinished work as there had been on Monday but enough to make me realize that having a system to deal with it was going to make everyone's life a lot easier.

But here's where I goofed. Wednesday is a minimum day, and my students go home at what is normally their lunchtime. It's always a bit of a frenzy getting them prepared to go home. Anyway, in the mad rush, I dismissed them all only to realize a while later that I had forgotten to meet with the students to give them back their unfinished math assignments. Dang! Now what do I do?

RICK

Having been there before:

> *Hey. It's okay. These things happen to the best of teachers.*
>
> *In fact, with just about any new technique that you're using for the first time, you're naturally going to run into highs and lows. You didn't really expect to be perfect the first time out of the gates, did you? (Well, yeah, you did. You're an overachiever for goodness sakes. That's one of the reasons you bought this book. Of course you expect perfection.)*
>
> *As I've stated elsewhere in this book: although it's important to have high expectations, it's essential that you maintain realistic ones. Forgive yourself when things don't go the way I've described them. It's all a part of the learning process.*
>
> *On Thursday, I would have met with the students who had placed an assignment in the box but didn't get it back. I'd apologize for not giving back their work. (I think it's healthy for students to hear their teacher apologize for mistakes.) I'd finish the dialogue by saying that I'd see them at the end of the day and take care of everything then. I'd keep it short and simple. "My bad. See you later. Love you guys."*
>
> *With a bit of time, though, I think you'll find yourself developing the habit of dealing with the unfinished assignments at the end of each day.*

Reality: Probably the toughest part of any new technique is "staying the course" until the technique becomes second nature. After that, it's a piece of cake.

Final Thought

If your FAK experience turns out to be like mine, you'll find yourself having to record twelve assignments on the first day you use it. For the most part, these will be the students who don't yet realize that you're serious. By the third day, though, you'll only have to deal with six assignments. And by the end of the week it will be down to four students who need to put an assignment in your First Aid Kit.

Since these are the students who are going to need your dedicated intervention and support anyway, you'll appreciate having a simple technique that will help you help them. Your consistency and firmness will really pay benefits in the long run. And, if these target students do end up needing additional out-of-the-classroom assistance, the Log you've been maintaining will really help to support your case.

Bear in mind: The First Aid Kit is not a guaranteed solution to every student's difficulties with completing work on time. However, it should take care of 95% of the problems you'll face, which makes it a very powerful technique indeed.

Lesson 10

Before We Begin

How It All Got Started

Numbering Your Students

Using Student Numbers

Timers & Sound Makers

Class Chart

Check Off List

Check Off Sheet

First Aid Kit

Grade Books

There is more than one path
that leads to success.

—Rick Morris

Grade Books

◆ ◆

Goals for this lesson:

☑ Learn how easy it is to record grades when you're using student numbers.

☑ Learn how to set up your first New Management grade book.

☑ Discover the ins-and-outs of computer grading programs.

◆ ◆

*T*his last lesson on grade keeping is going to be a rather short one. That's because keeping track of grades, when you're using students numbers, is just so easy. Toss in the number-crunching power of grading software—more on this later—and you'll find that the whole thing has become quite manageable.

Or at least it's a heck of a lot better than what I was up against my first five years of teaching.

Grade Keeping 101

Back in the day, my grade-keeping technique was rather crude. I started off on the wrong foot by using what I had been given at the school. It was a denim-covered, three-ring binder that was filled with about a dozen or so blank grade sheets. Since I was expected to use a separate sheet for each of the different subjects being taught, I had to write the names of my students—in alphabetical order by last name—on each sheet. Once that was done, I was good to go.

Step 1: Collect the papers.
I used a couple of different methods, but most of them were some kind of synchronous, pass-them-down-to-the-end-of-the-row, Old School kind of affair. (Little did I realize that some of my students quickly figured out that if you didn't put your paper in the stack going by, Mr. Morris wouldn't know right away. This actually created more problems than the misery of grade keeping produced; but, that was back in my pre-number days.)

Step 2: Do something with the collected assignments.

I'd stick them in my grade book. Granted, there was a good chance that there would be other assignments already in the grade book that I had collected previously and had yet to record. Nevertheless, this is where I kept them. It didn't matter if they were science papers or spelling assignments or math activity sheets or book reports. Everything was placed inside my little grade book which, all too quickly, began to look like a phone book.

Step 3: Correct the assignments.

Although recording grades is infinitely easier with student numbers, you are still faced with the herculean task of correcting the assignments before you can enter the grades. Unfortunately, there aren't many shortcuts, but you can rest assured that your diligence at grading assignments will pay off as the year progresses.

Step 4: Record the scores or grades.[†]

Here's where the wheels came off. I'd open my grade book to the proper page and record the name of the assignment at the top of the column. I'd then pick up the first assignment in the stack next to me, read the grade, and try to find the student's name on the grade sheet. I say "try" because the stack of assignments did not match the order of names on the grade sheet. It was my own little "Where's Waldo?" game.

MR. MORRIS
Feeling good that he's evaluated all of the book reports as he got himself ready to record the grades:

---*Okay, who's first? Brian. Brian got a B. Way to go, Brian. Let's see...*
Scanning down my grade sheet:
---*Brian...Brian...Brian......ah, there he is.*
Entering a B for Brian and grabbing the next book report from the stack:
---*Sarah. Sarah got a B. Alright, Sarah.*
Looking for Sarah's name:
---*Sarah...Sarah...............Come on, baby. Where are you? Oh, there you are.*

As I entered a B for Sarah, I thought: Well, that's two of them.

Twenty-nine more entries and I can get back to my life.

The mind-numbing tedium of locating students so that I could enter a grade eventually led to a reduction in the number of assignments I actually corrected and recorded.

---

†   For the remainder of this lesson—with the exception of the pages devoted to computer grading programs—I'm going to use the generic word "grades" whenever I'm referring to grade book entries. Basically, a score would be the number of points earned. The points are then converted to a percentage. The percentage, based upon the standard established for the subject, is then converted to a grade. So, whether you actually record the score or the percentage or the grade, I'm going to call them grades. You can translate as necessary.

The whole thing was such a painfully slow procedure that I got to the point where I just didn't record as many grades as I should have. I felt I was doing enough by just assigning the activities. A ridiculous position to take, I know, but that's how I ended up looking at it.

Consequently, I noticed that, over time, students did not seem to be putting the same effort into their assignments that they had at the beginning of the year. Since they weren't getting back very many of their papers with grades on them, they started to give up. They were probably thinking: *I'm going to put as much effort into my assignments as Mr. Morris does in correcting them.* To be honest, it's tough to fault their reasoning.

Once again, I found myself wondering if there wasn't an easier way to do things.

The New Management Grade Book

In the sixth year of my teaching career, when I switched to using student numbers, I was able to make a huge improvement in how I recorded grades.

For the first time, I actually had a stack of assignments that matched the order of students in my grade sheet.

What a night-and-day difference. And it was so easy. Here's the recipe so that you can cook up your own batch of grade-keeping goodness.

Ingredients:
    1 stack of assignments that are in numerical order
    1 grade sheet that is based upon numerical order

MR. MORRIS
    Feeling good that he's evaluated all of the book reports as he got himself ready to record the grades:
      ---*Okay, here we go. #1…A*
    Recording an A for Amanda, student number 1:
      ---*#2…B*
    Recording a B for Andrew, student number 2:
      ---*#3…B.*

Zoom City.

I can enter a grade as quickly as I can pick up an assignment.[†]

[†] *Reality:* During two-day seminars, when we have the time to actually do some hands-on activities, I've given teachers sets of corrected papers to record. One teacher is given the mixed-up stack of assignments and an alphabetical order grade sheet. The other teacher is given a collated set of papers and a numerical order grade sheet. On your marks, get set, go! In almost every case, the teacher using the Old School method has entered eight or nine grades as the teacher using the system based upon student numbers is calling out "Done!"

Grade Sheets

You'll find two main grade sheets in the appendix. One is your basic sheet for recording ten separate assignments. Using the blackline master designed for 36 students as a sample, we see this:

	1										1
	2										2
	3										3
	4										4
	5										5
	6										6
	7										7
	8										8
	9										9
	10										10
	11										11
	12										12
	13										13
	14										14
	15										15
	16										16
	17										17
	18										18
	19										19
	20										20
	21										21
	22										22
	23										23
	24										24
	25										25
	26										26
	27										27
	28										28
	29										29
	30										30
	31										31
	32										32
	33										33
	34										34
	35										35
	36										36

© 2007 New Management

FIG. 10-1
This is the standard grade sheet for a class of 36 students.

The other grade sheet is more of a daily log entry form. There are four sections of five columns. The blackline master for 20 students looks like this:

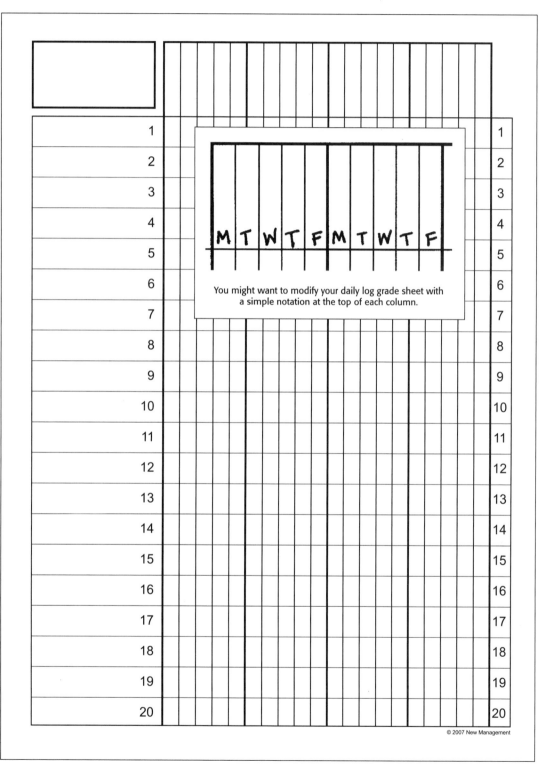

You might want to modify your daily log grade sheet with a simple notation at the top of each column.

© 2007 New Management

FIG. 10-2
This grade sheet for a class of 20 students can be used to keep track of daily activities.

Attention lefties: Did you notice that the student numbers are also written on the right-hand side of the page? A left-handed teacher told me that this would be convenient for the southpaws.

Preparing Grade Sheets

Like we've done with the other blackline masters, we're going to make a copy and then customize it before we make a bunch of copies.

1. **Make a xerox copy of the grade sheet found in the appendix.**

2. **Add the names of your students.**

    The first name is fine. If you have students with the same first name, just add the initial of their last names.

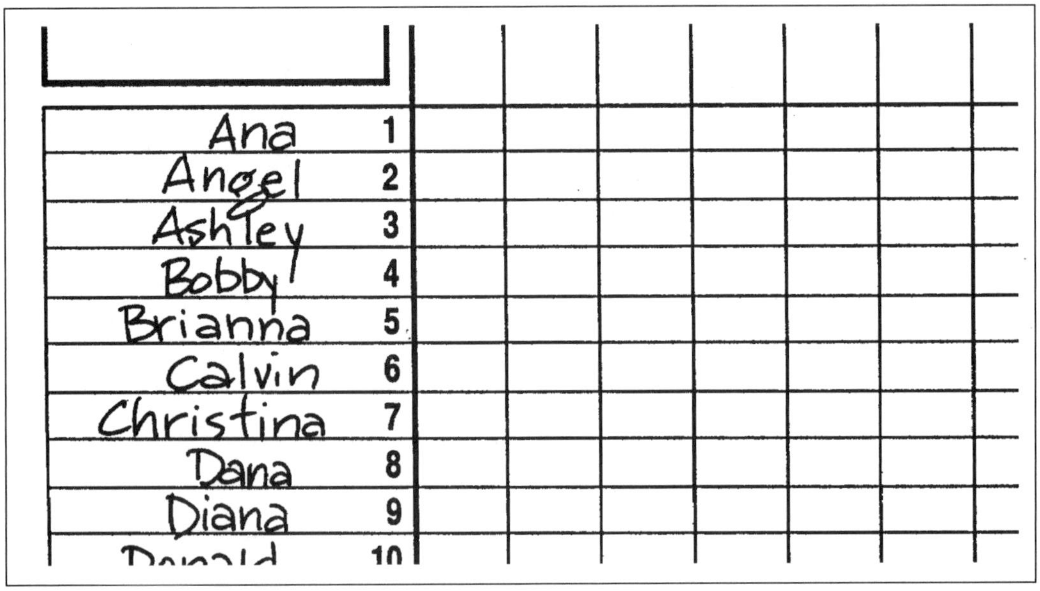

FIG. 10-3
Pencil in the names of your students before you make a bunch of copies.

Name	#							
Ana	1							
Angel	2							
Ashley	3							
Bobby	4							
Brianna	5							
Calvin	6							
Christina	7							
Dana	8							
Diana	9							
Donald	10							

3. **Mark your new blackline master.**

    When you are happy with the customized copy you've made, cut off a bit of the top right corner. (See page 7-7 for a reminder about why we do this.)

4. **Xerox a bunch of copies from your customized blackline.**

    Regular white paper is what you want to use.

5. **3-hole punch the sheets.**

    Since these grade sheets will be used in a portfolio—see next page—you'll need to use a 3-hole punch on them.

6. **Put away your blackline master.**

    Place a copy of your customized blackline master in your "NM Masters" file folder you created back in Lesson 7. You might want to put a second copy in the back pocket of your new grade keeping folio. This will make it easily accessible whenever you need to reproduce a few more.

Deciding on Grade Books

The portfolios that we used in conjunction with the Check Off Sheet are the ones I use for all of my grade keeping.

Although it may seem a bit overwhelming to use more than one grade book, there are a number of advantages that make it better than my original, one-book-holds-all-grades mini-binder thing.

1. **They come in different colors.**

   I've designated a color for each of the subjects I teach. The colors, of course, enable me to quickly grab the folder I need from a stack of them. I don't need to try to locate a title box or read a label; the color of the folder says it all.

Red	Literature
Orange	Daily Oral Language
Yellow	Science/Health
Green	Spelling
Blue	Math
Violet	Social Studies
White	Citizenship
Black	Homework
Brown	Written Language

Secondary Teachers	
Red	Period 1
Orange	Period 2
Yellow	Period 3
Green	Period 4
Blue	Period 5
Violet	Period 6

FIG. 10-4
If this image were in color, you'd get a glimpse of the power and simplicity of color-coding.

2. They enable me to compartmentalize assignments.

As we saw with the folders in Lesson 8: Check Off Sheet, the individual grade books will keep assignments organized and in one convenient place. I never have social studies activity packets getting tossed in with math papers. Spelling vocabulary sheets don't get mixed up with last week's reading comprehension assignments. Each type of assignment goes into its own colored folder.

Bonus: Whenever a student brings me an assignment after I've already collected most of them, it's easy to pop it into the correct folder with the others. Without the folder to help keep the papers together, I might be tempted to toss the late-arriving paper into a growing pile of other loose assignments. Knowing me, there would be a real good chance that these "orphans" would end up in the trash after a week or so. The folder provides a simple procedure for dealing with the first issue—late papers—while avoiding the second—an unmanageable stack of random assignments.

3. They hold extra papers or blackline masters.

The folders I buy—2 pocket folders with fasteners, details shown on next page—have a pocket in the front and back. These spots are a great place to keep lesson sheets, blackline masters, or any number of items that could be kept in the folder for easy access.

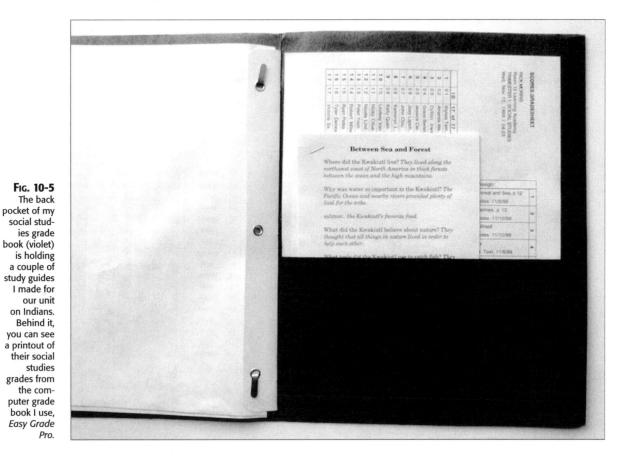

Fig. 10-5
The back pocket of my social studies grade book (violet) is holding a couple of study guides I made for our unit on Indians. Behind it, you can see a printout of their social studies grades from the computer grade book I use, *Easy Grade Pro.*

4. **They are handy for holding assignments until I want to return them to the students.**

> I've gotten into the habit of placing assignments in the back of the folder after I've evaluated and recorded them. This makes it that much easier to return them to the students the next day.
>
> *Important factor:* I feel that it's beneficial for my students to receive their last assignment before they begin the new one. Mistakes they may have made can be corrected on the new assignment.
>
> *Reality:* Speaking from experience, I know that I always wanted to get back my papers, projects, and reports as quickly as possible when I was in grad school. I always looked forward to going to class when I knew that the professor would be handing back our last assignment. It's just human nature to want to know what someone else thought of your hard work and effort.

FIG. 10-6
The five colors in this pack were: red, yellow, green, blue, and violet.

Here's the label from the last set of folders I bought. I think the cost was under two bucks.

You can find these types of folders at Staples and Office Depot.

Bargain shoppers: Target almost always has these on sale at the end of August. I got a bunch of them a couple of years ago for just ten cents each.

Notice how they call the fasteners that hold the papers "Tangs." Weird.

5. They make it easier to evaluate papers.

This may be just my take on it, but I've found that, in a psychological sense, seeing a stack of grade books with assignments in them waiting to be corrected makes the task ahead seem more manageable. Due to the individuality of the grade books, I can take on the grade-keeping task one folder at a time.

If, for example, I had ten minutes before heading off to an after-school staff meeting, I'd be more likely to grab one of my grade books and begin checking papers than if I had to reach into a towering stack of loose papers. The color of the folder alone would tip me off as to how time consuming the activity inside is going to be for me to evaluate and record. With only ten minutes, I might pick up the green Spelling folder or the orange Daily Oral Language folder. Both of the assignments in these gradebooks are relatively easy to correct. As I zip through one set of papers, I might be inclined to squeeze in one more set before leaving for the staff lounge.

Advantage: How nice that the grade book that was holding the assignments is at hand when I go to enter the grades. All in all, it makes for one convenient package.

It's Your Call

As usual, you don't have to use these folders. You could use a normal 3-ring binder and have separate sections for each subject. You'd lose out on the ability to compartmentalize, etc., but, hey, the choice is, and always will be, yours.

Preparing Your Grade Books

For the purposes of this lesson, I'm going to assume that you have wisely decided to use two-pocket folders as grade books. Way to go. I'm proud of you.†

The rest is simple.

1. Grab one of your colored folders and decide which subject this one is going to handle.

2. Insert four or five copies of your customized grade sheet into your new grade book.

3. Pop a blackline master of the grade sheet in the back pocket.

4. Decide what grades you are going to keep for this subject.

---

†   If you're just not sure if this is right for you, maybe you should try an experiment. Try a folder with just one of the subjects–or classes–you teach. I'd be willing to bet that you'll quickly convince yourself it's a good way to go.

Which Grades to Keep

When it comes to entering grades, I recommend you don't do what I did my first five years of teaching. In a nutshell, I would start recording grades in the first column of my grade sheet and then go across filling in the spaces until the entire sheet was full. I'd then grab a new sheet and start in the first column.

This seemed like a logical thing to do, but there was a flaw to this procedure. The flaw was that, at report card time, it was tough to get a handle on how my students had actually done. The string of grades I had recorded represented different types of activities within one particular subject. The challenge was to pick out the critical grades so that each student was given a fair evaluation.

Flipping through two or three sheets trying to synthesize the information I had so painstakingly recorded turned out to be no easy task. I was eventually given some suggestions from other teachers. The main one had to do with highlighting the more important columns of grades so that they stood out from the others. Alright, I thought, I can do that; but, come on, isn't there an easier way?

There is and it's so simple you're going to slap yourself in the forehead and ask yourself why you didn't think of it. Or maybe you've already figured it out and I'm the last one to arrive at the party. Either way, here goes.

A Better Way to Record Grades

Let's use math as our demonstration subject.

1. **Get a copy of your report card.**

2. **Look at the section that deals with math.**

3. **Determine which components make up the math grade.**
   A typical examination at a typical school might show that the subcategories for math are:

   Problem solving
   Computation
   Group activities
   Homework

4. **Label four different grade sheets with the four titles above.**

5. **Record math grades on the appropriate grade sheet.**
   If, for example, you had just evaluated an activity sheet that reviewed two-place subtraction, you would record the grade on the Computation grade

sheet. Actually, any type of computation assignment would be recorded on this sheet. It really doesn't matter whether the assignment dealt with addition, subtraction, multiplication, division, fractions, decimals, percentages, or whatever. Computation is computation, and that's what the report card is reporting.

There are a couple of advantages to using separate grade sheets for different types of activities.

Advantage One

It will enable you to more fairly evaluate your students. For example, the A's that Calvin earned from his math homework assignments—the ones his older sister is doing for him at home—won't overwhelm the C's he's getting on his in-class quizzes and tests. The separate sheets will clue you in to this odd disparity.

Advantage Two

You'll be able to quickly spot weak points. If I'm keeping grades for math problem solving on its own sheet, the low grades or small dots—a symbol I use to indicate an unfinished assignment—that Calvin received for these assignments will really stand out. They'll be sitting side-by-side on the Problem Solving grade sheet.

FIG. 10-7
Calvin's dismal record for our math problem solving activities fairly cries out for help.

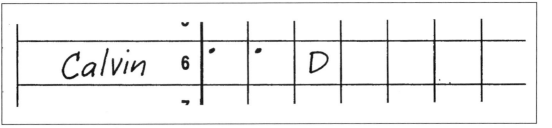

If I were still using my old method in which one grade followed the next regardless of category, the low grades and dots would only appear every four or five grades. It would be more difficult to spot the pattern and, thus, more difficult to remediate.

FIG. 10-8
In this example, the grades for Calvin's problem solving activities seem to hide among the other math grades.

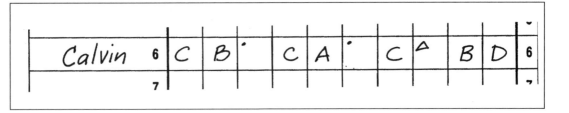

Comparing these two samples leads me to believe that grouping grades on separate grade sheets (Fig. 10-7) is preferable to the Old School method (Fig. 10-8.)

Entering Grades

So far, so good. We've made customized grade sheets, have 3-hole punched them, and inserted them into colored folders. The colors have been assigned to different subjects, and the grade sheets have been dedicated to different categories within the subject. We now need to decide what to enter: grades or scores.

As it turns out, the answer is: It depends.

For the most part, I like to record grades.[†] It's much easier at report card time to quickly evaluate progress by looking at a row of grades as opposed to a row of scores. Since the grades provide a more visual form of the evaluation information, I'm able to process them at a quicker pace.

Raw scores, though, require that I perform a series of calculations. The four steps are:

1. Add up the student's scores.
2. Add up the possible scores.
3. Divide the student's total by the total possible to find the percentage.
4. Translate the percentage into a grade.

Here's the difference in picture form.

FIG. 10-9
I don't know about you, but I find grades easier to digest than scores.

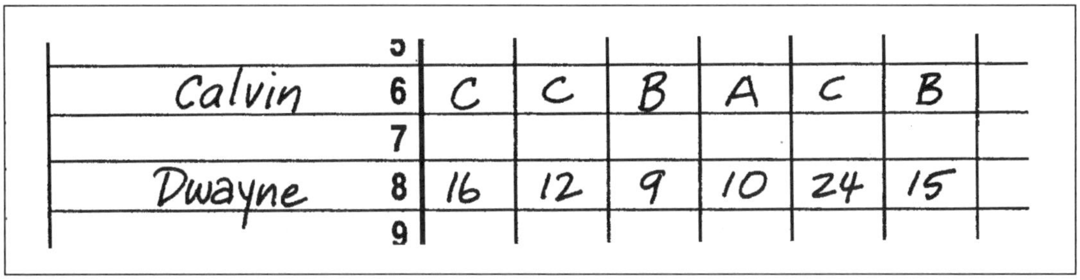

	5						
Calvin	6	C	C	B	A	C	B
	7						
Dwayne	8	16	12	9	10	24	15
	9						

Although we can quickly calculate that Calvin is pulling a B/B-, Dwayne's overall grade is not as readily apparent. To make my life easier, and to spare me from an extreme amount of work at report card time, I've learned to translate scores into grades as I enter the results of each assignment.

An attractive alternative, as shown on the next page, is to enlist the students' support.

---

†   Actually, I don't. I use a terrific grade-keeping program called Easy Grade Pro that does it for me. (See page 10-20.) All I need to do is feed it raw scores and the program does the rest. I can then print a copy of the results and place it in the front pocket of my grade book.

I've tried a bunch of grade-keeping programs and have found Easy Grade Pro to be the best. It's extremely easy to operate and offers a lot of flexibility, especially when it comes to adding notes or comments to progress reports. It's available for both the Mac and the PC. You can even download a demo copy from their website. Check it out; I think you'll be happy with their product. Orbis Software: www.easygradepro.com.

How to Have Your Students Calculate Grades

Here's how my students calculate their own grades based upon the score I've given them.

1. I start by writing their scores on their papers as a fraction. (They then know to do this whenever they've corrected their own assignments.)

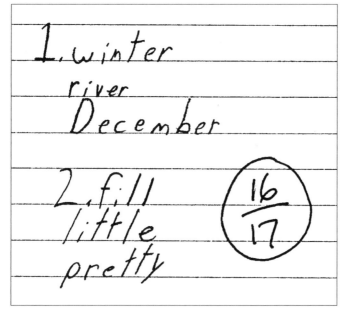

FIG. 10-10
On this spelling assignment, of which you can only see a portion, the student had a score of 16 points out of a possible 17.

2. Using calculators, the students change the fraction into a decimal. (Believe it or not, they love doing this. Whenever I pass back a corrected assignment, they all grab their calculators. And these are third graders, mind you.)

FIG. 10-11
I usually post this calculator formula on a bulletin board.

The formula is:

student score	divided by	possible score	times 100	equals

3. After determining the percentage, they use our grading chart and translate the percentage into a grade. (This part usually requires a bit of rounding which adds another element to the math that's being reinforced.)

FIG. 10-12
Here's our grading chart for most assignments.

D 50 to 69	C 70 to 79	B 80 to 89	A 90 to 100

4. The final equation is written on the assignment and then brought back to me. It only takes a second to record the grade which enables the student to post his assignment on the Wall of Fame. (See next page.)

Here's the finished equation for the score in Figure 10-10:

FIG. 10-13
Using the fractional score, this student calculated the percentage and the letter grade.

$$\frac{16}{17} = 94\% = A$$

Extension Idea:

26
Tools & Toys

If the percentage on a student's paper is 80 or higher, the student is allowed to add it to our **WALL OF FAME** bulletin board. A part of the board is devoted to a number line that shows percentages from 80 to 100. The students figure out where their paper belongs and then staple it in the proper location on the board. To keep it fresh, all of the posted work is removed every two to three weeks.

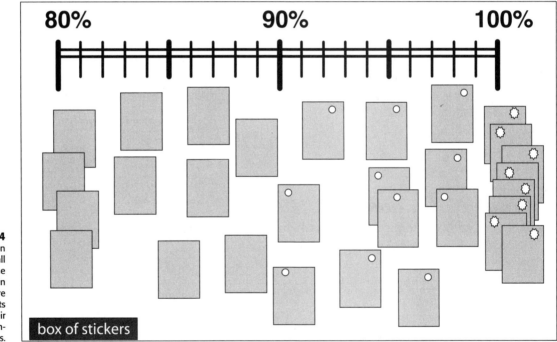

FIG. 10-14
A portion of our Wall of Fame bulletin board where students post their own assignments.

Added Bonus:

power
love
fun
freedom
safety

If the percentage was 90 to 99, the student gets a sticker from our sticker box and puts it on the assignment before stapling it up. The sticker box sits on the shelf near the Wall of Fame.

Perfect Papers:

power
love
fun
freedom
safety

If the student had a perfect paper, he would come to me for a sticker. I have a box of special ones I save for the 100% papers.

End Result:

I end up with grades in my book. My students learn how to use calculators and also validate their own achievement. It's a great thing to hear one of my underachievers exclaim, "Man, if I had gotten *one more point,* I would have had a B!" That kind of self-motivating awareness will eventually lead to increased achievement.

Speaking of motivation, allow me to make a point about letter grades versus number grades.

> *General rule:* The report cards we use at my school use number grades for the academic part of the assessment. The numbers range from 1 to 6. A 1 is equal to an A and a 5 is equal to an F. A 6 means that the subject was not evaluated during the reporting period. Numbers are okay but they lack the impact that letter grades provide. Letter grades have been a part of our culture for a hundred years; and the subconscious assimilation of their importance that has occurred over that period of time is not something that can be lightly dismissed. Therefore, I use letter grades for our daily work because of their motivational value but support our school plan by using number grades when it's time to fill out report cards.

Right now, I'd like to show you a couple of things about how I actually record grades in my grade books. After that, I'm going to present a few ideas that might help to make the entire grade-keeping process a bit easier. And then, we're going to draw this book to a close.

Whew.

Grade Notations

In addition to the basic grades I enter for each student, there are a few other marks that I use in my grade books.

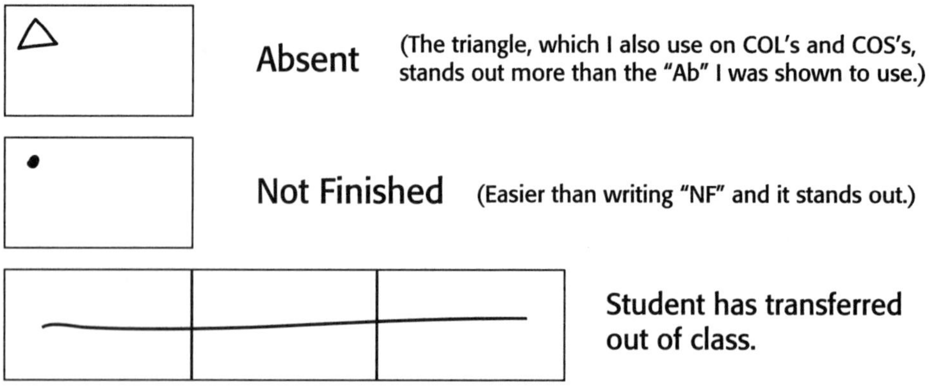

FIG. 10-15
Here are a few of the symbols I've developed to record what's going on.

Absent   (The triangle, which I also use on COL's and COS's, stands out more than the "Ab" I was shown to use.)

Not Finished   (Easier than writing "NF" and it stands out.)

Student has transferred out of class.

On the next page, you can see these symbols being used to tell different stories.

Absent
Whether or not the student is asked to complete the assignment is up to me. It mainly depends upon the assignment *and* the student's skill level.

MATH ACTIVITY SHEETS		#1 9-8	#2 9-15	#3 9-22
Amanda	1	A	B	A
Andrew	2	△	B	B
Ashley	3	C	•	C
Brad	4	A	B	B
Brandon	5	A	A	A
Calvin	6	•C	C	B
Colleen	7	B	A	A
Danielle	8	B	A	A
Eric	9	B	•	•
Evan	10	A	—	—
Fabian	11	C	ᴰB	B
Felix	12	B	B	B
Heather	13	ᴰ	C	C
Jesus	14	A	A	△

Not finished
The little dot is easy to make and stands out. I put it in the corner so that there is room to record a grade when the assignment has been completed.

Not finished
Now finished
Assignment was completed and handed in at a later date. Credit was given although the grade was lowered from a B to a C.

Not finished
Not finished
Looks like it's time to talk to someone. I usually talk with the student several times before flagging in the folks.

Transferred out
I'll draw a line through the boxes until a new student arrives and is given Evan's old student number, 10.

FIG. 10-16
This is a portion of the grade sheet I'm using to record grades for the math activity sheets. And, no, I don't have 14 students.

I do the same thing with D's and F's that I do with the "not finished" dot: I write it in the corner. The student is then encouraged to redo the assignment to not only improve his grade but master the skill.

Grading Programs

As I mentioned in the footnote at the bottom of page 10-15, I use Easy Grade Pro to make grade-keeping even easier. There are a couple of reasons why I use it over the other programs I've tried.

Student ID

Easy Grade Pro has a column that allows you to enter an ID number. (The sample below shows student numbers in the ID number column.) The beauty of the ID column is that it's sortable. This one simple feature makes the program very student-number friendly.

Before entering scores, I sort them by their ID numbers. Since the students are now in the same order as the stack of assignments,[†] grade entry is a snap. After I'm done, I like to resort them by overall grade and print out a copy. I'll then know which students deserve some appreciation and which ones need to hear a bit of concern.

Here are a couple of screenshots showing numerical order (left) and last name order.

FIG. 10-17
I love the fact that I can sort my students by their student numbers or by their last names.

	ID	20 of 20 Students	Overall
1	01	Matt Guerra	80 B-
2	02	Aliyah Ouro-Akondo	78 C+
3	03	Alric Thompson	95 A
4	04	Briann Curran	87 B+
5	05	Brittany Mendiola	93 A-
6	06	Cassandra Pollock	79 C+
7	07	Jack Kimbril	82 B-
8	08	Karena Josefosky	70 C-
9	09	Katie Gogo	99 A
10	10	Keir Havel	84 B
11	11	Kevin Del Angel	97 A
12	12	Lauren Seymour	92 A-
13	13	Marwa Elgazzar	100 A+
14	14	Michael Garner	92 A-
15	15	Nui Grube	89 B+
16	16	Peter Valdez	67 C-
17	17	Samantha Booker	93 A-
18	18	Shane Clites	86 B
19	19	Sta'phon Smith	91 A-
20	20	Waleed Areiquat	92 A-
21	ADD STUDENT +		

	ID	20 of 20 Students	Overall
1	20	Waleed Areiquat	92 A-
2	17	Samantha Booker	93 A-
3	18	Shane Clites	86 B
4	04	Briann Curran	87 B+
5	11	Kevin Del Angel	97 A
6	13	Marwa Elgazzar	100 A+
7	14	Michael Garner	92 A-
8	09	Katie Gogo	99 A
9	15	Nui Grube	89 B+
10	01	Matt Guerra	80 B-
11	10	Keir Havel	84 B
12	08	Karena Josefosky	70 C-
13	07	Jack Kimbril	82 B-
14	05	Brittany Mendiola	93 A-
15	02	Aliyah Ouro-Akondo	78 C+
16	06	Cassandra Pollock	79 C+
17	12	Lauren Seymour	92 A-
18	19	Sta'phon Smith	91 A-
19	03	Alric Thompson	95 A
20	16	Peter Valdez	67 C-
21	ADD STUDENT +		

† Working your way through a stack of assignments as you enter grades is one way to do it. Another way is to use a Check Off List with the scores written next to the student numbers. (See the top of page 10-22 for an explanation.)

You Can Customize Progress Reports

Several of the grade-keeping programs I tried didn't allow for a lot of flexibility when it came to progress reports. I remember one that automatically included the phrase, "If your records differ from what is shown, please see me."

Well, most elementary school students don't keep records. Couple that with the fact that the language seemed a bit stilted and you could end up feeling somewhat reluctant to hand out reports to your students. I've always felt that one of the true advantages of most grade-keeping programs is the ability to do just that. However, unless you get to say what you want to say, the advantage is lost.

Here's a copy of a progress report I sent home one day regarding homework assignments.

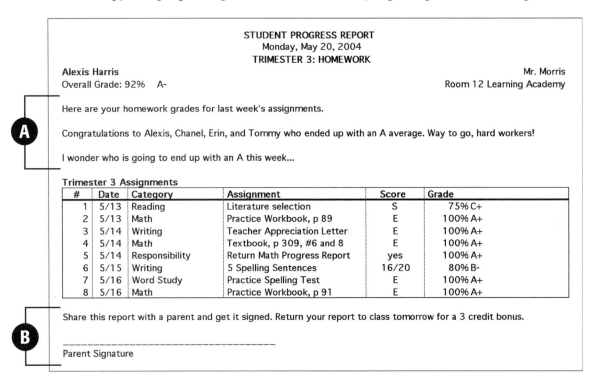

STUDENT PROGRESS REPORT
Monday, May 20, 2004
TRIMESTER 3: HOMEWORK

Alexis Harris   Mr. Morris
Overall Grade: 92%   A-   Room 12 Learning Academy

A

Here are your homework grades for last week's assignments.

Congratulations to Alexis, Chanel, Erin, and Tommy who ended up with an A average. Way to go, hard workers!

I wonder who is going to end up with an A this week...

Trimester 3 Assignments

#	Date	Category	Assignment	Score	Grade
1	5/13	Reading	Literature selection	S	75% C+
2	5/13	Math	Practice Workbook, p 89	E	100% A+
3	5/14	Writing	Teacher Appreciation Letter	E	100% A+
4	5/14	Math	Textbook, p 309, #6 and 8	E	100% A+
5	5/14	Responsibility	Return Math Progress Report	yes	100% A+
6	5/15	Writing	5 Spelling Sentences	16/20	80% B-
7	5/16	Word Study	Practice Spelling Test	E	100% A+
8	5/16	Math	Practice Workbook, p 91	E	100% A+

B

Share this report with a parent and get it signed. Return your report to class tomorrow for a 3 credit bonus.

_____

Parent Signature

The comments in sections A and B are ones I made. The program contains a settings page so that you can type whatever you want. That's something you'll come to appreciate.

FIG. 10-18
Customizing the reports with my own comments is easy for me to do and motivating for them to see.

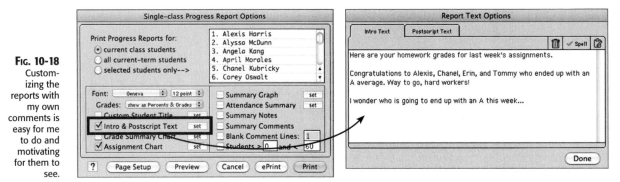

Easy Grade Pro Grade Entry Tip

Having the assignments in numerical order really helps to speed up grade entry. The only drawback is when you're missing an assignment. Unless you take the time to check each name as you enter the score, you're going to end up at the bottom of the class list without a score to give to the last student. That's because the missing assignment will have thrown off your input at some point in the entry process. What a bummer.

Tip: Write the scores on a Check Off List before entering the scores into the program.

Granted, it's an extra step; but, you'll fly down the list since you're not having to work your way through a stack of assignments. Also, the missing score will stand out on the Check Off List alerting you to skip that student when you get to him.

Tip for the Tip: Have a student transfer the scores from a set of corrected assignments to the Check Off List for you. It's going to require that you find someone you can trust but will definitely be worth the effort of doing so.

On-Line Grading

Most districts have made the switch to on-line grade entry. It's by far the most convenient way for parents to stay apprised of their children's progress. As a parent, you just enter your email address, type in your password, and Bingo! You can see all of the assignments and the corresponding grades for your child. What could be easier?

Unfortunately, it's not quite so easy for the teacher because most on-line grade programs are slaves to alphabetical order by last name. I've yet to find one that will allow you to enter a student's number along with his name information. And as much as I understand what a monumental programming task that would be to incorporate this feature, it sure would be nice if one of the companies stepped up and did it. They'd have my heartfelt appreciation, I can tell you that.

So, what are the options?

Emotional Response
You could cry about it. You could complain to someone. You could even gnash your teeth and tear your garments if you're so inclined. None of these, of course, will resolve the issue.

Rational Response
You could accept the fact that life presents problems and not everything is going to go your way. Above all, you know not to stress out about stuff you can't control.

Practical Response
Solve it. On the next page I've presented two suggestions to get you thinking about possible solutions to the pain-in-the-butt clunkiness of on-line grading.

Suggestion 1: Create a Fake Assignment

If this works you're golden. The problem's solved and life is one big mocha frappuccino.

*Create a non-graded assignment and
enter their student numbers as their scores.*

Although these "scores" won't appear anywhere but on your computer screen, you'd be able to use this assignment to sort your students by their numbers. After entering scores for an actual assignment, you can then post them the way you normally would.

Suggestion 2: Create a New Record Sheet

This one is going to seem like more work but, with just a bit of practice, I think you'd find yourself saving a lot of time.

The sample below shows a modification of the basic score sheet that can be found in the appendix. The student numbers in the right-hand score sheet represent the order of your students when they are alphabetized by last name. By transferring the scores from the left sheet to the right sheet, you'd end up with a set of scores that could be quickly keyed into your on-line grading program.

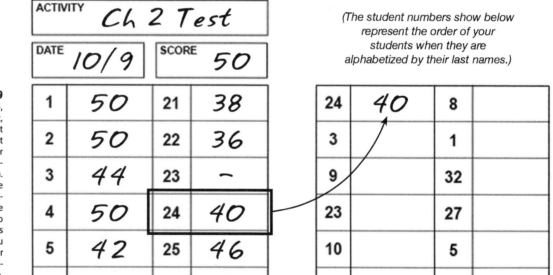

FIG. 10-19
Student 24, Rico Alvarez, is the first student listed in your on-line grading program. You'd use the right-hand score sheet to enter scores when you open your on-line grading program.

Again, it may seem like more work. Before you make that assumption, though, you should give it a try. You just might be surprised at how much it speeds up the process.

Suggestion: Similar to what I suggested about a student transferring scores from an assignment you corrected to a Check Off List, you could do the same thing with the double-entry score sheet. You could do the left side and a student could do the right.

Your Turn: If you come up with a slick solution, email me. I'll pass it along.

On Beyond Zebra

Here are a couple of other ideas that you can use to help with the grade-keeping work load.

Use a Mini-Grade Sheet (Appendix, Blackline Masters)

Mini-Grade Sheets are ideal for temporarily recording grades until you can enter them in the actual grade book. Anytime I find myself without my grade book at hand, I just snatch up a Mini-Grade Sheet, label it appropriately, and record the grades. I can then toss it into my Red Basket where it will wait until I am able to place it in the proper grade book.

I use these little grade sheets so often that I've learned to wait until I have four or five of them before I enter the grades. After I've accumulated a number of them for one grade sheet, I just lay them out, side-by-side, and record grades in bunches.

Another way to go is to have students record grades for you. All you have to do is hand a student a stack of corrected papers and a Mini-Grade Sheet. Without too much training they'll know to fill in the assignment and date labels and then record the grades next to the student numbers. It's just another one of these New Management no-brainers and a real relationship builder.

Stick Tally

Stick tallies are an easy way to show the amount of effort students are expending for different activities.

Tools & Toys

For instance, my students like to do the **BONUS BOX.** It's a one-problem, extra-credit math activity that reinforces basic skills while boosting accuracy and quality of work. My underachievers love it because it's so manageable.

After the students have submitted their answers—which are written on small pieces of note paper—I check them, pass out a coupon to the ones who got it correct, and then give the answer sheets to a student helper.

The helper then goes through the papers and records the results on a grade sheet. Correct answers receive a point; incorrect answers receive a minus.

Note: A minus mark—which means that the student did not answer the question correctly—is better than no mark at all. No mark means that the student did not even attempt to solve the problem. At least the student who received the minus was making an effort, and that's something to be acknowledged.

power
love
fun
freedom
safety

On the next page you can see the results of five Bonus Box math questions.

MATH BONUS BOX		9-18	9-19	9-20	9-21	9-22
Ana	1	+	+	+	−	+
Angel	2		−			
Ashley	3					
Bobby	4	+	+	+	+	+
Brianna	5	+	+	−	−	−
Calvin	6	−				
Christina	7	+		+		
Dana	8					
Diana	9	+		+	+	−
Donald	10		+			
Elise	11	+		+	+	
Jancarlo	12					
Jeff	13			−	−	−
John	14					
Kelly	15	+	+			+
Kira	16	+	−	−	−	−
Kyle	17				−	
Letticia	18		+	+		
Liliana	19	+	+	−	+	+
Lindsey	20		+			+
Nestor	21					
Nicole	22	+	+	+	+	+
Paul	23	+	+	+	+	+
Rene	24	+	+	+		+
Ryan	25	+	−	−		−
Sean	26		+			
Shandelle	27	−	−		+	
Steven	28	+	+	−	−	−
Tony	29	+	+	+	+	+
	30					

FIG. 10-20
This tally sheet, maintained by a student, provides me with the ability to counsel students about the effort they are putting forth.

I can use information in this form to motivate my students. Here's how I would do it:

1. **Meet with the students who have been doing a great job.**

MR. MORRIS

Picking a time when the students are working independently on math:

I'd like to see the following students outside, please: Ana, Bobby, Liliana, Nicole, Paul, Rene, and Tony.

I'd walk outside and wait for the students I had just called to join me.

Showing them the Bonus Box tally sheet:

You guys have done a fabulous job of answering the Bonus Box questions. Each of you has either four or five points this week. Way to go. Keep up the hard work. Tell your parents tonight what smart kids you all are.

2. **Meet with the students who had been doing a good job.**

I'd like to see the following students outside, please: Brianna, Diana, Elise, Kelly, Kira, Ryan, and Steven.

Once again, I'd walk outside and wait for the students I had just called to join me. I've got a smile on my face in case some of them are a bit nervous about being called outside.

Showing them the Bonus Box tally sheet:

You guys have really been trying hard on the Bonus Box questions. Each of you has tried to answer at least three of the questions this week. Even though you haven't answered them all correctly, I'm proud of the fact that you don't quit. Keep up the good work. And if you need any help with the next question, come see me. I'd love to help.

3. **Meet with the students who are making almost no effort.**

I'd like to see one more group of students outside. Ashley, Dana, Jancarlo, John, and Nestor, would you kindly join me for a moment?

Showing them the Bonus Box tally sheet:

I realize that Bonus Box is extra credit, but surely you can do one of them during the week. I can't imagine your day is so busy that you can't squeeze in one math question.

Pausing to make sure I have their undivided attention:

If you're not sure how to solve the question, come see me. I like helping you guys. It's why I come to school each and every day. So, what do you say we stop hiding from the Bonus Box and go after some of those questions?

Waiting for the sad faces to lighten up a bit:

All I'm asking you to do is give it a try. If you need help, please ask.

As you can see, grade books are more than just collections of records to be passed along in one evaluation form or another. They can be used to encourage students to make an effort, to try just a bit harder, to see education as something that is important and vital and in need of their dedicated attention.

Even something as simple as a tally sheet—as we saw with the Bonus Box record sheet—can be used to get students to be the best they can be. Imagine what you'll be able to do when you employ all of the New Management strategies to support your students.

Other Grade Books

There are a number of office products on the market that can be integrated into your student number system. The ones to look for are the ones that have been built around a monthly calendar. Since some months of the year have thirty-one days, you'll find tabbed folders, dividers, and other record-keeping devices that go from 1 to 31.

The one shown below is being used in a fifth grade classroom to record comments and observations after individual teacher/student conferences. The tabs down the right side make it easy to locate students while the convenience of having all of the reading conference records in one spot will help to keep the teacher focused and aware of what's going on.

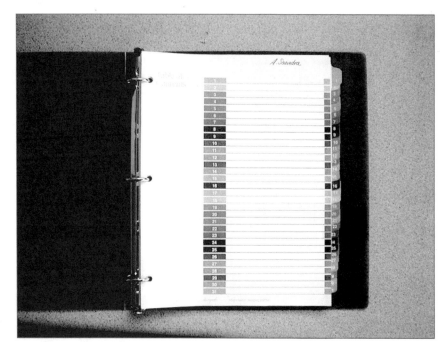

FIG. 10-21 This folder with numbered tabs is a handy tool for recording individual information about your students. It's made by Avery.

Bonus: How nice to be able to pull out the Reading Conference binder when one of the parents drops in to find out how things are going. The fact that you'll look so organized will add credibility to the comments you make regarding the progress of that parent's child.

The Clip Case

As the name implies, it's a combination of a clipboard and storage case. Like the binder on the previous page, this incredibly handy item can be found at Staples. They cost about eight bucks and are worth every penny.

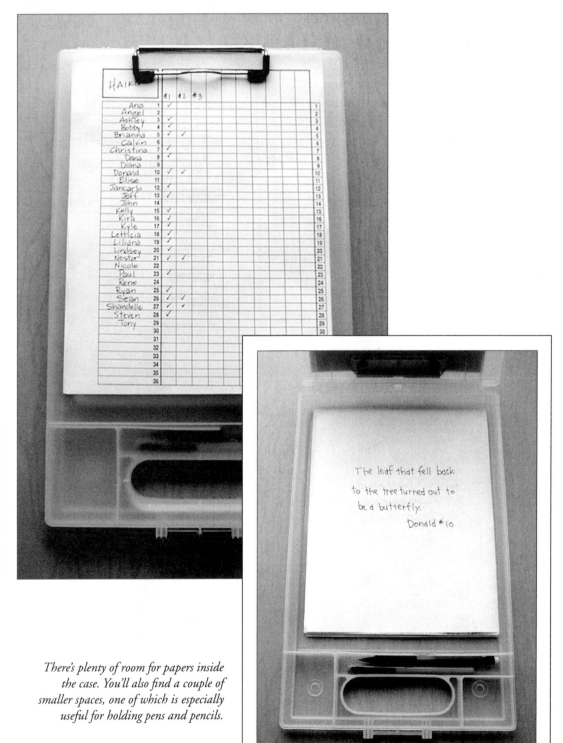

FIG. 10-22
The Clip Case combines a clipboard and storage case in one package. To access the inside compartment, you just lift up the hinged lid.

There's plenty of room for papers inside the case. You'll also find a couple of smaller spaces, one of which is especially useful for holding pens and pencils.

How to Use One

The Clip Case is ideally suited for taking care of a specific task or activity. To illustrate its effectiveness, I'll describe how I use mine to keep track of one of our writing activities.

Haiku in the Fall

Every year I teach a month-long lesson on writing haikus. Fall seems like an opportune time due to the seasonal awareness students develop at that time of the year.

In the Case

Before the first lesson, I check out a couple of small books of haiku and toss them inside the Clip Case. It's a reassuring thought to know that they'll be at hand when I'm ready to begin the lesson.

As students complete their first haikus and bring them to me, it's an easy matter to open the case and toss them inside. Later on, as I sit down to read them over, I know that I won't be inadvertently overlooking one because it was misplaced. Every single one of them will be safely inside the case until I'm ready to open it.

On the Clip

After reading the haikus and writing comments or evaluations, I place them on the clip. This will remind me to return them at the beginning of the next day's lesson. I think the students are motivated to write when they are given back their first efforts in a timely manner.

Under the haikus on the clip I keep a grade sheet. The grade sheet will enable me to monitor each student's progress. Although a grade sheet is normally thought of as an academic record, I like to use the first three or four columns as Check Off Lists. By having this information at my fingertips, I'll know who needs a bit of intervention and who deserves a well-earned pat on the back.

One Slick Package.

One of the greatest things about the Clip Case is that it's just so easy to use. With all of the hectic things going on in class, it's refreshing to know that all I have to do to get started with the day's haiku lesson is pick up the Clip Case. Everything I'm going to need is waiting for me. It's either inside the case or on the clip.

Suggestion: Since you're already at Staples, buy an extra Clip Case and give it to one of your teaching buddies. You'll hear about it for the next six months. Not only that, but I'm guessing that your buddy will come up with a few variations for using the Clip Case that you'll then be able to incorporate in your own classroom. Can we say, Win-Win?

Finis

Circa January, 2000
Here's what I wrote at the conclusion of the first edition of this book.

Well, that's it. I'm done.

Other than the appendix—which contains blackline masters, a collection of frequently asked questions, a class glossary, and a catalog of New Management products—that's a wrap.

A labor of love that started over ten years ago is finally at an end. In one way, I'm elated. In another way, I'm a bit sad. It always seems as if there is so much more that needs to be said.

To be quite honest, though, I don't think this book is actually finished. I don't know if it ever will be.

For one thing, teachers who have read it will take the ideas they've learned and move off in new directions. They will apply New Management techniques to new situations and new needs and end up creating their own wonderful system for running the classroom and involving students.

For another, I'm sure I'll come back to the book in a couple of years and write an updated, second version. I just hope it doesn't take another decade to complete like this one did. My wife, who has so patiently put up with my writing fugues, would never forgive me.

Circa January, 2007
Here are the closing comments to the second edition:

Upon further review...

> *I'm sure I'll come back to the book in a couple of years*
> *and write an updated, second version. I just hope it*
> *doesn't take another decade to complete like this one did.*

Well, yes and no.

Yes, I did come back to the book but it was seven years instead of "a couple of years."

No, it didn't take ten years to complete. More like three months.

But, holy cow, it still seems as if there is so much more to share. I guess I'll just have to include those extra thoughts in the next edition.

Circa June, 2010
And here it is. I hope you enjoyed reading this book as much as I enjoyed writing it. And I wish you nothing but the best as you attempt to recreate the techniques and strategies contained in this third—*and final*—edition of the New Management Handbook.

Appendix

Blackline Masters

Frequently Asked Questions

Class Glossary

Modified Sets of Blacklines

If you are teaching in a classroom that has a population that doesn't fit the 20-student model or the 36-student model, you can get a modified set of blackline masters that will be easier for you and your students to use.

I currently have sets of blackline masters for the following class sizes:

16, 18, 20, 24, 27, 30, 36, and 40

To obtain a set of masters for your particular group, visit my website and download them.

www.NewManagement.com
(click on the download files link)

Other Languages

If you would like a copy of something in a language other than English, just email me about it. I might already have it on file. If not, maybe you could provide me with the translation. I'd then be able to create a new form and email it back to you. Just let me know what you need.

UNIVERSITY SEMESTER CREDIT OPTION

One, two, or three semester units
of post-baccalaureate professional development credit.
(Except in CT, NJ, OH, PA and WI.*)

Additional $62 per credit fee required.

Follow-up practicum projects require 15 hours per credit.
Acceptable where local school districts approve and applicable
to state licensure where such activities are approved.

For additional information,
call Dr. Allan Lifson at (800) 762-0121
or visit www.TeacherFriendly.com

* CT, NJ, OH, PA and WI teachers, call 800-479-1995.

Blackline Masters

Large Class Set (36 students maximum)
Check Off List
Check Off Sheet (days of the week)
Check Off Sheet (generic)
Grade Sheet (individual assignments)
Grade Sheet (daily entries)
Mini-Grade Sheet

Small Class Set (20 students maximum)
Check Off List
Check Off Sheet (days of the week)
Check Off Sheet (generic)
Grade Sheet (individual assignments)
Grade Sheet (daily entries)
Mini-Grade Sheet

Student Bulletin (English and Spanish)

First Aid Kit Log

Late Log

Permission to reproduce
the blackline masters
contained in this appendix
for individual classroom use
is hereby granted by the author.

Rick Morris

ASSIGNMENT	ASSIGNMENT
DATE DUE	DATE DUE

1	19		1	19
2	20		2	20
3	21		3	21
4	22		4	22
5	23		5	23
6	24		6	24
7	25		7	25
8	26		8	26
9	27		9	27
10	28		10	28
11	29		11	29
12	30		12	30
13	31		13	31
14	32		14	32
15	33		15	33
16	34		16	34
17	35		17	35
18	36		18	36

finished (#) not finished [#] excused /#\ absent

finished (#) not finished [#] excused /#\ absent

ASSIGNMENT:

MONDAY _____   **DUE BY** _____

1	2	3	4	5	6	7	8	9	10	11	12
13	14	15	16	17	18	19	20	21	22	23	24
25	26	27	28	29	30	31	32	33	34	35	36

ASSIGNMENT:

TUESDAY _____   **DUE BY** _____

1	2	3	4	5	6	7	8	9	10	11	12
13	14	15	16	17	18	19	20	21	22	23	24
25	26	27	28	29	30	31	32	33	34	35	36

ASSIGNMENT:

WEDNESDAY _____   **DUE BY** _____

1	2	3	4	5	6	7	8	9	10	11	12
13	14	15	16	17	18	19	20	21	22	23	24
25	26	27	28	29	30	31	32	33	34	35	36

ASSIGNMENT:

THURSDAY _____   **DUE BY** _____

1	2	3	4	5	6	7	8	9	10	11	12
13	14	15	16	17	18	19	20	21	22	23	24
25	26	27	28	29	30	31	32	33	34	35	36

ASSIGNMENT:

FRIDAY _____   **DUE BY** _____

1	2	3	4	5	6	7	8	9	10	11	12
13	14	15	16	17	18	19	20	21	22	23	24
25	26	27	28	29	30	31	32	33	34	35	36

ASSIGNMENT:

Mon	Tue	Wed	Thur	Fri		DUE BY	
1	2	3	4	5	6	7	8	9	10	11	12
13	14	15	16	17	18	19	20	21	22	23	24
25	26	27	28	29	30	31	32	33	34	35	36

ASSIGNMENT:

Mon	Tue	Wed	Thur	Fri		DUE BY	
1	2	3	4	5	6	7	8	9	10	11	12
13	14	15	16	17	18	19	20	21	22	23	24
25	26	27	28	29	30	31	32	33	34	35	36

ASSIGNMENT:

Mon	Tue	Wed	Thur	Fri		DUE BY	
1	2	3	4	5	6	7	8	9	10	11	12
13	14	15	16	17	18	19	20	21	22	23	24
25	26	27	28	29	30	31	32	33	34	35	36

ASSIGNMENT:

Mon	Tue	Wed	Thur	Fri		DUE BY	
1	2	3	4	5	6	7	8	9	10	11	12
13	14	15	16	17	18	19	20	21	22	23	24
25	26	27	28	29	30	31	32	33	34	35	36

ASSIGNMENT:

Mon	Tue	Wed	Thur	Fri		DUE BY	
1	2	3	4	5	6	7	8	9	10	11	12
13	14	15	16	17	18	19	20	21	22	23	24
25	26	27	28	29	30	31	32	33	34	35	36

1											1
2											2
3											3
4											4
5											5
6											6
7											7
8											8
9											9
10											10
11											11
12											12
13											13
14											14
15											15
16											16
17											17
18											18
19											19
20											20
21											21
22											22
23											23
24											24
25											25
26											26
27											27
28											28
29											29
30											30
31											31
32											32
33											33
34											34
35											35
36											36

1																										1
2																										2
3																										3
4																										4
5																										5
6																										6
7																										7
8																										8
9																										9
10																										10
11																										11
12																										12
13																										13
14																										14
15																										15
16																										16
17																										17
18																										18
19																										19
20																										20
21																										21
22																										22
23																										23
24																										24
25																										25
26																										26
27																										27
28																										28
29																										29
30																										30
31																										31
32																										32
33																										33
34																										34
35																										35
36																										36

ACTIVITY

DATE	POSSIBLE SCORE	
1	19	
2	20	
3	21	
4	22	
5	23	
6	24	
7	25	
8	26	
9	27	
10	28	
11	29	
12	30	
13	31	
14	32	
15	33	
16	34	
17	35	
18	36	

ACTIVITY

DATE	POSSIBLE SCORE	
1	19	
2	20	
3	21	
4	22	
5	23	
6	24	
7	25	
8	26	
9	27	
10	28	
11	29	
12	30	
13	31	
14	32	
15	33	
16	34	
17	35	
18	36	

ACTIVITY

DATE	POSSIBLE SCORE	
1	19	
2	20	
3	21	
4	22	
5	23	
6	24	
7	25	
8	26	
9	27	
10	28	
11	29	
12	30	
13	31	
14	32	
15	33	
16	34	
17	35	
18	36	

ASSIGNMENT

DATE DUE

1
2
3
4
5
6
7
8
9
10

11
12
13
14
15
16
17
18
19
20

✎ finished ⊛ not finished △ absent

☐ excused

ASSIGNMENT

DATE DUE

1
2
3
4
5
6
7
8
9
10

11
12
13
14
15
16
17
18
19
20

✎ finished ⊛ not finished △ absent

☐ excused

ASSIGNMENT

DATE DUE

1
2
3
4
5
6
7
8
9
10

11
12
13
14
15
16
17
18
19
20

✎ finished ⊛ not finished △ absent

☐ excused

ASSIGNMENT:

MONDAY _____   **DUE BY** _____

1	2	3	4	5	6	7	8	9	10
11	12	13	14	15	16	17	18	19	20

ASSIGNMENT:

TUESDAY _____   **DUE BY** _____

1	2	3	4	5	6	7	8	9	10
11	12	13	14	15	16	17	18	19	20

ASSIGNMENT:

WEDNESDAY _____   **DUE BY** _____

1	2	3	4	5	6	7	8	9	10
11	12	13	14	15	16	17	18	19	20

ASSIGNMENT:

THURSDAY _____   **DUE BY** _____

1	2	3	4	5	6	7	8	9	10
11	12	13	14	15	16	17	18	19	20

ASSIGNMENT:

FRIDAY _____   **DUE BY** _____

1	2	3	4	5	6	7	8	9	10
11	12	13	14	15	16	17	18	19	20

ASSIGNMENT:

Mon	Tue	Wed	Thur	Fri	_____	DUE BY	_____
1	2	3	4	5	6	7	8	9	10
11	12	13	14	15	16	17	18	19	20

ASSIGNMENT:

Mon	Tue	Wed	Thur	Fri	_____	DUE BY	_____
1	2	3	4	5	6	7	8	9	10
11	12	13	14	15	16	17	18	19	20

ASSIGNMENT:

Mon	Tue	Wed	Thur	Fri	_____	DUE BY	_____
1	2	3	4	5	6	7	8	9	10
11	12	13	14	15	16	17	18	19	20

ASSIGNMENT:

Mon	Tue	Wed	Thur	Fri	_____	DUE BY	_____
1	2	3	4	5	6	7	8	9	10
11	12	13	14	15	16	17	18	19	20

ASSIGNMENT:

Mon	Tue	Wed	Thur	Fri	_____	DUE BY	_____
1	2	3	4	5	6	7	8	9	10
11	12	13	14	15	16	17	18	19	20

1											1
2											2
3											3
4											4
5											5
6											6
7											7
8											8
9											9
10											10
11											11
12											12
13											13
14											14
15											15
16											16
17											17
18											18
19											19
20											20

1																					1
2																					2
3																					3
4																					4
5																					5
6																					6
7																					7
8																					8
9																					9
10																					10
11																					11
12																					12
13																					13
14																					14
15																					15
16																					16
17																					17
18																					18
19																					19
20																					20

ACTIVITY		
DATE		**POSSIBLE SCORE**
1		11
2		12
3		13
4		14
5		15
6		16
7		17
8		18
9		19
10		20

ACTIVITY		
DATE		**POSSIBLE SCORE**
1		11
2		12
3		13
4		14
5		15
6		16
7		17
8		18
9		19
10		20

ACTIVITY		
DATE		**POSSIBLE SCORE**
1		11
2		12
3		13
4		14
5		15
6		16
7		17
8		18
9		19
10		20

ACTIVITY		
DATE		**POSSIBLE SCORE**
1		11
2		12
3		13
4		14
5		15
6		16
7		17
8		18
9		19
10		20

STUDENT BULLETIN

Name _____   Date _____

BEHAVIOR

- ❑ Demonstrated leadership
- ❑ Set good example
- ❑ Strived to improve
- ❑ Sometimes forgot self-control
- ❑ Placed on restriction
  for one day

- ❑ If checked here,
  please sign & return.
- ❑ Note on back of bulletin.

WORK HABITS

- ❑ Worked independently
- ❑ Showing improvement in
  work skills and study habits
- ❑ Needed some guidance to
  complete class assignments
- ❑ Needed constant guidance to
  complete class assignments
- ❑ Easily distracted
- ❑ Distracted others

EFFORT

- ❑ Excellent effort
- ❑ Very good effort
- ❑ Good effort
- ❑ Is improving
- ❑ Needs to improve

Conference requested
- ❑ by teacher
- ❑ by parent

Teacher signature _____   Parent signature _____

BOLETIN ESTUDIANTIL

Nombre _____   Fecha _____

CONDUCTA

- ❑ Demostró Liderazgo
- ❑ Puso un buen ejemplo
- ❑ Se esforzó por mejorar
- ❑ A veces olvidó controlarse
- ❑ Se le puso en restricción
  por un día

- ❑ Si se marcó aquí,
  por favor firme y devuelva

HÁBITOS DE TRABAJO

- ❑ Trabajó Independientemente
- ❑ Muestra mejoría en conocimientos
  básicos y hábitos de estudio
- ❑ Necesitó guía para completar
  sus trabajos de la clase
- ❑ Necesitó guía constante para
  completar sus trabajos en clase
- ❑ Se distrae con facilidad
- ❑ Distrae a los demás

ESFUERZO

- ❑ Excelente esfuerzo
- ❑ Muy buen esfuerzo
- ❑ Buen esfuerzo
- ❑ Está mejorando
- ❑ Necesita mejorar

Solicitó entrevista
- ❑ el maestro(a)
- ❑ el padre/madre

Firma del maestro(a) _____   Firma del padre/madre _____

First Aid Kit

#						Miscellaneous

LATE LOG • PERIOD

#	Assignment

#	Assignment

Frequently Asked Questions

Lesson 1: Before We Begin

You mentioned Bill Glasser's book, The Quality School Teacher. Should I read it?

Once you've finished reading this one, have at it. It's a good book with some deep insight and well worth reading if you've got the time. You should know, though, that its primary audience is the inner-city high school teacher.

If you're looking for a great book on discipline, read Robert MacKenzie's *Setting Limits in the Classroom*. It is without a doubt the best book I've ever read on discipline. It will literally change the way you interact with your students.

Here are some other books worth reading:

> *Setting Limits in the Classroom*, Robert MacKenzie (a must-read guide for discipline)
> *Between Teacher and Child*, Haim Ginott (a classic)
> *Conscious Classroom Manageemnt*, Rick Smith
> *Right-Brained Children in a Left-Brained World*, Jeffrey Freed
> *Dream Class*, Michael Linsin (You'll find a link on my website.)
> *The Bible*

I read in this lesson that you offer New Management workshops. How can I attend one?

The best way to go is to have me come to your school or district and conduct one. For this to happen, though, you'll have to be the one to pass along the information to your administrators. We do very little promotion or marketing ourselves; it's all done by teachers who have attended workshops that I present at conferences or through university extension courses. If you'd like a brochure that you can share with your administrator, just email me—rick@newmanagement.com—and I'll send you one.

If you'd like to find out how you can attend one by yourself without involving your school or district, check out the New Management website (www.newmanagement.com) and click on the Conferences/Workshops link. You'll be shown a list of offerings, dates, and locations that are open to anyone who wishes to attend. It's not an extensive list because most of the workshops are contracted by schools and districts and are limited to just their staff members.

My current teaching position doesn't match any of the ones you described on page 1-8. It's completely different. What do I do?

Do what you can. Not every idea is going to work in every classroom. One of the beauties of teaching, though, is that you can modify new ideas to fit your needs and the needs of your students.

Here's something you might want to keep in mind: Teaching positions sometimes change over time. Ideas you may not be able to use in your current position might come in handy later on when you switch to a new one. In other words, keep this handbook in a safe spot. You just never know when you're going to find yourself facing a brand new teaching situation.

I am team-teaching with another teacher. We share students and lesson responsibilities.
Unfortunately, my partner does not want to use the student number system. What can I do?

Even though your partner is not yet ready to go with the New Management system, don't feel you need to limit yourself. Apply the ideas you've learned to your core group of students. The benefits you'll gain from using the system with just those students will be well worth the time you spend developing it.

Also, there's a really good chance that, within a month or so, your partner will begin to see the light. More than the words you could use to convince your teammate that it's a great program will be your nonverbal enthusiasm of its merits and the ease of management you'll be able to display.

Spiral-bound teacher's guides or manuals in 3-ring binders are so much easier for me to use.
How come you didn't use either of those formats?

Cost, shipping concerns, and binder quality were the main issues.

However, the redeeming value of a paperback book—such as this one—is that you can easily turn it into a spiral-bound book or one that fits in a 3-ring binder on your own.

Check out page 1-15 for suggestions on how to do this.

I teach at the secondary level. Many teachers are already using the number system. Won't the
students get confused by having different numbers for each class?

It's actually no harder for them to keep the different numbers separate than it is for them to remember the different rooms in which the classes are conducted. It's one of those it-takes-a-bit-of-time things. Also, they'll have a notebook in which to record their student number information, and you'll have a Class Chart on the wall as a reference tool.

If you've decided to go with using colors to help keep your classes organized—page 1-13—I think your students will find it even easier to stay on top of things.

Lesson 2: How It All Got Started

I'm a new teacher. What do I do when veteran teachers at my school question the wisdom of
the student number system?

For the most part, I've found that teachers are an incredibly supportive group. For anyone who does have concerns, hand him this book with the invitation to read the first few chapters. If they're really interested in discussing the advantages and disadvantages of using student numbers, they'll read the pages and then get back to you. If they're still not convinced, that's okay. Everyone is entitled to his own opinion.

If, however, they decline your offer to read the lessons you suggested, it would appear that they are more interested in passing judgement than they are in gaining insight into something that is unfamiliar to them. There's not much you're going to be able to do in this situation except make the best of it. One month with student numbers should convince you, though, that you've made the correct decision.

What do I do with the parent who just doesn't like the student number system?

Let me reassure you that, based upon my somewhat extensive experience at using student numbers, it's the rare parent who complains. Most of them love how organized the classroom is and how involved their children are.

If someone does object, schedule an appointment and listen to their concerns. Many times, that's all people need: an opportunity to share their feelings so that their input seems valuable.

During your discussion, make an effort to portray the student number system as an almost invisible part of your classroom structure. If it helps, call the numbers "desk numbers," "book numbers," "cubbie numbers," or any other designation that will emphasize the fact that student numbers were never designed to take the place of students' names.

No matter how you handle it, try to leave the impression that you appreciate their insight. Let them know that they are welcome to share their concerns whenever they wish. Your willingness to listen will sometimes speak louder than anything you end up saying during your conference.

Lesson 3: Numbering Your Students

At my school, I am required to submit report sheets to the office every two weeks. Since the report sheets are in alphabetical order by last name, should I number my students the same way so that they are already in that order?

It's always best to filter the ideas presented in this handbook through the sifter of your own school requirements. Thus, an alphabetically ordered report form that needs to be sent to the office every two weeks mitigates in favor of you taking the same approach.

There will come the time, however, when you will receive a new student. Putting the new student at the end of the list will mess up your order somewhat. Nonetheless, the majority of your list will be in the correct order. It will only be a matter of looking at the bottom of your grade sheet to find the grades for your new student when you come to his name on the report form. No sweat.

The Other Side of the Coin: Most of the recording, evaluating, and assessing is done in-house. And although you will need to export things to the office on a regular basis, the volume and extent of the reporting is not even close to the amount work you do in your own room on a daily basis. I'd concentrate on making your classroom as efficient as possible.

I teach a combination class: half of my students are third graders and half of my students are fourth graders. Should I keep the two groups separate when I number them?

If you're talking about having the third graders use numbers 1 to 18 and fourth graders using numbers 19 to 36, I wouldn't recommend it. Although it may seem like the natural thing to do, it's only going to add to the already divisive atmosphere of the combination class. Whenever possible, you want to try to break down that feeling of having two separate groups and bring them together as one class. Commingling the numbers will help you to achieve that goal.

Of course, the advantage to grouping the numbers is that it would enable you to more clearly focus on the two separate grade levels. The Check Off List example on the left shows the grouping method. The example to the right shows how an integrated system still enables the teacher to maintain a grade level specific awareness.

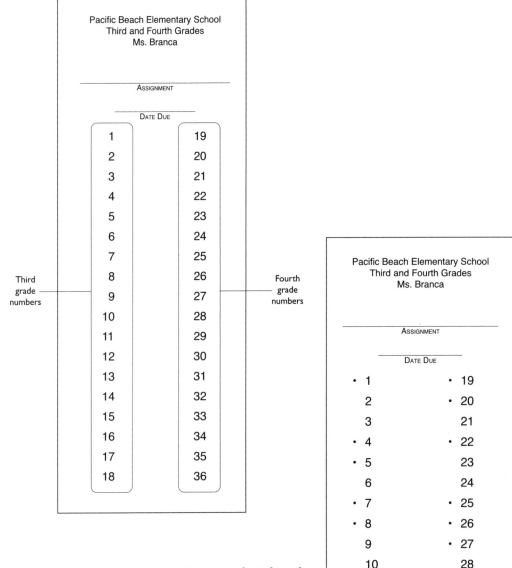

Pacific Beach Elementary School
Third and Fourth Grades
Ms. Branca

ASSIGNMENT

DATE DUE

Third grade numbers

1	19
2	20
3	21
4	22
5	23
6	24
7	25
8	26
9	27
10	28
11	29
12	30
13	31
14	32
15	33
16	34
17	35
18	36

Fourth grade numbers

Pacific Beach Elementary School
Third and Fourth Grades
Ms. Branca

ASSIGNMENT

DATE DUE

• 1	• 19
2	• 20
3	21
• 4	• 22
• 5	23
6	24
• 7	• 25
• 8	• 26
9	• 27
10	28
• 11	29
• 12	30
13	
• 14	
15	
• 16	
• 17	
18	

By putting a dot in front of the numbers being used by third graders, this teacher was able to focus on just those students when she collected an assignment that was only given to her third graders.

The numbers without a dot—fourth grade students—were not given the assignment and could be ignored.

I had my students get in an alphabetical order line according to their first names in order to receive a student number. A month later, a new student enrolled in my classroom. Should I re-alphabetize everyone and assign new numbers?

First of all, congratulations on allowing your students to become involved in the "get a number" procedure. I think it's important that we promote participation in as many ways as possible.

Second, don't even think about renumbering your students so that you can maintain alphabetical order. I realize that having students in order by their first names makes it easier to learn a student's number or locate the name in a grade book; nonetheless, it's not so important that you'd want to make it your top priority.

When a new student enrolls, you can do one of two things.

1. Reassign any number that is no longer being used. This is usually the case when a former student has transferred out of your room.

2. Add the new student to the bottom of your list.

I know this messes up that carefully crafted order you established on the day the students received their numbers, but it's just not that big of a deal. Within a week, it won't bother you at all.

Lesson 4: Using Student Numbers

I'm concerned that students at the back of the line, the ones with the higher numbers, might resent the fact that they are always at the back of the line. How do I make sure that all of the students are being treated fairly?

Your concern is a well-founded one, and I'm glad to see that you are being sensitive to the needs of your students. After all, we don't want any students to see their numbers in a negative light.

Probably the best thing you could do to ensure equal treatment would be to adjust the order of your students by the date. This means that instead of always having student number 1 at the front of the line or always asking for student number 1's assignment first, you start with the student whose number matches the date. Thus, if today was the 8th, you could start your line with student number 8. The line would then go 9 to n, n being the last student in class. Following the last student would be students 1 through 7.

Should I be concerned about calling upon students by number?

It's okay in certain situations, but I'd be careful about overdoing it. If, for example, you're looking at a Check Off List and verbally identifying the group of students who have completed the assignment, I don't see why you couldn't read a list of numbers. Not only do most students love their numbers but they also know how you feel about them. The strong relationship you've created with your students is more meaningful and important to them than the fact that you sometimes call upon them by number. Also, in their minds, their numbers are synonymous with their names.

Remember, though, that we're trying to avoid the perception that student numbers are going to replace student names. Calling upon students by number when it might be more appropriate to use names might argue against our vow to keep things name-based.

Rule of thumb: If you're identifying a large group of students, numbers are okay. If you're calling upon one student or a small group of students, use names.

Lesson 5: Timers & Sound Makers

Where do you keep all of your sound making toys?

I keep most of them on, or in, my desk. I use a student desk, one of the double-sized ones normally used by two students. On top of the desk you'll find: 1) a digital timer or two; 2) my hotel bell for passing out papers; 3) my dog squeak for getting attention; and 4) my set of Class Cards.

There are certain toys, though, that are kept on a student's desk. For example, the tone bars that we use to remind students to put "name, number, date" on their papers is held by a student. All I do is nod my head in his direction when I want the three-note tune to be played.

However, when trying to figure out where to place tools and toys, don't limit yourself to flat surfaces. You could hang a sound maker from the ceiling so that it is within reach of your raised hand. Or maybe you could get some double-sided tape and attach a small toy to the wall of your room.

Whatever you decide, the daily practice you'll receive at using your tools and toys will make their eventual location and placement a natural part of how you use them. In other words, don't allow yourself to get too frustrated when they're not immediately at your fingertips the first few weeks. You have to live with things for a while before you understand where they should be kept. Also, it takes a bit of time to develop the habit of returning them to the proper place so that they're at hand the next time you need to use them.

And if the sound maker you need is across the room, don't worry about it. Enjoy the ten-second walk.

How many different sounds can students differentiate?

Depending upon their grade level and general ability, most students can easily learn the meanings to a dozen different sounds. (Just stop and think about all of the musical slogans and jingles you've assimilated over the years. It's got to be close to one hundred. Granted, you wouldn't be able to think of that many. You would have to hear them before you were able to identify them.) All it takes is a bit of time and patience on your part.

Suggestion: Start with the basics—"Stop, look, listen" and "I need to pass out materials"—and live with those for a month before you begin to add other sounds with other messages.

What do I do when the timer beeps and <u>none</u> of my students are finished with the assignment they were given to do?

This happens every now and then, especially when you first begin to use a digital timer to keep track of how much time students have to complete an assignment. There are two ways you can go.

1. If you become aware of the fact that the time frame you established is not going to allow enough time for your students to complete the assignment and the timer hasn't beeped yet, stop the timer, get their attention, and make an announcement. Tell them that you goofed and need to add more time. By doing this before the timer beeps, you'll be reinforcing the fact that the beep means that it is time to stop working.

2. If you become aware of the situation after the timer has beeped, you should probably just tell your students that the timer is telling us that it's time to stop. Tell them that they'll be able to work on the assignment tomorrow in class.

Either way you go, it's important to be flexible. It's okay to adjust the time limits as long as you don't make a habit of it. Too much flexibility will cause your students to see every time standard as something to be ignored.

Lesson 6: Class Chart

My students all know each other's names and numbers. Do I really need a Class Chart hanging on the wall?

No. The Class Chart is just a reference tool for anyone in class who needs to know someone else's number. So, if you and your students know them all, you can forego this tool.

If, however, you plan on receiving new students during the year, or you have volunteers who work in your room, you might want to think about how helpful a Class Chart would be to these people.

I teach at the secondary level and have five different groups of students. How do I make a bulletin board-sized Class Chart for each group?

You don't. All you really need is the information available in some form.

Probably the easiest thing to do would be to dedicate a bulletin board to this task and attach class rosters that have been printed on regular paper. These 8 1/2 by 11 mini-charts will provide all of the information your students will need. Using printer paper will also make it easier for you to adjust a mini-chart whenever a new student adds or drops one of your classes. All you'll have to do is print out the newly adjusted roster and staple it over the old one.

Lesson 7: Check Off List

What do I do with a Check Off List after I've used it to collect an assignment?

Why not toss it? Although I suppose you could add it to your record keeping paper trail, I don't really think you need to hold onto it. Your grade book(s) will maintain a history of your students' work skills and study habits anyway.

Teacher idea: I was visiting a teacher's room and saw that she had stapled the used Check Off Lists around the perimeter of the room. She used the space above the bulletin boards. This collection of COL's was a graphic reminder of how many things the class had taken care of that month. It was rather striking.

What do I do when a student marks off another student's number?

This sometimes happens when you first begin using student numbers and the collection tools based upon the number system. Rest assured that it won't last very long. It has more to do with the novelty of marking off numbers than anything else.

If it does occur, try to keep things low key. You might want to make an announcement about only marking off your own number. Tell them that although it may seem like a student is being helpful by marking off someone else's number, it actually confuses things a bit.

Tell the student who told you that someone had marked off his number to just mark off the number again. Tell him not to worry; it won't continue for very long.

Lesson 8: Check Off Sheet

I drew a circle around a student's number because he wasn't finished with the assignment I was collecting. Do I go back and draw a line through the circled number when the student finally finishes the assignment and gives it to me?

I don't think this is necessary. After all, you have a record on your grade sheet—a dot in the assignment space—which indicates that the assignment was initially late.

The Check Off Sheet is primarily a collection tool that provides a quick summary of the assignments that were turned in on time. Your grade book is where you want to keep the permanent records for your students.

Notice how this grade sheet shows both "completes work on time" status and the grade each assignment earned. To go back through Check Off Sheets and update them seems like a lot of work for a little gain.

FIG. 11-1
The dot in the grade space will remind you that the student did not have the assignment finished on time.

MATH ACTIVITY SHEETS		#1 9-8	#2 9-15	#3 9-22
Amanda	1	A	B	A
Andrew	2	A	B	B
Ashley	3	C	•	C
Brad	4	A	B	B
Brandon	5	A	A	A
Calvin	6	• C	C	B

The grade sheet not only keeps track of who didn't have an assignment in on time, it also provides a reminder as to who still needs to get it done.

In the sample to the left, we can see that Calvin's taken care of his but Ashley hasn't taken care of hers.

How do I decide whether I should use a Check Off List or a Check Off Sheet?

The general rule is this:

A Check Off List is for a one-time application.

A Check Off Sheet is used for assignments or activities that you will collect on a daily basis.

When in doubt, use a Check Off List. It's quick, easy, and can be attached to what is being collected with a paper clip.

Lesson 9: First Aid Kit

Calvin has a spelling assignment in the First Aid Kit because it wasn't finished on time. Later on in the morning, he found himself with some extra time to finish assignments. Would it be okay for him to retrieve his spelling paper from the First Aid Kit to work on it?

The reflexive answer is: "Sure, why not?" Unfortunately, though, we haven't had our FAK meeting yet, which means that his assignment won't be listed on the log sheet in the First Aid folder.

As it stands right now, I've got the finished spelling assignments sitting in my spelling grade book and the unfinished ones sitting in the First Aid Kit. I've got them all. If Calvin, with whatever good intentions he's displaying, gets his spelling paper out of the FAK, it's no longer under my control. The big question then becomes: How do you track this assignment?

You could, of course, have him bring you his assignment and the First Aid Kit Log so that the assignment could be stamped and recorded. That might work. Granted, it wasn't the end of the day when you normally meet; nonetheless, you still had the opportunity to stamp and log the assignment. You could have also added your insights and motivational spin to the situation. Having taken care of FAK business, he'd be able to work on the assignment, and you'd still be able to follow up on it later.

One other concern I have regarding this adaptation of the basic FAK procedure—and I'm all for adapting any process in order to maintain its efficacy—would be the effect it might have on Calvin's dedication to bearing down on his spelling assignments during your scheduled time for spelling. If he knows, in the back of his mind, that he might be able to finish it later during social studies time because he plans to finish his social studies assignment early, there's a good chance that he may be less inclined to complete the spelling assignment sitting in front of him at the moment. "Ah," he thinks, "I'll finish this later during social studies." This is not the way you want your students to plan their day.

My feeling is this: once it goes in, it stays in.

I'm standing at the door of our room collecting assignments in numerical order. As soon as I've collected them all, we're going outside for P.E. Should I have the students who weren't finished work on their assignments while the rest of us play?

As much as you might feel this intervention is justified, I don't think it's a good idea. For the most part, your daily activities—especially the fun ones—shouldn't be used as weapons in the war against poor work skills. Consequences need to fit the situation, and I'm not sure how vocabulary is connected to P.E.

> For a better explanation of how behavior and consequences are connected, read Robert MacKenzie's seminal work, *Setting Limits in the Classroom.* He has an entire chapter devoted to appropriate interventions. Do yourself a favor. Read this book. Enough said.

One of the great things about the elementary environment is that you are with one group of students all day long. Consequently, you have the advantage of being with your students through good times and bad. By playing with the underachievers during P.E., I'm able to build a bond which I can then use to motivate them during spelling. If, on the other hand, they're denied entry to the fun stuff due to their inability to complete activities they think are not fun, they might end up seeing the day as a never-ending string of unpleasant experiences. This may be overstating it a bit; but, that's how kids think.

Nonetheless, for those situations in which you have a student who has developed a pattern of not having certain assignments done on time, it would be appropriate to invoke consequences. One of the first steps I take with the hard-core non-finishers would be a loss of freedom. (You may recall that, in our room, freedom is just the opportunity to make choices.)

MR. MORRIS
Speaking to Calvin who, once again, does not have his spelling finished:
Calvin, if you continue to make bad choices, I'll have to make the choices for you. My choice, next time you're not done with spelling, is that you'll work on it during P.E. I'm going to let you play today. I know how much you enjoy playing kickball. I like it when you're out there playing with us. Unfortunately, though, you're going to have to spend P.E. time finishing spelling if you can't get it done on time. Do yourself a favor and have it done tomorrow.

If you're going to restrict students from what is normally a regular part of your day, make an effort to warn them before you act. That way, no one can complain that you were not being fair.

What do you do with the student who doesn't bring back a First Aid Kit assignment?

The basic procedure is:

1. Circle the assignment in the log sheet.

2. Have the student state his agreement to complete the assignment and return it to class the next day.

After one week, the student receives an "incomplete" for that assignment. You should make a point of apprising the student—and if possible, the parents—of this action. A simple way to keep the parents aware of these situations would be to prepare a standardized note with blanks to fill in for the student's name, the date, the incomplete assignment, etc. By having a ready-made communication tool, kind of like a form letter, you'll find yourself using it more than if you had to hand write a letter to the folks each time there was an incomplete assignment.

Although you may feel frustrated with the student who seems to be doing nothing, you're actually preparing the way for a more formal intervention. By using the First Aid Kit Log to keep track of his lack of effort and your attempts at remediation, you'll eventually find yourself with the documentation you need for a parent conference or a consultation meeting with the school counselor. Without the daily documentation, you'll just end up feeling frustrated.

What do I do with an assignment that was turned in on time but shows poor quality or lack of effort?

Pop that bad boy back in the First Aid Kit. Although the FAK is normally reserved for assignments that are not finished on time, there's nothing wrong with using it to boost quality.

Let's not forget, though, that the first step in the accountability process is getting kids to accept the fact that they are responsible for completing assignments on time. Once that's been established—and for some students, this step takes a long time—you can then focus on doing a quality job.

Reality: Poor quality, not much effort, or handwriting that looks like Sanskrit? First Aid Kit, please.

May I leave assignments in there for a couple of days and then pass them back for students to finish during Friday Free Time?

Feel free to use your First Aid Kit any way you wish. After all, that's what's going to make it work for you and your students. (By the way, what's Friday Free Time? It sounds like fun.)

Lesson 10: Grade Books

Do you grade every assignment?

Not really. I've learned to grade the essential assignments and just spot check the ones designed for practice. It takes a bit of experience to develop an eye for what is critical and what isn't. Although some teachers might say that every assignment is critical, I don't know how realistic that actually is.

If you're asking because you're concerned about your assignment correcting work load, think about focusing more on quality than quantity.

For example, instead of asking your students to write one spelling sentence for each of their twenty spelling words, why not ask for just five sentences? Since they're only going to be writing five sentences, you'll be able to ask that the sentences be high-quality, well-written ones.

This reduction in volume will do two things. It will: 1) cut down on the amount of sentences you'll have to check; and 2) lead to an improvement in your student's writing ability. With only five sentences to write, they'll focus more on writing and less on just getting done with the assignment.

Is it okay to have students correct their own assignments?

There are benefits to doing this. However, the assignment has got to be one that is easy for them to correct. Anything that required extensive writing or accuracy of spelling and grammatical convention are not appropriate activities for students to correct.

Appropriate activities for them to correct would include: 1) multiple choice; 2) fill-in-the blank; or 3) any activity that is more objective than subjective. Math assignments that were computational would be a good example of an objective activity that would be relatively easy for students to correct.

For multiple choice correcting, write the answers on the board as you say them. If you don't, you are most likely in for umpteen variations on, "What was the answer to number 7?"

Additional Questions

Hey, buddy. I didn't see the question I wanted to have answered.

Feel free to email me any questions you may have that weren't covered in this section of the book. I'd be happy to share my thoughts. Just be prepared for the fact that it sometimes takes a week or two to get back to you with a response. I'm on the road a lot.

Another option—not that I'm trying to shirk my responsibilities, mind you—would be to seek out other teachers at your site who are currently using New Management strategies. It's amazing how helpful someone else's insight can sometimes be.

Bonus: Your helper will end up feeling like a hero which never hurts when you're trying to cultivate professional relationships.

2010 Update: I now have a section on the website called Got Questions? You'll find answers to a lot of the questions teachers have emailed me over the years. The link is on the main page and looks like this:

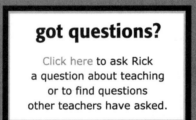

Class Glossary

Here's a sampler of some of the language I've used with students over the years that helped us create a happier, more productive classroom.

activity sheet

The term we use for work sheets. "Activity" is a more positive descriptor. It also has a better ring to it than "work" does.

appropriate

I teach my students this word within the first week of school and then use it throughout the year. It's the perfect word for not only eliminating negative emotion from teacher-student dialogues but for setting the tone for the freedom the students will have in the classroom. (See *freedom*, page 357.) For example, my students know that when it comes to sharpening a pencil or getting a drink, they may do so as long as it is an appropriate time. This will require that students engage in some decision making before they undertake either of these behaviors. Seems simple, I know, but it's just another problem-solving moment. (These moments do occur without the teacher being involved.) If, on the other hand, I make them come to me for permission to sharpen a pencil or get a drink, they're missing out on an opportunity to develop the awareness of when it's appropriate to do something.

choice

This simple word is extremely helpful in getting students to understand and improve their behavior. To tell a child, "That was not a good choice," focuses on the behavior instead of the child. You're basically saying that the child is okay but the action was not. The word "choice" implies a variety of options while avoiding any unintended damage to a student's self-worth.

Used in a more positive way, the word "choice" can become a meaningful communication tool for helping students develop responsibility and self-direction. Imagine we were about to take turns reading aloud from our social studies book. Since the reading selection was already listed on the board, I might say, "A good choice is that you're looking at page 88 and you're ready to read out loud. That's a good choice." By clearly defining expected behaviors, students are more capable of exhibiting them.

collate

I use this word when I want a student to put a set of assignments in numerical order. For some reason, students have a very difficult time with this term. Fortunately, the more I use it, the better they get at understanding it. Here's a typical interaction.

MR. MORRIS
  Handing a student a stack of collected assignments:
  Would you collate these, please?

STUDENT
  Obviously confused by the term:
  Huh?

MR. MORRIS
  Patiently:
  Would you put these in numerical order?

STUDENT
  Starting to catch on to what is being asked:
  You mean like number order?

MR. MORRIS
  Smiling:
  Yes. Numerical order. Collate them, please.

STUDENT
  Pleased to be asked:
  Oh, sure.

It takes a while.

"Could you do a sample?"

This specific question is asked in class whenever a student is not understanding the concept being taught at the moment. It's a much better way to ask for clarification that the time-honored, "I don't get it!" (The problem for teachers when they hear this phrase is that they sometimes think it's the student's fault and are less inclined to either offer help or find out what' wrong.)

The message behind the phrase, "Could you do a sample?" basically means: "Hey, Mr. Morris. Stop talking and start showing. Or, could you model or demonstrate or act out what you're trying to explain. The words aren't makin' it for me." Although it takes a bit of time for your students to ask for help in this fashion, I've found I'm much more likely to help them when they do ask in this way.

Counseling Center

The Counseling Center is a place—a student desk set against one of the side walls of our classroom—where I can send a student who is having a difficult time paying attention to a lesson or working independently. The advantages to using a location inside the room for an isolation spot are: 1) the student can still participate in the lesson; and 2) they stay under my direct supervision. Having a student sit outside your room meets neither of those two critical needs.

discipline

According to T. Berry Brazelton, Director of the Harvard Board of Pediatrics, discipline is teaching, not punishment. I make sure my students and their parents are aware of this definition. Otherwise, whenever you use the word, it will take on negative connotations.

"Echo!"

This word is spoken by a student who has not heard what another student had just said. Check out the chapter on echoing called, "Confessions of a Former Echoer." You can find it in *Eight Great Ideas: Simple Ways to Transform Your Teaching.*

fair

"Fair is not always equal, fair is what's right." This definition is especially helpful whenever a student is complaining that my treatment of another student wasn't fair since he didn't receive that treatment. I can counter his claim by stating that I did what I did because I thought it was the right thing to do.

freedom

"Freedom" is just the opportunity to make choices. And, according to the research, it's the choices children make that help to build their character.

Max

The name of our digital timer. Giving the timer, or other items in your room, a name makes them a bit more user-friendly. Max is described in Lesson 5: Timers & Sound Makers.

paper folders

Each student in class is given two paper folders. The folders are the accordion type that can hold a number of papers without them spilling all over the top of the desk. Although both folders go home each day, the papers inside the two color-coded folders are treated differently.

Papers in this folder go home but come back to school the next day.

Papers in this folder go home and stay home.

pod

The name we use for the group of desks a team uses. The standard formation, created from three double-desks, looks something like this:

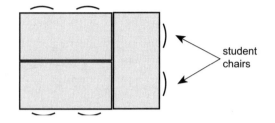

Red Basket

I have a red wire basket that sits on my desk. The basket holds items I need to take care of. The students also know that if they have something they want me to have, they can put it in the Red Basket. In this way, notes from home, volunteer slips for the PTA, and the countless other bits of detritus that would otherwise clutter up my desk or fill my pockets end up in the same place. If I don't have a place for the students to put these things, I make them come to me with each and every one of them. That kind of stuff wears me out. It's so much better to say to a child trying to hand me the note from Mommy, "Just put that in the Red Basket, please."

staff meeting

The term we use for class meeting. Since we normally talk about administrative things—turning in forms for the office, collecting permission slips, announcing assemblies or meetings—I felt that staff meeting had a better ring to it. As Thoreau stated: "Language is a volatile truth." Call your five minutes of info sharing a staff meeting and it sounds rather significant.

study areas

power
love
fun
freedom
safety

Places where students can relocate themselves for studying, reading, or completing assignments. We use our Counseling Center, the conference tables, and an outside desk for alternate study areas. It's their choice if they wish to move or not. However, if they move but get off-task, I have them return to their normal seats. It's just another opportunity to learn about appropriate behavior.

study hall

Study hall refers to students working in the classroom during Thursday's morning recess. I've found that it doesn't do much good to have students work during recess unless they are under direct teacher supervision. If they sit outside against one of the buildings where the other students are playing, the worker is resentful and the work is poor quality. So, I set aside Thursday morning as a time when I work in the room on administration item—stuff in my Red Basket—while students work on late or unfinished assignments.

"Take a risk."

I use this phrase during class discussions to elicit a response from reluctant students. Normally, after I've asked a question, I'll get a number of answers from overachievers which is then followed by an awkward pause. Instead of filling this void with my own summary conclusions, I'll either rephrase the question or encourage my students by saying, "Take a risk. You're among friends." It's amazing how this little comment and a bit of patience on my part can empower the underachievers to offer their thoughts.

In fact, there was a study done on this phenomenon called "Wait Time: Slowing Down May Be a Way of Speeding Up." The researchers discovered that teachers need to wait through the awkward pause. While waiting, teachers need to: 1) rephrase the question; and 2) encourage students to think and respond. They found that if you do this, responses from underachievers go up 400%! So relax, take your time, and let your students know it's okay to "Take a risk."

"Take two."

We have a little stick-on digital clock in the room. It's attached to a wall in an out-of-the-way location. Whenever a student is in need of a short "time out" in order to calm down, I'll tell him to "Take two." He then heads over to the clock and stands there for two minutes. (It's digital: they can read it.) After the two minutes are up, he can then return to his activities.

This technique is just one of the many interventions we use to keep things running smoothly. "Take two" is simple, effective, and does not require documentation or follow-up of any kind. Its effectiveness comes from the fact that I don't overuse it: once or twice a day at the most.

"Talk Radio."

During lessons and discussions, my students will raise a hand in the form of a sign language "c" to show me that they would like to make a comment. If, however, I see that more than half of the class wants to make a comment, I say, "Talk Radio." This means: *turn to your neighbor and share whatever it was you wanted to say.* By doing this, everyone's comment is made in a short amount of time, and we are then able to move on.

teams

Teams are groups of students who work together at a pod throughout the year. We have six teams and identify them with rainbow colors: red, orange, yellow, green, blue, and violet. The teams can be great sources of information and support. (If you're not sure about something, you can always check with your team. Someone will help you find the answer.) This is not to say that we are constantly working in a cooperative fashion. It's just nice having people you've come to trust there for you when you need them.

whiteboard

Although they're nothing like Promethean boards, whiteboards are far superior to the Old School chalk-on-slate. The only drawback is that the students always want to draw on them. To avoid the annoyance of them asking and me having to say "Nope," I came up with a simple definition. "The whiteboard is a tool, not a toy."

> STUDENT
> Looking for something fun to do:
>> *May I draw on the whiteboard?*

> MR. MORRIS
> Smiling but firm:
>> *The whiteboard is a tool, not a toy. Remember?*

> STUDENT
> Bowing to the inevitable:
>> *Oh, yeah. I forgot.*

Before too long, they stop asking. Ah, ain't that nice.

Create Your Own Culture

This short glossary piece was offered to stimulate your thinking. After all, we're in the business of communicating. If we can codify, and thus clarify, some of that communication, everyone wins.

So, see what you can do along this line. Not only will your students benefit from your efforts in this regard but your sanity will as well.